THE POWER OF INNOVATION

What the world's decision makers have to say about Min Basadur's Simplex Process for Creative Problem Solving:

'A highly effective process that can provide senior management with a unique tool to tap into a massive organizational resource. Learning to leverage the creative thinking skills of every individual, regardless of their level, creates the sustainable competitive advantage every corporation is striving for.'
Jim O'Neal, President and Chief Executive Officer, PepsiCo Foods International – Europe Group

'The Simplex process is the best fundamental program for defining and solving problems I've ever used . . . A language for CEO and sales teams alike, the most important tool in the tool-kit.'
Richard M Routhier, President, Sales & Merchandising Division. Bantam Doubleday Dell.

'The process has helped us to unleash the hidden creativity within the organization. It provides a common problem solving language that has been useful in crossing departments, functions, and business units. The "How might we?" and "What's stopping us?" never fails to put the group in a positive frame of mind. The problem solving wheel provides an excellent structure for getting at solutions to those "fuzzy" problems.'
Randy Jensen, Vice President Operations Resources, McCormick & Company Inc. Corporate Division.

'So often I see packages that do not seem to provide much more than a "slogan of the month". This is not the case with Creative Problem Solving, we have continued to use it as an essential tool of our Total Quality Management efforts. It has, in fact, become part of our culture and so continues to payback year after year.'
Tom H. Artes, McCormick & Company Inc., McCormick/Schilling Division

'We have found the Simplex CPS process to be effective not only in removing the "fuzz" from problem definition but in helping us to assign ownership of problems and, therefore, responsibility for implementing solutions once developed.'
Olga Delvecchio, Manager, Quality Systems Development. Stelco Inc.

'Creative Problem Solving has taken confrontation out of the creative process. It has become an integral part of every meeting. Whenever seeking solutions to major issues, we almost automatically go to the Min Basadur diverge/converge process. We've used this process to prioritize training objectives, marketing objectives and organizational objectives.'
John F. Gabriel, President, Pepsi-Cola Bottlers' Association

'These skills have enabled our work teams to discover and eliminate root causes of problems while enhancing corporate profits. Aside from hard-core savings and new future investments, we have experienced more employee tolerance for ambiguity and unstructured challenges, increased desire to initiate new ideas and commit to an action plan and increased self-confidence.'
Nicholas Pollice, Manager, Organizational Development. E.D.Smith

THE POWER OF INNOVATION

How to make innovation a way of life and put creative solutions to work

Dr Min Basadur

Center for Research in Applied Creativity

FT
PITMAN
PUBLISHING

PITMAN PUBLISHING
128 Long Acre, London WC2E 9AN

First published in Great Britain 1995

Published by Pitman Publishing
under license from
The Center for Research in Applied Creativity.
Principal, Dr. Min Basadur

British Library Cataloguing in Publication Data
A CIP catalogue record for this book can be obtained from the British Library.

ISBN 0 273 61362 6

3 5 7 9 10 8 6 4

Typeset by PanTek Arts, Maidstone, Kent.
Printed and bound in Great Britain by
Biddles Ltd, Guildford and King's Lynn

*The Publishers' policy is to use paper manufactured
from sustainable forests.*

This book is dedicated to:

Eleanor, Bob, Steve and Tim
Anica, Bosko and Irene
Patti, Michelle and Craig
Bruce

Foreword: My Own Flight to Creativity—How the Simplex Process Came to Be

I like to begin any creative problem-solving seminar or application session with a small exercise that tells participants a little bit about myself.

I explain that 'Min' is actually a nickname and invite participants to guess my real name. After exhausting all their guesses—Minnesota, Minister, Minneapolis, Benjamin, Administrator, Dominic—I proceed to tell a little story that goes like this:

My parents emigrated to Canada from Yugoslavia and settled in a little town called Kirkland Lake, where in those days, a lot of Yugoslavians worked the gold mines. When I was born, my parents decided to give me a Yugoslavian name: Marijan.

After writing the name on the chart, I ask everyone to guess how it's pronounced. After a few tries, someone gets it right: 'Mah-ree-YON.' This is a very common Yugoslavian name that translates nicely into English as Marion, perfectly acceptable as a boy's or girl's name. I would have been perfectly happy with this name. But right from the start, my parents called me by a slightly different name: Marino. Italian, not Yugoslavian.

My Italian-sounding Yugoslavian name wasn't a problem, until we moved to Toronto when I was about five years old. There were no Yugoslavians mining in Toronto, in fact, there were very few Yugoslavians there at all. When they learned my name, people assumed I was Italian. And no one had even heard of Yugoslavian. Thanks to my name, I learned early what it meant to be different.

Hoping to eliminate the problem, I actually encouraged nicknames, but none of them stuck. Except one.

Unlike most of the kids I grew up with, who wanted to become hockey players, my real love was baseball. Back then, the New York Yankees dominated the game. Almost every year they won the American League pennant and the World Series. Baseball fans really had only two choices: they could *like* the New York Yankees, or they could *hate* the New York Yankees. I chose to hate them, partly because it was boring to watch a team that just won over and over again, and partly because New York always seemed to have more money than anyone else to buy the players they needed.

In the American League, only two teams were able to beat the Yankees once in a while for the pennant—the Chicago White Sox and the Cleveland Indians. One player whom they used to trade back and forth was named Minnie Minoso.

As I relate the story to the seminar group, I show off my Minnie Minoso baseball cards. One card dated 1976 shows Minnie at age 54. That was the year he set a baseball record for becoming the oldest player to hit safely. The Chicago White Sox had allowed him to bat in a regular season game that year and he'd managed to get a base hit. In 1980 they let him bat again. He failed to hit safely that time, but he still set another world record, becoming the first player to play in a regular season game in each of five decades. In 1990 the White Sox announced they were going to give Minnie a chance to make it six decades. I thought it was a great idea, but the baseball commissioner vetoed it as nothing more than a publicity stunt. Now in his late 60s, Minnie is still working out with the White Sox, ready to play whenever he gets a chance.

Minnie was a fun-loving, excellent ball player who seemed able to play any position and do whatever it took to help the underdogs against the Yankees. While the other kids were rooting for Mickey Mantle or Yogi Berra, I rooted for Minnie Minoso. People started to call me Minnie Minoso, then Minnie, and then just Min. The name has stuck ever since. (By the way, my three sons are named Steve, Tim and Bob, for obvious reasons.)

That's where my name came from. So where did Simplex come from? That's another story, one that I'm still compiling as I continue to teach, consult, research and learn. It probably starts in 1957 when I enrolled in engineering physics at the University of Toronto.

While I wouldn't say I hated *every* minute of the next four years, I did hate *almost* every minute of them. Every day was the same: the professor wrote on the board all kinds of equations full of x's and y's and z's, which we all copied as fast as we could. The name of the game: to make all of the x's and y's and z's come out to zero. During examinations at the end of the year, the goal was to show you could regurgitate everything you'd copied down in the classroom. If you did a good job of making the x's and y's and z's come out to zero, you passed. I never fully understood why I was doing these x's and y's and z's, just that I had to. Nearing the end of my fourth year, I remember saying to myself, 'Please God, let me get a job where I don't have to do any more x's and y's and z's.'

My wish was answered. One company in Hamilton, Ontario called Procter & Gamble Inc. didn't say anything about x's and y's or z's. They seemed to be more interested in how well I could think and communicate, and in my general knowledge. They seemed very people-oriented, keen on teamwork, and had excellent profit sharing plans and pension schemes. They offered me a choice: work in the plant or work in something called research and development. Not having a clue about what research and development might be, that's what I chose. There I had to do many different things, few of which had anything to do with what I'd learned at engineering school: show initiative; solve all kinds of problems with other people; start and finish projects; and work with varied employees in sales, manufacturing, market research and advertising. I enjoyed developing new products and helping other people to get things done.

About six years later, my boss asked me to transfer to a new division called Industrial Products at company headquarters in Cincinnati. Unlike the company's retail divisions, whose customers were mostly supermarket patrons buying soap or laundry detergent, Industrial Products had all kinds of products for all manner of customers from industrial laundries and automatic car washes to hospitals and manufacturers.

But after two or three years, our division was falling short of expectations. One day, a senior manager said, 'The Industrial Products division needs to be more creative.' None of us really knew what that meant. What did creativity have to do with industry? Out of the blue, somebody received a brochure for a creative problem solving seminar being held by the Creative Education Foundation at the State University College at Buffalo. I and another colleague went along to see what we might learn for our division to use.

It was a wonderful week. I was introduced to concepts that immediately fell into place for me: balancing divergent and convergent thinking skills; addressing problems that lacked single, correct answers but required imagination and a fresh pair of eyes. These were concepts I hadn't learned in school, where we had learned how to converge on the one 'correct' answer for most problems. It seemed to me that these concepts were the things that people had to use in order to succeed in their jobs and their lives—including the people in our division.

I began to weave what I'd learned into my job whenever I could. When I worked on projects involving other departments, I talked them into using the same concepts. It wasn't long before people in other departments started asking me to lead problem solving sessions, even on tough, technical issues. I remember standing up before a roomful of extremely bright chemistry and engineering PhDs, and saying to myself, 'What right have I got to be telling these people how to think?' However, I found that I was actually able to help them. While they had great knowledge of their fields, very few of them knew much about creative thinking processes. My little knowledge about such processes made me more of an expert than them, and they appreciated my help.

I was seen more and more as an 'internal consultant' in helping people through the creative process on all kinds of problems. And I began to sense that there were two parts to being effective in an organization. One part was being versed in *content*—knowledge about your job. Most of my colleagues dealt in content, the 'what' of their jobs. The other part was being versed in *process*—having skills in 'how' you do your job. I had something to offer my colleagues, not because I knew more about any single problem or area, but because I was gaining expertise in processes that helped others think their way through problems. I was becoming a process consultant, facilitator and coach.

The key word seemed to be 'simplicity.' In fact, that's where the name Simplex came from. Keeping things simple, and keeping an open mind are fundamental to the creative process. I found my co-workers wasted a lot of time by plunging into solving problems without ensuring they were tackling the right ones. Projects were delayed because people ignored simple but vital facts. They felt that if a problem was worthwhile, it had to be complex. The secret, I believed, was to think as much as possible like a child or like the guy who just got off the boat, without feeling embarrassment about asking 'simple' questions or digging for facts that others took for granted. You had to start without preconceived notions about solutions to problems—and about what problem you were really trying to solve. Part of what I was doing at Procter & Gamble was simply helping people to think in the way children do, in simple terms, without preconceived notions.

The 1970s were a decade of unprecedented change for Procter & Gamble as well as everyone else. We saw double-digit inflation, an Arab oil embargo that made raw materials scarce, and anti-trust laws that thwarted our normal practice of growing by acquiring and developing small companies. We couldn't depend only on R&D's new products to meet the company's goal of doubling its business every 10 years. Until then, Procter & Gamble had worked mostly on a functional basis. Solving these new, complex problems would require teamwork and interfunctional co-operation. Most important, we had to become more creative. I was offered a job as a full-time creative process consultant to help the corporation learn to use creativity, to use creative processes in teamwork, and to use teamwork to meet these challenges. I developed many different processes that worked within my evolving Simplex creative problem solving model: fact finding; problem definition; teamwork . . .

I realised it wasn't good enough just to have an effective process. There were also process skills that people could perfect in order to make these processes work better. Wanting to learn more about process and process skills, I enrolled on a course in organizational behaviour at the University of Cincinnati, with minors in educational psychology and social psychology. In 1977 I undertook my doctoral dissertation, a two-year experiment involving creativity training of engineers at Procter & Gamble. I developed a scientific model that showed how creativity training worked and demonstrated that training in the creative process and process skills—specifically Simplex—improved job performance. My work won the American Psychological Association's S. Rains Wallace award in 1980 for the best industrial and organizational psychology dissertation.

With my doctoral work, I had only begun to explore the range of research possibilities. Other corporations that had heard about my successes were inviting me to consult with them to improve processes like employee involvement and product innovation. I found the idea appealing: I could draw on my academic and business experience to consult with companies, which would then become 'crucibles' in which I could test and expand my own knowledge of creative processes. It was time for a leap of faith.

By 1981 I found myself on the business faculty at McMaster University in Hamilton, back where I'd started with Procter & Gamble many years earlier. McMaster, known for its innovative practices, had been looking for someone to launch a course in organizational behavior and to help it establish ties with industry. My move to McMaster gave both of us what we needed.

Since then, I've had the freedom to experiment and consult with top corporations throughout the United States and Canada and around the world. And I've developed a network of associates across North America and abroad called the Center for Research in Applied Creativity. This book is an attempt to share what I've learned.

Twenty years after entering engineering school, I had finally realized what I wanted to do with my life. There existed a whole set of important skills that had not been identified in engineering school. These were creative process skills, skills you could learn only by experiencing, skills that weren't written down in books—which leads me to my own struggle throughout much of the eighties in writing this book . . .

Like others, I had learned by doing, experiencing, discovering. In running training workshops or problem solving application sessions, I'd been able to transfer most of this knowledge to participants by getting them involved in learning. But how to permit an invisible reader to experience the concepts of the creative process and creative process skills? And with a book designed to satisfy millions of readers, how to focus on providing precisely the help they want? Fortunately I achieved a process breakthrough of my own. Why not use the same methodology that I planned to impart in the book in the actual writing of it? I decided to separate the book's content—in a nutshell, the explanation of process and process skills—from the process of writing it.

I believe that by following the same route—by separating process from content—organizations can gain enormous competitive edge in our global marketplace. And I believe the same holds true for every individual within the organization. You can take the lead in overcoming problems without waiting for the boss's say-so. You can vastly improve your performance and stature in your organization by learning the processes and process skills in this book. By focusing your efforts on process and not just content, you can distinguish yourself without other people even knowing how you're doing it.

This book is designed for anyone who wants to develop his or her own personal performance, in whatever endeavor. For many readers, the most obvious and appealing use is to dramatically improve their work performance. Thus, I've relied throughout on examples from the world of work. But 'organization' can mean just about anything: businesses; volunteer groups; sports teams; your family; society itself. In any of these arenas, the secret to success is to separate management of content from management of process.

One important process skill that I hope to share is the ability to adapt this book's ideas from one arena to another. If keeping things simple is the most important process skill, perhaps the second most important is the ability to adapt. The worst way to learn is to confront every new idea with the words: 'I'm different, that won't work for me.' The best way to learn is to say, 'I'm different but so is everybody else. How might I adapt this information so it *will* work for me?' Adaptation is the secret of learning.

ACKNOWLEDGEMENTS

Having reached this stage in my own creative development, I would like to acknowledge and thank a number of people who helped me along the way. Their names are almost too numerous to mention, and I hope that those whose names are not included here will recognize that their contributions have been no less valuable to me.

First, my early teachers who shared their secrets of helping others discover their personal creativity: Roy Jones, Sid Parnes, Bob Barnett, the late John Demidovitch, Charlie Clark, Sid Shore, Ruth Noller and Angelo Biondi.

Second, Keith Staples, Ted Logan, Bruce Paton and Delaine Hampton, who encouraged me to emphasize my creative talents in my work and to help my co-workers and others to unleash their own creativity.

Third, those people who have allowed me to bring my processes into their organizations and become partners in a mutual learning process about how to make their organizations more creative. This has permitted me to deepen my learnings and share those learnings with people in other organizations, with my students and colleagues at McMaster University, and with my associates: Jim O'Neal, Bruce Paton, the late Charlie Cotton, Wayne Calloway, Max Wright, Jim Jarratt, Pete Carrothers, Bill Elston, and the core group, including Ken Fessenden, Frank Prince, Bob Moreland, and Dave Morrison, that I trained and who helped to launch the great 'Off$et' effort at Frito-Lay; Randy Jensen, who spread the word to Rick Frattali and others at McCormick; Ken Dowling, Larry Bruno, Ray Sauers and others who helped me transfer Simplex to the employee involvement training group at Ford Motor Co.; Jim Thyen, Gene Recker and Joe Dedman among others at Kimball, who, with Sue Ellspermann's help, made Simplex so meaningful; Harry Whaley and others, who nurtured the process at Woodstream with Janet Getto; Les McLean, Wayne Hill, Ezra Rosen and Bob Milbourne's steering committee, who made the process a way of life at Stelco Inc.; John Thyne, John Gabriel, Rick Routhier, Ron Tidmore, Denny Larabee, Joe Maurer, Jerry Donais, Jim Reddinger, Roger Barker, Bill Moore, Charlie Thomas, Craig Weatherup, Brenda Barnes and others who have made practical use of Simplex at Pepsi-Cola; Steve Semmer, and Philippe Lemaitre, Russ Catania and Pat Banks, who helped introduce the process to accelerate thriving reengineering and organizational development processes at Pillsbury and TRW; Dick Denoyer, who has continually used Simplex in trying to improve community life in the Princeton School District of Cincinnati, Ohio; Dave Swedes, Bill Ulmer, Bob Gibson, Mike Sipple and Dave Wilson, who provided encouragement in the early days in Cincinnati; George

Graen, my mentor at the University of Cincinnati, who helped me to capitalize on the opportunity provided by Jim Ott, Bill Flack, Larry Pettett, Pres Grounds and Geoff Place to conduct my award-winning doctoral research at Procter & Gamble; Mitsuru Wakabayashi and Jiro Takai, my research partners at Nagoya University in Japan; Angel Sanhueza, Rupert Brendon, Jack Price, Barb Pitts, Don Lawson, Jim Satterthwaite, Carl Finkbeiner, Naresh Agarwal, Chris Bart, Bob Cooper, Randy Ross, Bob Cunliffe, Jackie Wyer, Jim Campbell, and Tony Vercillo, who have supported me in many ways; Andrew Vowles, Paul Mattioli, and my associates Larry Crase and Dave Connell, who helped me to write and illustrate this book; and Sue Ellspermann, Janet Getto, Susie Robinson, Gwen Speranzini, Nick Pollice, Richard Hamlin, Kathy Kleindorfer, Garry Gelade, and K.T. Connor, my other associates, and Marg Forrest, in the Center for Research in Applied Creativity.

CONTENTS

Foreword: My Own Flight to Creativity—How the Simplex Process Came to Be.   v

1 Unleash Your Creativity—And Boost Your Performance   1

NEXT YEAR?!? WHAT ABOUT NEXT WEEK?!?   1
Summary of learnings   2

    Creating change deliberately   3
    Is your organization effective?   6
    Creativity: The key to making change   8
    How we suppress our natural creativity   9
    A process for unleashing your creativity   16

2 Making Innovation a Way of Life   19

BUT WHAT IF WE FAIL?   19
Summary of learnings   20

    Toward more complete thinking   22
        HOT NEWS ABOUT HOT WAX:
            Chemists discover they were working on the wrong problem   22
        AHA! GREEN STRIPES NOT THE PROBLEM:
            Product development team goes for refreshment instead   24
        SMALL DETAIL PAYS OFF:
            Breakthrough comes from unlikely source   25
        TURF WARS TERMINATED:
            Interfunctional team stops bickering over solutions;
            agrees instead on common problem definition   25
        A GOOD IDEA TRASHED
            Haste makes waste for household products company that
            throws out innovation 'pizza box' trash container   26
    Recurring patterns that show our lack of process skills   28
    Your three key challenges   30

3 The Big Secret: Separating Process From Content   42

PROGRESS GETS LIP SERVICE   42
Summary of learnings   43
    How to distinguish process from content   44
       PROCESS, NOT JUST CONTENT:
          Workers motivated by opportunity to spread creative wings   47
       'BURNING THE FURNITURE':
          Company forced to re-hire layoffs as higher-priced consultants   48
    The 'big secret'   52

4 Simplex: A Process for Making Innovation a Way of Life   54

SHORT-TERM GAIN, LONG-TERM PAIN   54
Summary of learnings   55

    Problem solving: A creative process   56
    Eight steps to solving problems   57

5 Getting Starting: Problem Finding and Fact Finding   60

WHY DIDN'T YOU SAY SO?   60
Summary of learnings   61

    Step 1: Problem finding   63
       LITTLE QUESTIONS THAT CHANGE THE WORLD:
          You can't solve a problem—or invent a phonograph—without
          finding a problem first   63
    You can be a better problem finder   66
       SCIENTISTS IN SALES?:
          Company's 'sell, then create' approach ensures that researchers
          keep customers in mind   67
       LOOKING FOR GOLDEN EGGS:
          Seeking problems creates opportunities at this firm   68
    Step 2: Fact finding   68
    Seven strategies for finding facts   68
       IS THAT *REALLY* A FACT?:
          Young engineer turns up 'new' information; offers way to get
          rail efficiency back on track   70
    Six fact finding questions   71

6 If You Define It, The Solutions Will Come   77

GREAT PRODUCT, NO MARKET   77
Summary of learnings   78

Step 3: Problem definition   80
'How might we?'   80
    'WE CAN'T BECAUSE. . .':
      'Negative thinking' number-one killer of good ideas, says study   81
The 'why-what's stopping' analysis   84
    MORE THAN JUST A LEAK:
      The 'why-what's stopping' analysis: From repairing a leak to
      fixing a company   86
    MY PROBLEM IS OUR PROBLEM:
      Employees fit themselves into bigger corporate picture   89
    FROM ONE THING TO ANOTHER:
      Engineer discovers right question; ignites energy
      conservation program   92
Keep the 'why-what's stopping' *analysis simple*   93

7 More—And More Creative—Solutions   95

OF ALL THE HARE-BRAINED IDEAS . . .   95
Summary of learnings   96

Step 4: Idea finding   97
Four ideas for generating ideas   98
Step 5: Evaluate and select   101
Criteria of choice: The criteria grid method   103
Blended criteria: Paired comparison analysis   105

8 Putting Creative Solutions to Work   110

ALL TALK, NO ACTION   110
Summary of learnings   111

Step 6: Action planning   112
Psychological roadblocks to action   112
Step 7: Gaining acceptance   117
How to sell ideas   117
Step 8: Taking action   120
How to prompt yourself to act   121

9 Three Process Skills for Making Innovation a Way of Life 125

MAKING A BAD DECISION WORSE 125
Summary of learnings 126

    Quality results = Content + process + process skills 127
      IT'S NOT JUST *WHAT* YOU DO, BUT *HOW*:
        Buying a training program won't change the way you do things 127

10 The Three Process Skills: Diverging, Converging and Deferring Judgment 133

IF YOU GET YELLED AT EVERYTIME . . . 133
Summary of learnings 134

    Divergence and convergence: The two-sided thinking process 135
    Between divergence and convergence; Deferral of judgment 136
    Killer phrases 138
    Toward better ideation 139
    Valuing and creating different points of view 141
    Toward better evaluation 155

11 A Fourth Process Skill: Follow the Simplex Process 159

AREN'T YOU SUPPOSED TO BE THE EXPERT? 159
Summary of learnings 160

    Vertical deferral of judgment 161
    Simplex from start to finish 163
    'I want to improve my poker game' 179

12 Follow the Process with Others 188

A MEETING WITHOUT THE MINDS 188
Summary of learnings 189

    Meetings: Tools for solving problems 191
    The groundwork for a good meeting 192
    The meeting process and process skills 196
    Debriefing: Toward better meetings 198

13 Follow the Process in Teams 201

MONKEY SEE, MONKEY DO? 201
Summary of learnings 202

The problem with teamwork 203
WHY CAN'T WE JUST GET ALONG?:
Team members need to check egos and go-it-alone attitudes
at door 204
Toward more productive teams 206
Interpersonal skills for better teamwork 208
Team skills for better teamwork 209
WHOSE SIDE ARE YOU ON?:
Bargaining team takes 'win-win' approach to contract
negotiations 214
DREAM TEAM?:
'Foes' team up in creative approach to improve bottom line 217
TAKEN TO TASK:
Task force maps out key challenges; breaks long-time impasse 219

**14 Alignment: Follow the Simplex Process to Define Your
Key Challenges** 224

THE MISSING LINK 224
Summary of learnings 225

How to define your key challenges 226
Defining your key challenges: An example 227
WHAT CAN I DO?:
Purchasing director goes beyond the call to involve others in
innovation 236

**15 Alignment: Follow the Process to Define Your
Organization's Key Challenges** 238

HEAD OFFICE SAYS WE HAVE TO DO IT THIS WAY 238
Summary of learnings 239

Link your challenges with your customer's challenges 240
STICKHANDLING FOR CUSTOMER SATISFACTION:
Bank trains employees to find creative ways to cut costs—
and make customers happy too 240
Strategic planning: How to identify key external challenges 247
Creating the strategic action plan 250

16 Alignment: Follow the Process to Empower Others   254

WORKING NINE TO FIVE   254
Summary of learnings   255

How to involve others in solving key challenges   256
CONTINUOUS CREATIVITY IS KEY:
Japanese suggestion system stresses means, not ends   258
SEEING THE BIGGER PICTURE:
Japan's suggestion systems force employees to think big   260

17 Get Going: Start the Simplex Process Yourself   262

IT'S ALL IN HIS HEAD   262
Summary of learnings   263

A plan for implementing your solutions   264
How to create—and sustain—your action plans   265

18 Get Going: Involve Others in the Process   267

THEY SAY THEY WANT INNOVATION, BUT . . .   267
Summary of learnings   268

The creative process: Rise above your differences   270
Helping customers through the innovation process   273
'Together, we can carry out the process'   274
Organizational roadblocks to creativity   276
NEVER MIND THE MEETING:
Managers trying to think long-term find themselves penalized 277
NEW PRODUCT OUT TO LUNCH:
Failure to check assumption proves costly   279
How to involve others in implementing innovation   284

19 Get Going: Build Your Skills in the Process   287

BUT I DID MY TRAINING OBJECTIVE!   287
Summary of learnings   288

Training improves employee creativity   290
NURTURING THE CREATIVE SPARK:
Training improves creativity, process skills   290
Training improves use of process skills   292

THE TEAM THAT TRAINS TOGETHER . . . :
 Intact work groups transfer training back to job   292
Training improves process skills, no matter who you are   293
 FROM OFFICE TO SHOP FLOOR:
 Training benefits white- and blue-collar workers alike   293
Training improves use of active divergence—and how   294
 ANY MORE BRIGHT IDEAS?:
 'Best' idea often saved for last: Study   294
Training improves use of active convergence   294
 I'LL BE THE JUDGE OF THAT:
 Training yields more ideas, and better ways to judge them   294

20 What's an Easy Next Step?   297

WHAT'S THE NEXT STEP?   297
Summary of learnings   298

Integrate Simplex, or implement it from scratch?   299
The secret to total quality management   301
 TQM TAKES TIME:
 Total quality no overnight success   301
Using Simplex as a 'total quality process'   302
 WHAT CAN I DO?:
 Employees learn to help company adapt to change   302
Using Simplex to involve all employees   304
 TOP-DOWN TRAINING:
 How one company pushed a training program through
 the ranks   304
Using Simplex to expand a cost improvement program   307
 WHAT ARE WE ABOUT?:
 Company defines niche, appoints teams to roll out
 cost improvements   307
Using Simplex to empower employees   308
 WHAT DO YOU THINK?:
 Employees forced to look inward for answers to problems   308
Using Simplex to flatten costs   312
 A PROCESS FOR PROFITS
 Company uses creative process to reap cost savings   312
Using Simplex to regain business   314

MAKING UP LOST GROUND, AND THEN SOME:
How one company used creativity to make up for lost business   314
Your next step   316
It's up to you   317

Appendix   321
Index   323

1

Unleash Your Creativity—And Boost Your Performance

Next year?!? What about next week?!?

We'd just reached cruising altitude, and the fellow next to me had introduced himself as Harry, the operations manager for a manufacturer.

'Continuous improvement programs,' he repeated, sighing and shaking his head. 'The trouble is, they all sound great but implementing them is a whole new ball game. At our company, we know we need to continuously change our products and procedures to stay ahead. But getting people to actually do things differently is tough.'

'What do you mean exactly?' I said.

Harry sighed again. 'Well, take the front-line people. What frustrates me is that I can't get them to look at next week's problems and solve them before they actually happen, let alone plan for big changes for next year. Even when they *know* about a problem that is sure to occur next week, most can't do anything about it. They just wait for it to happen. And when the problem finally crops up, they act as if they'd had no prior knowledge of it.'

'Are you saying they just ignore problems?'

'Not really. In all fairness, they *are* good at solving problems that I hand them. And if I define what I want, they'll give it to me. They're also good firefighters. They know how to react to sudden problems. But that's not the kind of problem I'm talking about. They just don't seem to have the skill to look ahead and handle new, fuzzy kinds of situations on their own. They're not anticipating problems, partly I think because they don't know what to do about them anyway.'

'Join the crowd.' I shook my head. 'I've seen this sort of thing before. What are you doing about it?'

'Well, what I'm trying to do is change our culture so we become more proactive,' Harry explained. 'What we need is a process people can follow and master for anticipating problems, not just handling whatever they're given. I'm looking for a continuous improvement program, one that will get everybody focusing not just on what they're doing today but thinking about tomorrow's problems and opportunities at the same time.'

'So you want them to look both short and long term, right?'

'Exactly. I know that when we talk about continuous improvement, we're talking about involving people in steadily improving things over the long term. But the need exists even in our day-to-day operations. They have to be able to anticipate and solve short-term problems on their own, and yet keep an eye on the long-term opportunities too. Keeping both eyes open—that's the key, that's what I'm looking for.' ■

Summary of learnings

✦ *Many people in organizations need to change but go about it wrongly. They institute crash programs that usually fail because nobody really changes how they think and behave.*

✦ *People who deliberately innovate, or make continuous changes in their products and processes, help their organizations win a competitive edge.*

✦ *People in competitive organizations display three specific characteristics simultaneously: efficiency, adaptability and flexibility. For most people, adaptability is the most difficult to mainstream, but it is the key to innovation.*

✦ *Adaptability requires creativity.*

✦ *Creativity is a continuous process of discovering good problems, solving these problems, and implementing the solutions.*

✦ *Everyone is born with creativity, but it's suppressed as we mature in three main ways: our attitudes, our behaviors, and our thought processes.*

✦ *By learning skills to unleash your innate creativity, you can dramatically improve your performance and make valuable change.*

Total quality. Empowerment. Reengineering. Intrapreneuring. Work flow. Time management. There's no shortage of continuous improvement, management development, and self-help programs and methods on the market today. What this book offers is a way to make sense of that jumble of programs and methods and a way to successfully apply them. How? By unleashing your own creativity, and the creativity of people around you. By learning the Simplex process of creative problem solving, you can dramatically improve your personal performance and lead your organization in making valuable changes.

CREATING CHANGE DELIBERATELY

No matter where you look around the world today, organizations face a common challenge: the need to improve their performance in order to adapt to rapid change. In North America, crash restructuring and downsizing have become a way of life as organizations struggle to regain market share from global companies producing higher-quality products. Companies try overnight to become more quality-conscious and customer service-oriented. In Eastern Europe, managers and employees struggle to establish new behaviors and procedures that will allow their companies to compete in the free market. Third World countries hungry for economic development look for growth markets around the world. In Japan, organizations that once had a clear target—to match and surpass North American quality and customer service—now lack a blueprint for further progress.

Whatever the case, the keys to maintaining competitiveness lie in the ability to change and improve what we do and how we do it. It's the ability to change that allows organizations to develop new products more quickly, to improve customer service and training, and to encourage people to assume more responsibility and to work in teams. These organizations continuously anticipate problems, trends, customer needs, and opportunities, and push themselves to develop and implement new processes and products. They don't wait to *be* pushed. They deliberately change.

Yet organizations still find it difficult to meet the challenge of adapting to change. What are organizations doing wrong? Plenty. Too many companies are preoccupied with short-term results. Their employees and teams fail to pursue common goals within the company, and with the company's suppliers and customers. Undervaluing their workers' skills, organizations neglect human resources. Too few companies can move new ideas quickly and efficiently from lab bench to market. And too many managers and workers cling to work patterns established at a time when North American companies could thrive simply by mass producing and selling standard commodities for a captive domestic market.

When these companies finally do get around to trying to change their ways, they often do so under pressure to produce quick results. They introduce quick-fix programs that are seldom more than Band-aid solutions employing tools and techniques to make short-term profits. They fail to gain real commitment for improvement from lower and middle managers, to offer necessary employee training, to establish reinforcement systems and to allow enough time for participation, buy-in and ownership. Without these fundamental changes, employees fail to understand how and why to integrate the new tools and techniques into their work, and view the programs as nothing more than extra tasks. When senior managers unilaterally set goals based on short-term costs and profits, middle managers get mixed messages about the importance of quality, customer service and shared goal-setting. Small wonder these programs sputter and die.

Making new programs work requires changing behaviors and attitudes in the office, in the boardroom and on the shop floor. It's one thing to state, for example, that improving customer service and developing human resources are top corporate priorities. It's another thing to turn words into actions. Tools and techniques alone won't do the trick. You won't encourage employees to accept a new 'philosophy' if they see no substantive change behind the rhetoric. Companies must change their management and organizational systems in ways that really alter long-term corporate behavior and structure. This means managers must lead, model and induce the behaviors and attitudes required to successfully implement these programs. It takes time. Developing these systems took the Japanese decades. For most companies, complete implementation of a successful improvement program like total quality management (TQM) will take between six and 12 years.

From a different perspective, this preoccupation with short-term results and quick fixes reflects a more fundamental problem: most organizations lack the skills needed for the process of making change. In fact, their bureaucratic functional structures discourage change. Organizations rely on specialized, well-defined jobs and tasks to attain maximum control, highest quantity and lowest per-unit cost. The organization views changes in technology, customer tastes and competition as irritating disruptions to its routine. Any changes that the organization does make are nothing more than quick fixes to handle emergencies. The idea of seeking out problems as part of a continuous process of change is foreign to a culture that works by the slogan, 'If it isn't broken, don't fix it.'

This attitude wouldn't be cause for concern if the world weren't changing so rapidly. In an unchanging world, of course, we could continue doing what we were doing, in the same way we'd always done it. But the only real constant is that change will continue to occur, and ever more rapidly (Figure 1-1). We must accept and accommodate change as a fact of life and develop skills to adapt to it. It's a challenging task. As we'll discuss later in this chapter, little of what we

Over the centuries, an adage has developed that there are two things in life that are permanent: death and taxes. Many years ago, Sophocles (400 B.C.) suggested a third: change. Today almost everyone agrees with him, because this state of change is much more in evidence than ever before. In his book 'Future Shock,' Alvin Toffler points out that we are living in an age not just of change but of rapid change. This acceleration is now so great that many people are unable to cope with it and are being, as it were, 'shocked.' Most of us have been trained to function in a more stable world than the ongoing state of instability and uncertainty we find ourselves living with today.

Science suggests that mankind has been on earth for about 50,000 years. This represents about 800 lifetimes. Amazingly, people did not 'emerge from the cave' for the first 650 lifetimes. Toffler suggests that, by the time a person reaches age 50, 97 per cent of everything known in the world will have been learned since the time he was born. We have enjoyed having the electric motor only for the last two lifetimes. Thus, the curve of knowledge development versus time looks like this:

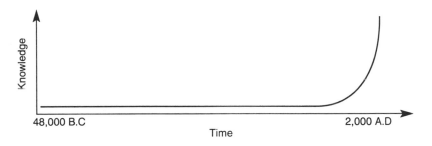

In other words, the rate of change in knowledge is in rapid acceleration. The amount of change one person might have experienced in a lifetime in the 1800s is experienced in about five years by a person in the late 1900s. Toffler illustrates this further by estimating the shrinking length of time it has taken to turn various technological concepts into practical executions of the concepts. One needs only to look at some common examples to underscore this idea: It took 140 years for the photograph to be invented (implemented) from the time someone actually conceived the idea of photography. It only took the radio 40 years; television 12 years; and finally the transistor two years. We are now becoming so sophisticated that we can make new ideas practical in almost no time at all.

What does all this mean? First, there are two postures a person or organization can take towards change. One is defensive—fearing change, reacting toward it reluctantly, and wishing it would disappear; in short, being controlled by change. The second is to treat change as something that is a fact of life and ask: "How might I adapt to change and turn it into an opportunity?" Thus change is life a knife, one can grasp the blade or the handle—view it as a threat or an opportunity.

Fig. 1.1 The accelerating rate of change

learn as we grow up has equipped us to cope with change. Rather, most of our formal education emphasizes maintaining the status quo.

IS YOUR ORGANIZATION EFFECTIVE?

Organizational research conducted by Dr. Paul Mott of the University of Pennsylvania suggests that an effective organization is one that displays three specific characteristics: efficiency, adaptability and flexibility (Figure 1-2).

Efficiency allows an organization to implement and follow routines. Every organization, large or small, continually turns out specific goods or services. The effective organization follows a well-structured, stable routine for delivering its 'product' in high quantities and high quality and at low cost. In yesterday's relatively stable world, organizations might have been able to concentrate on efficiency alone. If we still bought buggy whips, the organization's sole concern would be simply to produce lots of high-quality, low-cost buggy whips. But in a changing world, efficiency alone is not enough.

In a way, *adaptability* is the other side of the coin. While efficiency implies mastering a routine, adaptability means mastering the process of changing the routine. Adaptability is a proactive process: it allows the organization to deliberately and continually change its routines to improve quality, raise quantities and reduce costs. Adaptable people and organizations anticipate problems and opportunities, and develop timely solutions and new routines, such as higher-

---

1 EFFICIENCY (organizing for routine production)
   ● High quantity of 'product.'
   ● High quality of 'product.'
   ● Low cost of 'product.'

2 ADAPTABILITY (organizing to change routine)
   ● Anticipating problems and developing timely solutions to them.
   ● Staying abreast of new methods applicable to the activities of the organization.
   ● Prompt acceptance of solutions.
   ● Widespread acceptance of solutions.

3 FLEXIBILITY
   ● Organizing to react to unexpected emergencies quickly.

Adapted from Mott, P.E., Characteristics of Effective Organizations, Harper and Row, 1972

Fig. 1.2 Characteristics of effective organizations

quality buggy whips or, say, automobile self-starters. Adaptability requires looking outside the organization for new technologies, ideas and methods that may improve or completely change its routine. Adaptable organizations are willing to accept new solutions quickly. The most effective organizations are both highly efficient and highly adaptable.

While adaptability is a continual, proactive process of looking for ways to change, *flexibility* is more short-term and reactive. Instead of forcing change, flexibility allows the organization to react quickly to unexpected forces or disruptions without getting mired in organizational bureaucracy. It allows the efficient organization to stay on its feet to deal with the disruptions while maintaining its routines. Many companies are finding that it's no longer enough to rely solely on flexibility in order to cope with change. Instead of merely reacting to a competitor's product introduction, the organization must anticipate such a change by 'leapfrogging.' The organization must bring to market goods and services that meet a need that consumers themselves have yet to recognize, thus leading its customers.

The alternative is to be scooped by the competition. During the past two or three decades, many companies allowed themselves to be scooped by waiting for new ideas that they could have implemented themselves. Allowing a competitor to make the initial change, they found themselves playing catch-up. North American automobile tire manufacturers, for example, refused to make radial tires, even though the technology existed and the product had already proven enormously successful in Europe. Michelin had leapt in and revolutionized the market, leaving its domestic competitors scrambling to catch up. The latter had stubbornly refused to make the move for a variety of alleged reasons, including high capital costs, potential reductions in the replacement market, and supposed differences between European and North American consumers and cars. The real reason for their reluctance was their discomfort and lack of skill in the process of change. They just didn't want to change.

Earlier, Procter & Gamble once had the market for household cleaning products sewn up with its Spic and Span brand. While it had already developed a liquid cleaner, Lestoil had been first to enter the market with its liquid cleaner. Procter & Gamble was swift to market Mr. Clean in response, but the company had lost the opportunity to be the first entrant. It was only the company's concentration on marketing that allowed it to make up sizable market share later.

Adaptability is the name of the game. You must sense your customers' problems and find ways to address them. You must find potential customers with new problems, and find new goods and services, and processes to deliver them. You must find internal processes that do a better job of delivering today's goods and services.

When an organization actively anticipates problems and keeps abreast of new improvement methods, it demonstrates skills in the process of problem finding. When it develops timely solutions, it demonstrates skills in the process of problem solving. And when it willingly and rapidly accepts and implements new solutions, it demonstrates skills in the process of solution implementation. What drives problem finding and solving, and solution implementation—the process of deliberate change making—is creativity, roughly synonymous with adaptability.

CREATIVITY: THE KEY TO MAKING CHANGE

So what is creativity and what makes it such a vital part of the change-making process? The definition of creativity varies depending on who's talking. Some say creativity is independence, the ability to do the things you'd like to do. Many people associate creativity with a chameleon-like ability to change with a changing environment. To some, creativity is what lies behind longevity and endurance—the secret to the cockroach's staying power over millions of years. For those who believe there's nothing new under the sun, creativity is the ability to rearrange existing variables into new combinations. To others, creativity is the act of 'creating' or making something brand-new. Some believe creativity is a bolt from the blue, something that appears unexpectedly in a flash of insight. Others believe creativity results only from lengthy painstaking work, like the process of trial and error endured by the Wright brothers in making the first airplane (Thomas Edison once said that creativity is 99 per cent perspiration and 1 per cent inspiration.)

However you define it, the good news is that all of us *are* creative. Creativity is an inborn human faculty, one that we can nourish, cultivate and raise to extraordinary heights in virtually anything we try. Creativity is as much a part of you as your arms and legs. What matters is not what you call it but how you use it. As children, we allowed our creativity to flourish. We let our imaginations flow. We continually created new ideas and things. We delighted our parents with our freshness.

The bad news is that adults often worry that the development of their children's imagination might go too far. Because we value practicality, we are encouraged to exercise greater judgment and logic at the expense of imagination. By the time we become adults, we're armed with plenty of judgment and logic but precious little imagination. What's the problem with that? Anything we do, either alone or with others, is based on established customs, precedents, and historical and current practices. Without such precedents, however, new challenges leave us stumbling in the dark, lacking the light that imagination can bring.

While scientific research on creativity is wide-ranging, diverse and difficult to integrate, we can draw a few broad conclusions about this faculty:

- Creativity is not a gift for a chosen few. Virtually everyone is born with creativity and uses it extensively during childhood.
- While we don't all have the same amount or type of creativity, we have substantially more of it than we use. Most adults use no more than a fraction, perhaps 10 per cent, of their natural creativity each day.
- Creativity has little connection to IQ, sex, age or any other demographic factors.
- Most people can tap into more of their natural creativity by learning a few basic process skills—and by using these skills deliberately to 'uncondition' themselves.

HOW WE SUPPRESS OUR NATURAL CREATIVITY

Most of us undergo a conditioning process as we mature that suppresses our creativity (Figure 1-3). Our greatest learning and creativity spurt occurs between birth and age five (1). During this period, we question, experiment, explore, welcome new experiences, say what we think, and invent all kinds of ideas without fear of negative judgment or ridicule. The central question in our vocabulary becomes 'why.' Instead of making assumptions, we seek facts in order to understand and to formulate relationships.

Later, we begin to spend more time in the outside world where things we say and do are no longer always well-accepted (2). Other children, teachers and adults may ridicule our ideas if they fail to 'make sense' or are not 'what was expected.' We begin to make mental notes to take more care in what we say and do. We begin to prejudge what might be more acceptable, and shape our thoughts and ideas accordingly. Why risk giving the 'wrong' answer in class when only the 'correct' answer is rewarded?

Peer pressure to conform reaches its height during high school (3). Pity the 'oddball' who belongs to no particular group or who enjoys any activity viewed as 'different.' Why stand out if it means sacrificing our sense of belonging? During later high school years, the name of the game becomes not what we learn but what grade we get (4). The fun of learning becomes secondary to high marks, particularly if we want to impress a future potential employer or enter college or university.

In college, the game becomes one of 'psyche out the professor' (5). Because we believe that getting the grade is the ticket to a career, we concentrate on finding out what material is likely to be 'on the exam' and reviewing previous examinations in an attempt to predict this year's questions.

The questions become even more refined as we reach adulthood and the working world (6). The game here is called 'tell me what you want me to do and I'll do it.' We ask questions like: 'How do you get ahead around here?'... 'What does the boss want?'... 'Why doesn't someone tell me exactly what I'm supposed

Fig. 1.3 The conditioning process: how use of creativity is suppressed

to do?'... 'What can I get away with not doing?' By the time we become adults, we have become skilled in evaluating, analyzing and limiting the number of ideas and options, to the virtual exclusion of imagining more ideas and options.

We suppress our creativity in three major ways: by our attitudes, by our behaviors, and by our thought processes. Let's describe these three mechanisms by discussing learned fears, beliefs or values commonly encountered under each.

How our attitudes suppress creativity
(Figure 1.4)

- For many of us, the primary mission in life is to avoid being labeled an outsider. In an organization, this desire surfaces most obviously in meetings. Instead of trying to introduce fresh points of view, people do their best to go along with the group or the boss—hardly a recipe for original creative thinking. While collaboration is important in good problem solving, if we try too hard to get along merely for the sake of co-operation, we may not share enough new facts and points of view.

- Many people feel the need to account for their actions every waking minute of the day. Visualizing the future or playing with ideas that hold out no immediate payoff is considered a waste of time. But most of the 'great ideas' people, including inventors and problem solvers, spend a lot of time doing just that.

- We want to be seen as practical and economical at all costs. Yet people who are overly practical often exercise judgment too quickly, discarding less than perfect ideas rather than building on them.

- We worry about expressing doubt or ignorance, being too inquisitive, or asking 'why' about things that everyone accepts. We have been taught to be polite, to not rock the boat, and to accept things without question out of fear that others might view doubt as a personal attack. We don't know how to ask 'why' without placing others on the defensive.

1　We try too hard to get along with others instead of trying to introduce fresh facts and points of view.

2　We feel a need to account for all our actions instead of visualizing the future or playing with ideas.

3　Wishing to be seen as practical and economical, we often judge less than perfect ideas too quickly.

4　We worry about expressing doubt or ignorance, being too inquisitive, or asking 'Why?'.

5　We favour the adversarial approach to making decisions and resolving issues.

6　We desire the safety of the known and familiar instead of venturing new ideas.

7　Because we know too much about our work, we often squelch open-minded consideration of new ideas.

8　Reluctant to admit that others' ideas are better than our own, we reject attempts to improve our ideas.

9　We are unable to build on imperfect ideas.

Fig. 1.4 How our attitudes suppress creativity

- We have learned that the adversarial approach is the right way to make decisions and resolve issues. Think of the adversarial nature of the courtroom, the contract negotiating session, and the political arena. Developing a good solution becomes secondary to winning the battle. But we need creativity to tackle complex issues—we need creativity to determine the right problems and the right solutions, not how to win at all costs.

- Many people desire the safety of the known and familiar. New things are strange to us. Our discomfort prevents us from exploring potential solutions. For some people, pioneering is synonymous with gambling. How can you maintain security by doing something different? As a pioneer, you might fall flat on your face. But any new idea presents a growth opportunity. You'll venture few new ideas if you're afraid of growing.

- Sometimes we know too much about our work. Granted, if we don't know enough, then we cannot do our jobs well. But too much knowledge can squelch open-minded consideration of ideas. It's often the novice who tries a new idea without knowing why it can't work and discovers something completely unexpected in the process. Think of the Wright brothers. They were bicycle mechanics, not physicists, not mathematicians. What they brought to the untried notion of manned flight was untried knowledge. The leading mathematicians of the day were still trying to prove manned flight was impossible even as the Wright brothers were getting their craft off the ground.

- We don't want to admit that others might have better ideas than our own. So we reject attempts to improve or build on our ideas. Accepting an improvement would be like admitting that our original idea was wrong.

- Too often, we have to have a 'perfect' idea or we won't go ahead. We are unable to expand and build on earlier imperfect ideas.

How our behaviors suppress creativity
(Figure 1.5)

- Because we fear appearing foolish, our primary goal is to avoid making mistakes and looking bad. When we attend a meeting, we fear ridicule and are unwilling to chance saying what we are thinking—even if that thought might be a great idea.

- Sometimes we hesitate to share information or venture new ideas because we distrust others. Will they somehow use our suggestions against us, or take credit for our ideas? By holding back, we stifle our own creativity and that of others.

- We try to achieve success too quickly. Instead of looking objectively at a problem, we're drawn to the fast track. We go with the first solution that comes to mind—the 'ready, fire, aim' approach. Rather than solve the real

1 Because we fear appearing foolish, we do anything to avoid making mistakes and looking bad.

2 Our distrust of others' motives makes us hesitant about sharing information or venturing new ideas.

3 Rather than solve the 'real' problem, we go with the first available solution and fail to uncover better possibilities.

4 Believing there is one right answer to any problem, we are content to stop with a workable solution.

5 We try to solve a problem immediately; we lack the confidence to let the problem incubate for a time.

6 We feel compelled to solve a problem directly instead of taking apparently off-course detours.

7 After finding a workable solution, we fail to drive the problem solving process through to implementation.

8 We are too quick to assume that something cannot be done or that a problem cannot be solved.

Fig. 1.5 How our behaviors suppress creativity

problem, we go for the quick, feel-good answer. We fail to clarify and uncover possibilities that might take a little more time to implement but that may be more productive.

- Believing that there is only one right answer to any problem, we are often content to stop after finding one workable solution. Thus, we miss the chance to come up with better solutions.
- People often become uptight when they face unfamiliar problems. They feel that, if they don't solve the problem immediately, they have somehow failed. Often, when you set aside a problem for a few days, relax and let it 'incubate,' a solution pops up when you least expect it. A part of your subconscious works on the problem without your awareness. Studies show that, if you let your inner mind take over, you learn and solve problems up to 50 times more quickly. Top athletes master this skill: no matter how tense the game, they are able to relax. They know that if they 'think too much,' they will not succeed.
- Many people feel they have to plow straight ahead on a problem rather than take detours that appear to divert them from their target. Sometimes you have to follow the road and let it show you where you were meant to end up.
- Sometimes we think we're finished problem solving when we find a solution we think will work. But the real test of creativity comes when it's time to

drive the process through to implementation. Some of your greatest creativity comes out only at the implementation stage, when you discover things you hadn't considered that require you to modify your solution.

- Once we prematurely assume that something can't be done or that a problem can't be solved, we shut down our own creativity and the creativity of those around us. All that's left is to prove yourself right. However, making the opposite assumption immediately improves your chances. Research shows that, if you set your sights high enough and visualize a successful solution, you're bound to succeed. Avoid negative attitudes toward problems at all costs.

How our thought processes suppress creativity
(Figure 1.6)

- When evaluating a new idea, we often rely too heavily on our mental processes instead of physically trying out the idea. The two methods must be balanced. Our attitude toward something often changes when we try it (recall the old phrase, 'Try it, you'll like it'). When we experience a new idea, we often discover unexpected insights that permit us to develop the idea further or even change it. Sometimes we even find a new opportunity to try out an entirely different idea. Too often, we fear trying out a new idea because we mentally judge it as not perfect. We wait for a better idea to come along—a wait that sometimes turns into procrastination—when we could be making progress, experiencing the idea, and working with it to see where it leads. The real purpose of trying out a new idea is not so much to test and discard it, but to learn something in the process. Our experience base immediately broadens, allowing us to view other opportunities and ideas in a new light.
- Rather than strive for a clear interpretation of the facts, we often make assumptions about people and situations based on preconceived ideas, or categorize based on experience and hearsay. Better to leave aside assumptions, and start with the facts. Charles Kettering, former chief of research for General Motors in Detroit, Mich., and inventor of the automobile self-starter and the electric cash register, once said, 'It's amazing what people can do if they start out without preconceived notions.'
- We are often inflexible and rely too much on our own biased view of the world. This mental rigidity precludes creative solutions.
- In problem solving, we are often unable to isolate the underlying key facts from apparent symptoms, or separate cause from effect. Beware assuming that you 'already know the real problem.' Upon hearing news, our usual reaction is to quickly attribute the event to some cause. The creative process requires us to defer judgment, to take the time to get more facts, to interpret

1 We rely on thought in evaluating new ideas and not on physically trying out the ideas.

2 Rather than try for a clear interpretation of facts, we make assumptions based on preconceived ideas, or categories based on our experience and hearsay.

3 We are inflexible and rely too much on our biased view of the world.

4 During problem solving we are unable to separate the underlying key facts from the apparent symptoms, or separate cause from effect.

5 We discuss problems in language that we assume others will understand; we use jargon and ambiguous terminology.

6 We take on enormous problems without separating them into smaller components.

7 Hung up on the smaller components of a problem, we lose sight of the larger challenge.

8 If information lacks a clear connection to everyday activities, we prematurely discard it as irrelevant.

9 Believing that problem solving is complicated, we fail to see the obvious.

Fig. 1.6 How our thought processes suppress creativity

them clearly, and to use them to increase our understanding. When we are convinced we know the nature of a problem, we're reluctant to spend adequate time defining it before jumping to solutions.

● People often discuss problems in language that they mistakenly assume their colleagues understand. It's best to define exactly what you mean and take time to be clear when communicating. Avoid jargon or ambiguous terminology. For example, instead of using the vague word 'productivity,' why not use more precise terms like units per hour, defects per thousand, or cost per hundred? Use simple language to clarify, not to confuse. When working in teams, avoid the phrase, 'We all know what we mean.' This is a dead giveaway that different people have different understandings of the facts. Ill-defined facts lead to poorly defined problems and off-target solutions, meaning that problems must be solved again and again.

● Sometimes we make the mistake of trying to 'erase world hunger in two hours.' We take on enormous problems and jump to solutions that we hope will somehow help. We are unable to see the trees for the forest. Often a big fuzzy problem only yields fuzzy solutions. Large complex problems can always be separated into smaller components. Better to create focused solutions to each smaller component in turn.

- Sometimes we get hung up on the components of the problem and lose sight of the forest for the trees. Our view is overly narrow. We don't take the time to investigate the intent behind a challenge we are wrestling with. If we know the intent, we can create solutions to bypass the more narrow challenge. Perhaps I view my challenge as how to build a better mousetrap when my real intent is to get rid of the mice in my house. There are many more ways to eliminate the mice than there are to build a better mousetrap.

- If we fail to see a perfectly clear connection to our day-to-day activities, we prematurely discard information as irrelevant. Making connections between apparently unconnected things is a key to the creative process. Think of Alexander Fleming's discovery of penicillin: rather than discarding experimental material that appeared to have been contaminated, he asked himself how the mold might be used in combating disease. Instead of saying, 'Gee, I can't see what this new information has to do with my work,' why not say, 'I wonder what this new information *might* have to do with my work'? During the creative process, connections can be made between almost anything. By screening out seemingly irrelevant things, we often miss the opportunity to improve our problem solving.

- We often fail to see the obvious. We believe that problem solving should be difficult and that simple information cannot be useful because it's too evident. Children are excellent problem solvers because they see nothing as being too obvious. It is often the fresh, unfettered mind that comes up with the simple, powerful ideas that become solutions to tough problems.

A PROCESS FOR UNLEASHING YOUR CREATIVITY

These attitudes, behaviors and thought processes all suppress your creativity. As I mentioned at the beginning of this chapter, the purpose of this book is to help you learn to unleash your creativity. By learning skills in the creative process—by learning the Simplex process of creative problem solving—you can dramatically improve your personal performance and lead your organization in making change. There's just one major caveat. You have to *want to* dramatically improve your personal performance. Without your commitment, reading this book can't help you.

Maybe you're already involved in some program designed to improve your performance or to improve the performance of your team, department or entire company. The purpose of this book is not to replace these programs but to help you to successfully apply them. What's different about Simplex is that it's a process that concentrates on the 'how's,' not just the 'what's.' Instead of focusing on *what* you're doing (content), the book—and Simplex itself—addresses *how* you're doing it (process).

As its name implies, the Simplex process is a simple way to improve your performance. It embodies such complex management philosophies as total quality management, but it's simple. It draws on such elusive personal qualities as creativity, but it's simple. The key is to understand the distinction between process and content, to learn how to master process and not just content in everyday work and life.

It's a process you can take charge of and one that yields tangible results. You don't have to wait for a company program to give you the luxury of time in order to use Simplex. With enough desire, you can use the process without needing permission and even without anyone knowing you're using it. And you can immediately apply the techniques and ideas to your working life.

It's a process with a consistent, 20-year track record of success. Japan's success in implementing total quality control (TQC) stems from the focus on putting process before content. Here in North America, client companies that have implemented Simplex to help fuel adaptability programs have produced outstanding tangible results. Among its successes: Procter & Gamble saved 6 per cent of sales or $600 million a year in process improvements; Frito-Lay saved $500 million over five years. This book and the process are based on my own practical experience and research findings over the past two decades. The process itself comes under continual scrutiny for ways to improve it.

Just as the Simplex process itself is grounded in simplicity, so this book relies on simple, user-friendly explanations. It's designed for ready, continuous use as a handbook. You can use its chapters or sections immediately without necessarily taking the time to read all of it. We'll address the use of Simplex under seven broad themes.

First, we'll look at the 'big secret' of dramatically improving personal performance: separating process from content.

Then we'll look at the three key challenges you will face: how to better find and solve important personal and corporate problems; how to acquire the process skills you need to find and solve those problems; and how to demonstrate effective leadership throughout the process.

Naturally, the book discusses the Simplex process itself. You will learn the process of finding and solving important personal and corporate problems. The process includes defining your customers' challenges in improving their own performance, inventing creative ideas to foster that improvement, and taking action to help your customers improve.

It will discuss the process skills needed to put Simplex to work, explaining what process skills are and why they're important. It will impart the specific process skills contained in Simplex, and the specific process skills that drive Simplex.

Besides outlining process skills, the book explains how to apply them. You will learn how to use Simplex process skills in personal problem solving, in working more effectively with your colleagues, and in conducting productive meetings.

You'll also learn how to become an effective leader. How to take the lead in identifying and solving important corporate problems? How to define and manage your own critical challenges? How to empower your employees to act on their delegated responsibilities?

While the process is based on simplicity, it won't be implemented without a struggle. We'll talk about how to overcome the struggle—by learning how to take action to improve your own performance, how to improve meetings, how to demonstrate effective use of process skills to others, and how to train others in developing these process skills.

Besides attaining these specific goals, you will learn a number of generic skills, including: improving teamwork; creating effective teams; implementing total quality management correctly; satisfying customers; developing new products and services that meet customers' needs; attracting new customers; defining problems accurately; implementing effective decision-making and problem solving processes; conducting straightforward and usable strategic planning in one-tenth the time; and encouraging colleagues to acquire ownership of your challenges.

2

MAKING INNOVATION
A WAY OF LIFE

'But what if we fail?'

'And another thing,' said Harry, gesturing with his glass of soda water. 'Something else I can't get people to do is to take any kind of risk to improve anything. They'll only sign on to something if they're sure they won't make a mistake. For example, one of our marketing guys told me that people are so afraid of failure that they don't even want their names associated with new products in case they bomb during test marketing.'

'But I thought that was what test marketing was all about,' I said. 'To experiment and even to fail sometimes.'

'Well, that's the way it's supposed to be,' Harry said, nodding his head. 'But it's not the way it really works. The company doesn't seem to know how to reward people for taking chances with new ideas. Of course, it knows how to punish people for making mistakes. That's the problem. With that kind of reward system, people try to sniff out the winners so they can hop on the bandwagon. As soon as they smell a loser, boy, do they run.'

'Product development can't be much fun at all.'

'You're right. And it slows things down a lot too. Test marketing takes forever because managers grab every excuse they can find to put off a decision. It's like, "Well, you know, the overall results are good, but what about these murky results in the southwest. And up north, we're not really sure about the over-40 crowd. Better hold off for another three months while we clear up the grey areas." Seems to me what they're really doing is putting off taking a risk. It's like "paralysis by analysis". I'm sure some of them are even hoping they'll get promoted or reassigned before they have to make the decision, so they can leave it to the next person.' ⇨

'I've heard this kind of story many times,' I said. 'What's even worse than the delays and the indecision is what happens to people's creativity. It's awfully hard for people to be creative when all the company is worried about is avoiding mistakes. There aren't too many organizations out there that know how to encourage innovation. A few stand out, the ones that know how to take the risk of innovating and how to turn failures into lessons for next time. They're the ones that really understand the creative process.' ■

Summary of learnings

✦ *Many of us are plagued by incomplete thinking skills. While we may excel in analytical thinking and problem solving, we often show poor creative thinking and problem solving.*

✦ *We actually demonstrate inadequate creativity, a lack of awareness that creative problem solving requires a process and a set of process skills.*

✦ *This lack of awareness shows up in our organizations in six main ways or 'patterns,' as follows: getting bogged down; trusting myself and my colleagues; parlor discussion or applied action?; wanting a new management style but...; change: fearful or fearless; and sharing the risk.*

✦ *These six patterns relate to three key challenges an individual faces in attempting to improve his or her performance. These challenges are: learning and using the process of organizational creativity; learning critical process skills to effectively implement this process of organizational creativity; and learning to lead your organization in using this process and these process skills.*

✦ *The process of organizational creativity is actually a process of mainstreaming innovation, or continually finding important corporate problems, solving those problems and implementing the solutions.*

✦ *People in innovative organizations foster an environment that emphasizes the importance of innovation, rather than simply measuring, managing and rewarding efficiency.*

✦ *The innovation process consists of four creative problem solving styles: generating, conceptualizing, optimizing and implementing. Each corresponds to a discrete quadrant of the process.*

✦ *All individuals and organizations have peculiar blends of these four problem solving styles, defined as a creative problem solving profile. In order to succeed in innovation, a team requires members who learn to use their differing strengths in all four quadrants to complement one another.*

✦ *The creative problem solving process styles characteristic of each of the four quadrants correspond to two activities carried out in each quadrant. Together these eight activities make up the complete creative problem solving process called Simplex.*

✦ *In order to carry out innovation, individuals and organizations must learn and apply three specific process skills within each quadrant and within each of the eight activities that make up Simplex. These process skills include deferring judgment, active divergence and active convergence.*

✦ *An organization must establish structures and processes that encourage members to use the innovation process and process skills.*

———————————

The main purpose of this book is to show you how to unleash your creativity and thereby dramatically improve your performance. Few of us know how to do so. Unleashing your creativity and that of your organization requires you to meet three critical challenges. The first challenge is to learn and use the process of organizational creativity. The second is to learn critical process skills to effectively implement this process of organizational creativity. The third is to learn how to lead your organization in using this process and these process skills.

TOWARD MORE COMPLETE THINKING

A lack of complete thinking skills is evident in many North American organizations. While individuals in the organization may display excellent analytical thinking and problem solving, they often demonstrate poor creative thinking and problem solving. We're great at making short-term profit decisions—figuring out, for example, how many jobs a new piece of equipment can eliminate. That's the easy part. The hard part is convincing head office not to lay people off but to reassign them into other important positions. When decisions require more than mere mathematical calculations, we do a lot of poor problem solving.

Following are examples of these shortcomings and suggestions for overcoming them using the processes and skills shared in this book. Try to step into the minds of the individuals in these examples. Can you identify with their puzzlement, frustration or elation? Do their experiences remind you of examples from your personal or business life?

HOT NEWS ABOUT HOT WAX

Chemists discover they were working on the wrong problem

Procter & Gamble's fledgling Industrial Division had decided to go after a developing market for automatic car wash products in the early 1970s. In our product development department, a small team of chemists and engineers was rushing to fill out our existing product line. My boss asked me to take over the car wash section to speed up our product development efforts, especially in a floundering 'hot wax' project.

Fortunately for me, I could hardly spell hot wax, let alone profess to be an expert on the product. I rarely took my own car through an automatic wash; as a young engineer, I saved money by washing my car by hand. Why 'fortunately'? Because I knew nothing about hot wax, I was free to display my ignorance, keep an open mind, and ask lots of questions to try to get a handle

on what needed to be done and why the project had bogged down. Thus, my first question was a very simple one: 'What's hot wax?'

The team explained that hot wax was a relatively new but potentially profitable idea. It was a liquid spray applied as an optional service at the end of an automatic car wash. Automatic washes dispense all their products in water-soluble form and, of course, wax doesn't dissolve in water. However, a small competing company had found a way to combine wax from the South American carnauba tree with certain solubilizing ingredients and water, yielding a stable fluid that could be sprayed onto cars. (Carnauba wax already had gained a reputation as the best wax for polishing shoes.) The competitor had received a patent for its product.

When I asked why our team had been bogged down for 18 months, the members explained that they couldn't come up with a combination of carnauba wax, solubilizers and water sufficiently different from the competitor's to avoid violating its patent. The team had tried countless combinations, and had even recruited a carnauba wax supplier to help, without success. What gradually became evident to my outsider's mind was that the team had focused its efforts on a specific challenge: 'How might we develop a carnauba wax formula that does not violate the existing patent?'

Continuing my fact finding, I asked how well the competitor's product performed. To their response that it performed very well, I asked how they knew. They told me that, since the product was a hot seller, it was obviously doing a good job. When I asked what our test methods showed about the product's performance, they replied, 'What test methods?' It turned out that, because the team had been in such a headlong rush to enter the market, it had neglected to develop test methods. The team's understanding of the competing product's performance consisted of a single fact: a lot of people were buying it. I suggested that we quickly broaden our understanding.

Testing the competitor's product during lab simulations, we found no evidence that it adhered to car bodies. We got the same result when we tested the product in the automatic car wash. We had turned up a new fact: our team had been trying for 18 months to duplicate a product that didn't work. Inadequate fact finding had led the team to define its problem too narrowly. We redefined our problem to a broader challenge: 'How might we develop a hot wax product for a spray-on water system that will adhere to car bodies and provide a worthwhile benefit?'

AHA! GREEN STRIPES NOT THE PROBLEM

Product development team goes for refreshment instead

Still at Procter & Gamble, I was asked for help by a product development team also formed at short notice to respond to a competitor's new product. Colgate's green-striped Irish Spring had been the first striped soap bar introduced to North America. With its aggressive advertising campaign emphasizing 'refreshment,' Colgate's new product was finding ready consumer acceptance.

Procter & Gamble worked by the rule that, if we were the second entrant into a new market, we had to demonstrate a product's competitive advantage before we could carry out a market test. When I asked the team what was going wrong, they said that they had been unable to produce a green-striped bar that worked better than Irish Spring in a consumer preference blind test. The team had experimented with several green-striped bars, all of which merely equaled Irish Spring in blind testing. It became evident to me that the team had chosen to define its problem as, 'How might we make a green-striped bar that consumers will prefer over Irish Spring?'

During a creative problem solving meeting, one of our important processes was to develop alternative ways to define our challenge. Repeatedly asking why we wanted to make a green-striped bar that consumers would prefer over Irish Spring yielded many alternative challenges. The flash of inspiration came from an answer posed from a consumer's point of view: 'We want to make a bar that makes people feel more refreshed.' This led us to the new challenge: 'How might we better connote refreshment in a soap bar?'

This less restrictive challenge, which included no mention of green stripes, gave us more room for creative solutions. We broke this problem into three separate components—'How might we better connote refreshment in appearance, shape and odor?'—and then focused our imaginations on solutions. Beginning with the product's appearance, the team members visualized scenes, images and situations that suggested refreshment. One pictured himself at the sea coast. Another imagined sitting on a beach and looking at a blue sky and white clouds. Later, when the team sat back to evaluate its many solutions, these two ideas were selected and combined. The result was a blue- and white-swirled bar with a unique odor and shape. The product quickly achieved market success under the brand name Coast. Solving this problem once it had been properly defined took the team mere hours. By leaping prematurely into solutions, the team had wasted almost six months before coming up with that problem definition.

SMALL DETAIL PAYS OFF

Breakthrough comes from unlikely source

After solving the refreshment bar problem, we still weren't finished. We had to conduct another round of creative problem solving. Before we could sell the new soap formula, we had to overcome a patent problem in the machinery design. There were already no fewer than six worldwide patents restricting how you could blend blue and white soap pastes. We had to find a machine design in order to make our product without infringing on anybody else's technique.

We assembled diverse points of view in a small technical team of engineers, technicians, lawyers and even a few people who were unfamiliar with this technology. After the team had spent some time in fact finding, including discussing sketches of the patented processes, a breakthrough solution soon came from a simple observation by the team member with the least technical knowledge and education. This person noted a small detail that the others had completely overlooked in their search for more complicated solutions. The lesson: it's important to value the input of each member of a team, no matter their level of experience. Sometimes the best ideas come from people unencumbered by 'too much' knowledge, people who can ask the simple questions that the so-called experts overlook.

TURF WARS TERMINATED

Interfunctional team stops bickering over solutions; agrees instead on common problem definition

In a large potato chip manufacturing plant, almost 10 per cent of the employees spent their days manually packing bags of potato chips into cardboard cartons—a costly, mundane task. The company had assigned a team from sales, marketing, engineering, manufacturing and other departments to find a way to automate this packing process. A senior manager who had asked me to help the team said that, over the past year, it had developed several feasible solutions but had been unable to find the 'perfect' solution for everybody. In every case, at least one team member had found the solution unacceptable for his or her particular function.

For example, one excellent possible solution was to lay the bags flat in the carton instead of standing them upright. The technology needed to automate this process was available and affordable. Everyone on the team liked the solution, except for the sales representatives, who strenuously objected that it would reduce their productivity. Most sales transactions were conducted on a cash and carry basis: the salesperson carried the carton into the store, and the store owner paid for the goods only after counting the number of bags in the carton. But if the bags were laid flat, the store owner would take much longer to count them, and the salesperson would be able to make fewer calls per day. The team had dropped the solution and gone on to another, which had prompted fresh objections in turn.

I suggested to the team that, rather than continue to develop and argue over imperfect solutions, we focus on fact finding and problem definition. When we discussed the above option, we agreed on one key fact: by laying the bags flat in the cartons, we could automate the process. We also agreed on the fact that the buyer had to be able to quickly confirm the number of bags. Building on these two facts and remaining open-minded, the team members generated several optional problem definitions, without evaluating them. We were able to reach consensus on a single problem definition: 'How might we lay the bags flat yet still allow the buyer to quickly confirm the number of bags?' Having agreed on this problem definition, the team went on to solve the problem successfully.

Successful teams and individuals are not necessarily the 'smartest' or most 'gifted' or the 'best' problem solvers. More often, they're the ones that take the time to ask good questions and find exciting ways to define their problem before looking for solutions. They invest sufficient time and energy in creating fresh, creative definitions of the problem on which they can agree.

A GOOD IDEA TRASHED

Haste makes waste for household products company that throws out innovative 'pizza box' trash container

A grocery products company was looking for a way to help consumers better handle their household trash. The company felt it could improve upon the polyethylene bags that most people used. A product development team was assigned to the challenge: 'How might we improve the handling of household trash?'

One of several interesting and imaginative solutions that I had helped the team develop was a cardboard product that resembled a pizza box. Pushing its top made the box telescope into a free-standing trash container with several polyethylene bags nested inside it. This stand-alone device eliminated many of the disadvantages of single polyethylene bags. It hid the trash beneath a hinged cardboard top, and was convenient and decorative to boot. When one of the bags was filled, you simply pulled a cord to tie its top and took it out of the box, leaving the next bag ready to use. The team members appeared excited about this idea's possibilities. Before leaving the team for another assignment, I made a mental note to follow up later on its progress.

I asked myself, 'What would be a good way to evaluate this idea?' One possibility would be to make a prototype container for field testing with consumers. To my surprise, when I checked back with the team members, they told me they had dropped the idea. It had been evaluated through a standard company screening technique for new product ideas: the market research department had written a single-paragraph description of the idea and presented it along with several others to a group of consumers. The department had included in its description the fact that the new product would add about 10 cents to the cost of each bag. Asked for comments, consumers said the product sounded like a good idea but that they would probably balk at paying the 10-cent premium for it. Without further consideration, the group had abandoned the idea.

I was disappointed that, after putting so much effort into generating ideas, the group had put so little emphasis on the evaluation process. I said to myself: 'Suppose that back in the days of paper grocery bags that cost nothing, consumers had been asked whether they would buy a new kind of bag for 10 cents each. How many would have said no? Probably many. Under that scenario, we might never have seen polyethylene bags at all. However, given the chance to experience their advantages rather than just read about them, the answer would have been quite different.' I felt convinced that, had the market researchers had been as creative in evaluating this radical idea as the team had been in developing it, people might well have been willing to pay the extra dime and more.

In retrospect, I felt that the team members had been almost afraid of the idea, and had been relieved to find a reason not to proceed with it. Here, creative problem solving had been used to come up with a unique product solution, only to have untested assumptions and lack of imagination kill the product before it ever got a real test. This story demonstrates the importance of keeping an open mind both in developing new ideas and in evaluating them.

I could relate many more examples of inadequate problem solving. You probably could as well. These are actually examples of inadequate creativity. They illustrate lack of awareness of the process and process skills of creative problem solving. We demonstrate these shortcomings in many ways. We wait for problems to be identified for us rather than actively seek them out. Even when a problem has been identified for us, we fail to ask good fact finding questions. We fail to properly define problems or to open-mindedly create and evaluate options. We tackle the wrong problems, dealing instead with mere symptoms or with the first version of the problem that occurs to us. Team members argue over half-baked solutions, protecting turf instead of seeking common ground. In managing projects or solving problems, we argue over trivial details. New ideas hit bottlenecks, and we fail to obtain commitment to implementing them. We ignore common sense and research findings about how to encourage commitment to solutions.

In order to make up for these shortcomings, we need to develop process skills in creative problem solving, including learning the following:

- how to create support, communication and teamwork within and among departments, and with customers and suppliers;
- how to dispel fear of change;
- how to effectively chair, facilitate and participate in effective meetings;
- how to redefine challenges to make everyone a winner;
- how to broaden and transfer ownership of problems;
- how to blend individual differences;
- how to convince employees that all ideas have value;
- how to rely less on your boss and more on your colleagues in solving problems;
- how to build individuals' confidence to encourage them to make valuable improvements;
- how to encourage people to believe in their own creativity;
- how to convince people that individuals can make a difference;
- how to draw out new ideas.

RECURRING PATTERNS THAT SHOW OUR LACK OF PROCESS SKILLS

Individuals and organizations show their lack of awareness and skill in the process of creative problem solving in six patterns, as outlined below (Figure 2-1).

- Getting bogged down
- Trusting myself and my colleagues
- Parlor discussion or applied action?
- Wanting a new management style, but ...
- Change: fearful or fearless?
- Sharing the risk

Fig. 2.1 What happens without a creative process

'Getting bogged down'

The first recurring pattern is 'getting bogged down.' Interfunctional teams formed to tackle a common problem often bog down, for various reasons.

Suppose a team gathers years' worth of test results on a less costly shipping method, but varying conditions make it difficult to obtain conclusive data. Even after it becomes obvious that the team will never pin down all of the method's pros and cons, it continues to churn out data. The team finally defines its main problem not as how to collect more information, but as how to face up to its fear of having to make a recommendation with less than conclusive data.

'Trusting myself and my colleagues'

Another recurring pattern is 'trusting myself and my colleagues.' This one shows up in several ways, as follows:

- 'I fear asking for help as it might be seen as incompetence.'
- 'I don't dare mention my real problem before my fellow managers. That would be displaying weakness.'
- 'I don't think the group's members trust one another enough to share what is really going on.'
- 'What if this solution doesn't work?'
- 'This is too radical—what will headquarters say?'

'Parlor discussion'

A third recurring pattern I call 'parlor discussion or applied action?', which shows up as the following:

- 'What's the point of having a good solution if you are unwilling to implement it?'
- 'Talking about it is one thing; doing it is another.'

'Wanting a new management style, but...'

The fourth pattern I call 'wanting a new management style, but....' For example, a manufacturer's top management team once asked me to demonstrate the Simplex creative problem solving process. During the first stage in the process—problem finding, or anticipating, seeking and sharing opportunities for improvement—the team members were reluctant to venture their problems. Eventually, we were able to select an important recurring problem. An excellent solution emerged only after careful evaluation, something the team had never tried. But as we tried to develop a plan to implement the solution, some members began to back away from it. Under this new solution, non-management employees would have a chance to participate in developing the final solution. This worried the team members, even though they had often stated a desire to push down decision-making to lower levels. After some discussion, they realized they were actually afraid of straying into unfamiliar territory. They preferred the relative safety of the team's admittedly poor but more customary approach.

'Change: fearful or fearless'

Another recurring pattern I call 'change: fearful or fearless,' which appears as follows:

- 'We need more participatory management at all levels of the company.'
- 'We want employees to feel that they are also owners of the company.'
- 'How do we train senior management in this applied creative process and get them to use it on a daily basis?'
- 'I want employee involvement. But if I allow too much leeway for self-management and creativity, I don't know where employees will take it.'
- 'Deep down, we fear getting involved. We fear the unknown. We might not be ready for more innovation.'
- 'I'd rather stick with the unacceptable solution we've accepted for the last five years than take the risk of trying a new idea even though it looks good.'

'Sharing the risk'

The final recurring pattern I call 'sharing the risk,' which shows up as the following:

- 'I'm afraid to report to my manager without having everything pinned down.'
- 'My manager talks a good game about not killing ideas, but he challenges almost everything I say as soon as I've said it. I find myself choosing my words carefully every time we speak and getting ready to defend myself.'
- 'We have taken the problem as far as we can, but will senior management be happy with our results?'
- 'How might we get senior management to share the risk with us?'
- 'Good ideas and projects languish in this system because people feel they have to perfect their idea before they will share their project.'
- 'I don't want to be told I didn't do my homework.'
- 'Unless a senior manager is willing to visibly use this creative thinking process, no one else will.'

YOUR THREE KEY CHALLENGES

We can organize these six patterns under the three challenges mentioned at the beginning of this chapter. These challenges were: to learn and use the process of organizational creativity; to learn critical process skills to effectively implement this process of organizational creativity; to learn how to lead your organization in using this process and these process skills. If you can meet these three challenges, you will find yourself in a new recurring pattern: 'an abundance of solutions.' These solutions can help your company save money, involve employees in generating workable solutions more quickly, select better options for implementation, and zero in on key facts from among large amounts of random information (and misinformation).

Challenge 1: Learning the process

As we discussed in the first chapter, the process of organizational creativity is the process of continually finding important corporate problems, solving those problems, and implementing the solutions. This process is also called mainstreaming innovation. An effective organization goes beyond simply reacting to change or viewing change as an external irritant (Figure 2-2). It continuously improves its existing products and services, develops new products and services, and creates new customers. It continuously improves its internal processes and creates new processes to better deliver these products and services. In other words, the organization mainstreams innovation.

Innovation is not something you can turn on and off. To dramatically improve your performance, you must make it routine. And you must lead your organization in making innovation part of everybody's routine. Thus, your first challenge is to learn and use this process as part of your daily life. In this book, we will outline a set of process skills that any person or organization can use to improve their innovation ability.

Too few of us view innovation as important, and too few organizations mainstream innovation. In fact, many companies regard innovation as an irritant, something that gets in the way of the 'real work' of turning out standard quantities of standard products and achieving the sales, cost and profit goals for this month, this quarter, this year. Their response to greater competition is to cut staff, reduce costs, lower service and, in some cases, lower quality. Too few respond creatively.

Many companies still organize themselves almost entirely around functional efficiency—an easier concept to understand, manage and reward. They encourage employees to achieve narrow parochial goals with little awareness of broader company goals. They give fast-track promotions to employees who achieve hierarchical functional or departmental goals. Employees who perform best across functions (horizontally) to achieve overall company results often go unnoticed. Often organizations don't know how to assess and reward these team players, especially over the short term. In fact, their performance sometimes threatens managers whose own minds work vertically, whose thinking and problem solving works only within functional boundaries.

The syndicated columnist Sydney Harris tells the story of accompanying his friend to a newsstand. The friend greeted the newsman very courteously, but in return received gruff and discourteous service. Accepting the newspaper that was shoved rudely in his direction, the friend of Harris politely smiled and wished the newsman a nice weekend. As the two friends walked down the street, the columnist asked:

'Does he always treat you so rudely?'
'Yes, unfortunately, he does.'
'And are you always so polite and friendly to him?'
'Yes, I am.'
'Why are you so nice to him when he is so unfriendly to you?'
'Because I don't want him to decide how I'm going to act.'

Often we feel at the mercy of others. We let ourselves be angered, embarrassed or depressed by the actions of others or by unexpected events, and respond needlessly. When we do so, we are accepting problems to solve that really belong to others or that are beyond our control. When we pick and choose which problems we want to pursue and reject other problems, we are in control.

Creative problem solving skill begins with the same principle of control. Things are changing and new events are happening all around us. We can cope with change and new problems and challenges either by *reacting*, where we are fearful and at the mercy of change, or by *acting*, by adapting to change and actually taking advantage of it. By turning changing, shifting external events into exciting challenges to be solved and opportunities for improvement, we are being creative, we are changing ourselves, we are in control of our work and our lives. Change and problems are to be expected. They are permanent. If we accept them as such, we can absorb them into our everyday procedures as opportunities waiting to be turned into creative challenges and new ideas and solutions.

Fig. 2.2 Acting versus reacting

How many companies do you know that use innovation as a key performance appraisal criterion in rating managers and other employees? How many include innovation as a top corporate goal? How many have developed measures of their long-term adaptability? The number will likely be small. Yet innovation is hardly a mysterious thing. It can be achieved by any individual or organization. Innovative organizations create an environment that emphasizes the importance of innovation itself. They put in place processes to encourage creativity by hiring, training and rewarding people, departments and divisions for innovative performance.

Long-term thinking often becomes most visible only when a top executive forces a change throughout the organization. Sometimes this change only comes during a knock-down, drag-out fight with senior and middle managers who are unwilling to risk today's security on an uncertain tomorrow. C.J. Pilliod, the former chief executive officer of Goodyear, was profiled in numerous business publications during the late 1970s for his vigorous efforts to 'drag the company kicking, screaming, biting and scratching into the radial tire age.' Only in the nick of time did he succeed in preserving a portion of the company's share of the automobile tire market against the introduction of radials by France's Michelin. Other North American tire companies were not so fortunate.

Even earlier, the North American automobile industry had felt the impact of foreign innovation. The new model lead time in Japan is as low as three years compared to four to five years in North America and as high as seven years in Germany. One reason for this relatively short lead time is that the ratio of engineers per capita in Japan is considerably higher than what it is here; conversely, our ratio of accountants and lawyers per capita is considerably higher than what it is in Japan. As they redesign their cars every few years, the Japanese can react more quickly to market shifts and introduce technology more rapidly. New technology was hardly the hallmark of Japanese cars when they first entered North America. Since then, top car makers in that country have deliberately harnessed and encouraged employees' creativity to gain the edge in quality, customer service, choice and new features.

Datsun exported just over 3,000 vehicles worldwide in 1958, when the 'Japan Economic Yearbook' pinpointed the second-car market as the most likely source of American sales for Japanese cars. The vehicles themselves were utilitarian. But now, Japanese cars are purchased for many more reasons than their utility. In 1950, North America produced 79.4 per cent of the world's cars; by 1981, its share had slipped below 30 per cent.

These successful companies have learned to push innovation from top management through senior and middle management down to the shop floor.

Challenge 2: Getting the process skills you need

It's one thing to know about the innovation process. It's another to master the thinking skills you need to carry out innovation.

The innovation process consists of four parts or quadrants (Figure 2-3). It begins with quadrant 1, the generation of new problems and opportunities. It cycles through quadrant 2, the conceptualization of new, potentially useful ideas, and quadrant 3, the optimization of new solutions. It ends with quadrant 4, the implementation of the new solutions. Each quadrant requires different kinds of thinking and problem solving skills. If an organization hopes to mainstream adaptability or innovation, it must develop and blend employees' natural thinking and problem solving skills in all four quadrants.

In order to better understand these quadrants and to determine your own blend of problem solving skills, fill out the problem solving inventory as in

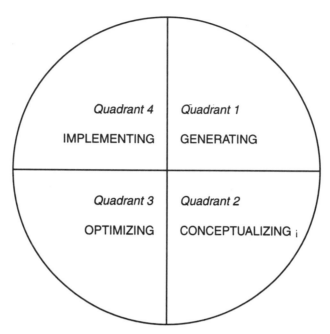

Fig. 2.3 The four quadrants of the innovation process

Figure 2-4. Then follow the instructions to score and interpret your creative problem solving profile. Connect the four points on the grid with curved lines to create your profile (Figure 2-5). If you have identical column scores—an extremely unlikely result—your profile will be a perfect circle. However, your profile is probably skewed toward particular quadrants. The largest of the four quadrants indicates your strongest orientation. The others represent your secondary thinking and problem solving styles. For example, if the area of the circle in quadrant 1 is larger than in the other three, you are oriented toward generating; if quadrant 2, then conceptualizing; if quadrant 3, then optimizing; and if quadrant 4, then implementing. Here's a description of each quadrant to help you further interpret and define your blend.

Generating

Generating involves getting the innovation process rolling. Generative thinking involves gathering information through direct experience, questioning, imagining possibilities, sensing new problems and opportunities, and viewing situations from different perspectives. People and organizations strong in generating skills prefer to come up with options, or diverge, rather than evaluate and select, or converge. They see relevance in almost everything and think of good and bad sides to almost any fact, idea or issue. They dislike becoming too

This inventory is designed to describe your method of problem solving. Give a high rank to those words which best characterise the way you problem-solve and a low rank to the words which are least characteristic of your problem-solving style

You may find it hard to choose the words that best describe your problem-solving style because there are no right or wrong answers. Different characteristics described in the inventory are equally good. The aim of the inventory is to describe how you solve problems, not to evaluate your problem-solving ability.

Instructions:
Eighteen sets of four words are listed horizontally below. In each horizontal set assign a 4 to the word which best characterizes your problem-solving style, a 3 to the word which next best characterizes your problem-solving style, a 2 to the next characteristic word, and a 1 to the word which is least characteristic of you as a problem-solver. Be sure to assign a different number to each of the four words in each horizontal set. Do not make ties.

	Column 1	Column 2	Column 3	Column 4
1	Alert	Poised	Ready	Eager
2	Patient	Diligent	Forceful	Prepared
3	Doing	Childlike	Detached	Realistic
4	Experiencing	Diversifying	Objective	Eliminating
5	Reserved	Serious	Fun-loving	Playful
6	Trial & Error	Alternatives	Pondering	Evaluating
7	Action	Divergence	Abstract	Convergence
8	Direct	Possibilities	Conceptual	Practicalities
9	Involved	Changing Perspectives	Theoretical	Narrowing
10	Quiet	Trustworthy	Irresponsible	Imaginative
11	Implementing	Visualizing	Modelling	Decisive
12	Hands On	Future-oriented	Reading	Detail-oriented
13	Physical	Creating Options	Thinking	Deciding
14	Impersonal	Proud	Hopeful	Fearful
15	Practicing	Transforming	Synthesizing	Choosing
16	Handling	Speculating	Fathoming	Judging
17	Sympathetic	Pragmatic	Emotional	Procrastinating
18	Contact	Novelizing	Impersonal	Making sure

Fig. 2.4 Basadur Creative Problem Solving Profile Inventory

SCORING: In each column, add up all the items except items 1, 2, 5, 10, 14, and 17 to get your column scores.

LEGEND: Column 1 scores indicate the orientation to getting knowledge for solving problems by Experiencing (direct personal involvement).
Column 2 scores indicate the orientation toward using knowledge for solving problems by Ideation (the generation of ideas without judgment).
Column 3 scores indicate the orientation toward getting knowledge for solving problems by Thinking (detached abstract theorizing).
Column 4 scores indicate the orientation toward using knowledge for solving problems by Evaluation (the application of judgment to ideas).

Post your total scores for each column on the appropriate axis below.

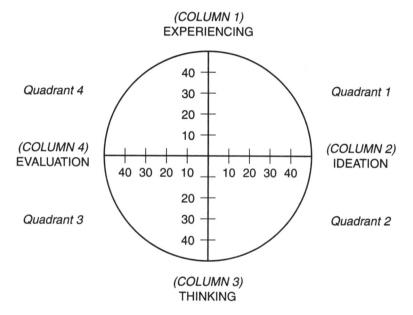

To develop your personal creative problem solving profile, simply connect the 4 points in sequence with 4 curved lines to make a 'warped' circle accordingly. (If you have identical column scores, you will have a perfect circle. This is unlikely.) The quadrant in which your profile is most dominant indicates your strongest orientation. The other quadrants represent secondary styles accordingly. Your profile is your own unique blend of the four quadrants.

Fig. 2.5 Basadur Creative Problem Solving Profile

organized or delegating the complete problem, but are willing to let others take care of the details. They enjoy ambiguity and are hard to pin down. They delight in juggling many new projects simultaneously. Every solution they explore suggests several new problems to be solved. Thinking in this quadrant includes problem finding and fact finding.

Conceptualizing

Conceptualizing keeps the innovation process going. Like generating, it involves divergence. But rather than gaining understanding by direct experience, it favors gaining understanding by abstract thinking. It results in putting new ideas together, discovering insights that help define problems, and creating theoretical models to explain things. People and organizations strong in conceptualizing skills enjoy taking information scattered all over the map from the generator phase and making sense of it. Conceptualizers need to 'understand': to them, a theory must be logically sound and precise. They prefer to proceed only with a clear grasp of a situation and when the problem or main idea is well-defined. They dislike having to prioritize, implement or agonize over poorly understood alternatives. They like to play with ideas and are not overly concerned with moving to action. Thinking in this quadrant includes problem defining and idea finding.

Optimizing

Optimizing moves the innovation process further. Like conceptualizing, it favors gaining understanding by abstract thinking. But rather than diverge, an individual with this thinking style prefers to converge. This results in converting abstract ideas and alternatives into practical solutions and plans. Individuals rely on mentally testing ideas rather than on trying things out. People who favor the optimizing style prefer to create optimal solutions to a few well-defined problems or issues. They prefer to focus on specific problems and sort through large amounts of information to pinpoint 'what's wrong' in a given situation. They are usually confident in their ability to make a sound, logical evaluation and to select the best option or solution to a problem. They often lack patience with ambiguity and dislike 'dreaming' about additional ideas, points of view, or relations among problems. They believe they 'know' what the problem is. Thinking in this quadrant includes idea evaluation and selection, and action planning.

Implementing

Implementing completes the innovation process. Like optimizing, it favors converging. However, it favors learning by direct experience rather than by abstract thinking. This results in getting things done. Individuals rely on trying things out rather than mentally testing them. People and organizations strong in implementing prefer situations in which they must somehow make things work. They do not need complete understanding in order to proceed, and adapt quickly to immediate changing circumstances. When a theory does not appear to fit the facts, they will readily discard it. Others perceive them as enthusiastic about getting the job done, but also as impatient or even pushy as they try to turn plans and ideas into action. They will try as many different approaches as necessary, and follow up or 'bird dog' as needed to ensure that the new procedure will stick. Thinking in this quadrant includes gaining acceptance and implementing.

All individuals and organizations have peculiar blends of these four distinct orientations. In which quadrant is your organization dominant? What blend does it exhibit? How appropriate is this blend? Have you seen your organization's blend change over time or from one situation to another? With rapid changes in markets and technologies, for example, some organizations now have to balance their traditional emphasis on optimizing and implementing with more generating and conceptualizing.

In order to succeed in creative problem solving, a team requires strengths in all four quadrants. Team members must learn to use their differing styles in complementary ways.

For example, generating ideas for new products and methods must start somewhere, with some individuals scanning the environment, picking up data and cues from customers, and suggesting possible opportunities for change and improvement. Thus, the generator raises new information and possibilities—usually not fully developed, but in the form of starting points for new projects. Then the conceptualizer pulls together the facts and idea fragments from the generator phase into well-defined problems and challenges and more clearly developed ideas worth further evaluation. Good conceptualizers give sound structure to fledgling ideas and opportunities. The optimizer then takes these well-defined ideas and finds a practical best solution and well-detailed efficient plans for proceeding. Finally, implementers must carry forward the practical solutions and plans to implement them. This includes convincing colleagues or customers of the worth of the changes, and adapting the solutions and plans to make them fit real-life situations and conditions.

Skills in all four quadrants are equally valuable. Teams must appreciate the importance of all four quadrants and find ways to fit together their members' styles.

This creative problem solving profile inventory is not a personality test. Some companies ask their employees to take personality tests to determine their individual thinking and problem solving styles. However, employees fear the potential uses of the test results. They wonder whether they will be shuffled around or asked to change their personalities if their test shows them to be a poor fit for their job. Constructing a creative problem solving profile is much less formal and less threatening. It is merely a tool to help an individual, team or organization to mainstream innovation in a supportive environment. If the profile is administered through a human resources department, employees should receive a thorough explanation of how and why it works. One major goal is to capitalize on an individual's strengths, thus making his or her work more satisfying. Another goal is to tap resources in all four quadrants to help the individual, team or organization cycle through the complete innovation process.

Thus, each of the four quadrants in the creative problem solving profile is characterized by two activities:

- Generating: problem finding and fact finding
- Conceptualizing: problem definition and idea finding
- Optimizing: idea evaluation and action planning
- Implementing: gaining acceptance and implementation

These eight activities make up the complete Simplex creative problem solving wheel. Whenever we refer in this book to the 'process' you must learn to use in your daily work, or the innovation process you must mainstream, we are referring to this Simplex process (Figure 2-6).

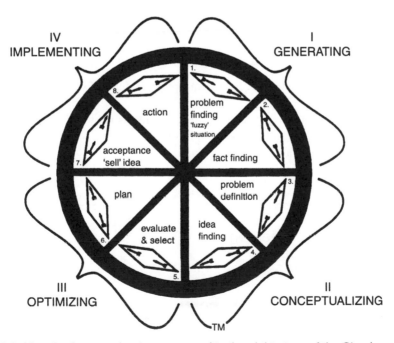

Fig. 2.6 *How the four quadrants correspond to the eight steps of the Simplex innovation process*

In order to make this innovation process work, individuals and organizations must learn and apply several specific process skills within each of the four quadrants and within each of the eight steps. These specific process skills include attitudes, behaviors and thinking skills.

One process skill is deferring judgment (Figure 2-7). Your skill in deferring judgment shows up in several ways, as follows:

- an open-mindedness to new opportunities;
- deferral of action on a problem in order to seek out facts;
- willingness to look for alternative ways to define a problem;
- willingness to try unusual approaches to solve a problem;
- open-mindedness to new solutions.

Another process skill is active divergence. This skill shows up when you demonstrate the following:

- continually seek new opportunities for change and improvement;
- view ambiguous situations as desirable;
- seek potential relationships beyond the known facts;
- show awareness of gaps in your own experience and tolerate situations in which things are less than clear-cut;
- realize that the early stages of innovation require the patience to discover the right questions before seeking the right answers;
- extend yourself to seek out additional possible solutions to problems and additional factors for evaluating solutions beyond the obvious.

The third process skill is active convergence. This skill shows up when you:

- take reasonable risks to proceed on an option instead of waiting for the 'perfect' answer;
- show willingness to help your team reach consensus by viewing differences of opinion as helpful rather than as a hindrance;
- follow through on implementation plans;
- do whatever it takes to ensure successful installation.

- DEFERRAL OF JUDGMENT
- ACTIVE DIVERGENCE
- ACTIVE CONVERGENCE

Fig. 2.7 The three critical process skills

Challenge 3: Demonstrating effective leadership

You may understand the innovation process and the need to mainstream it. You may even learn the process skills required to mainstream innovation and do a good job of executing the process. There's still one more step: you must learn to demonstrate effective leadership in implementing the process and process skills.

Your organization must put in place structures and processes that encourage employees to use the innovation process and their process skills. But most organizations lack such structures and processes. In most organizations, the 'innovation system' can be depicted as an hourglass. The grains of sand collected at the top represent the organization's business challenges. The narrow portion is the bottleneck where business challenges, if solved and implemented, would make the organization's products and services stand out from its competitors'. How to 'widen the neck' or ensure that enough breakthrough ideas get through becomes the challenge.

In order to take the lead, and thereby dramatically improve your performance, you must gain the commitment of fellow employees to help you widen the neck in the hourglass. Leading by example, you must encourage your organization to challenge employees to identify breakthrough opportunities in the top of the hourglass. Those employees must then be encouraged to concentrate on implementing solutions for these opportunities, resulting in breakthrough innovations. You must lubricate the bottleneck by educating others in the innovation process and process skills. A good way to begin is to involve other employees in finding opportunities. The next step is to involve your customers and suppliers as business partners in finding new challenges. Then you must seek out new customers and business partners, and involve them in turn in converting mutual challenges into breakthrough innovations.

Now instead of the hourglass, imagine a wheel. Its shape is a symbol for the continuous process of generating and selecting breakthrough challenges, conceptualizing new ideas, optimizing new solutions, and implementing new products, services and procedures. Circling around the wheel—following the Simplex creative problem solving innovation process—takes you forward to generating yet more new opportunities. You must learn from your actions and reinvest what you've learned into discovering new breakthrough challenges. You must mainstream innovation.

3

THE BIG SECRET: SEPARATING PROCESS FROM CONTENT

Progress gets lip service

It looked like the in-flight movie was going to be a real yawner. I turned back to my seatmate and said, 'So what do you do, Harry?'

'Well, my business cards say head of merchandise planning,' he said. 'But I like to think it's a bit more than that. Too bad other people don't.'

'What do you mean?'

'In our group, we tend to think of ourselves as part of the company's larger marketing team,' he said, spreading his hands in front of him to emphasize the point. 'We're not just the merchandise planning group, we're a support service for the other marketing groups. In fact, just recently we thought there were some real opportunities for improving how we work with these other groups. So I arranged for a meeting involving my people and theirs. We even included our outside advertising agency.'

'So what happened?'

Harry nodded. 'Well, we got some really good business solutions and recommendations out of it. What I thought was even more important was that we turned up a lot of good problems that get in the way of our working together effectively. We can always come up with good solutions, that's the easy part. The hard part is identifying what the real problems are and then being willing to do something about them. The trouble is, nobody's following up now on any of those good problems.'

'Why not?'

'What seemed like good problems to me just didn't seem so important to the other groups,' Harry said. 'Either that, or they just weren't willing to recognize that the problems even exist. They'd say things like, "These are minor problems. We have more important things to deal with, making plan, fending off the regulators, that kind of thing." From my point of view, they're stuck in the trenches.'

'Tell me more.'

'Seems to me that if we have problems in how we work together, then it's a question of process, and it's more important and fundamental to tend to these problems than to the daily nitty-gritty. In fact, I'll bet that if we could tighten up our processes—really work hard at working together—a lot of these other problems would just blow away. That was the whole point of the meeting. But these people feel they don't have the time themselves to iron out the kinks in our procedures. And they're unwilling to hand off any of the recommendations to their subordinates. Maybe it was my fault for not briefing them well enough on what exactly I wanted to accomplish. But I don't think that's the issue. I can't count the number of times we've gone to them with ideas and initiatives to improve our procedures and processes. But every time, they either ignore us or just pay lip service to the ideas. It seems like, if they can't see an instant payoff, they can't be bothered.' ■

Summary of learnings

✦ *To distinguish yourself from the pack, you must understand the crucial difference between content—'what' you're doing—and process—'how' you're doing it.*

✦ *Quality results = Content + process + process skills*

✦ *Simplex is a learnable technology for managing process in your job and in your organization.*

✦ *Managing process using Simplex is synonymous with innovating.*

✦ *Just as organizations created formal R&D departments to mainstream innovation for their products, organizations must now formally mainstream innovation for their processes. When every member's job includes innovating, then innovation has been mainstreamed.*

The main purpose of this book is to show you how to unleash your creative process and thereby dramatically improve your performance. In the previous chapter, we identified the three main challenges you will face in doing so. The first challenge is to learn to continuously find and solve important problems—the process of creativity you can use to mainstream innovation. The second challenge is to acquire the process skills you need in order to mainstream innovation. The third challenge is to learn how to demonstrate effective leadership in mainstreaming innovation—in your own work and in leading the organization. In this chapter, we will reveal what I call 'the big secret' that you must master in order to meet these challenges.

When you concentrate on continuously finding and solving important problems, you concentrate on process. Most of us, however, ignore process and focus only on content. Simply defined, content is *what* you're doing, and process is *how* you're doing it. When you focus all of your attention on content, you achieve no better than mediocre results. In order to distinguish yourself from the pack, you must understand the crucial difference between content and process, and learn to focus on both.

HOW TO DISTINGUISH PROCESS FROM CONTENT

How to distinguish process from content? Let's take an example from an automobile assembly plant. A good company will put a lot of thought into the elements of an efficient and effective assembly line. The assembly line itself is

how (*the process*) all the parts (*the content*) are put together to make the automobile (*the result*). If the parts are flawed, or if the workers lack the technical knowledge to run the machines, the result will be poor quality. If the line itself (*the process*) is flawed, the result will again be lower quality (Figure 3-1).

Perhaps both the parts and technology, and the assembly line, are high quality. But if the assembly line workers and their managers lack teamwork skills (*process skills*), the result will be the same: a poor-quality automobile (Figure 3-2). What you need for a high-quality result is a combination of good content, a good process, and good process skills (Figure 3-3). We can express this idea as the quality results equation (Figure 3-4).

Similarly, if the plant managers focus only on content and lack skills in managing process, poor quality will result. It is not enough, for example, for managers to concentrate only on the number of cars produced and the associated costs. If they neglect to maintain and upgrade the auto assembly process, and neglect to develop their skills in co-operating with their fellow managers, employees, customers and suppliers (*their process skills*), what will result are poor-quality cars and poor sales and low profits. When the managers pay equal attention to maintaining quality parts, machinery and technical skills, creating and maintaining efficient assembly lines, and ensuring that people are motivated and co-operative, then they are managing both content and process.

For world-class managers, in this assembly line or anywhere else, today's quality results are never good enough. These managers strive to improve both

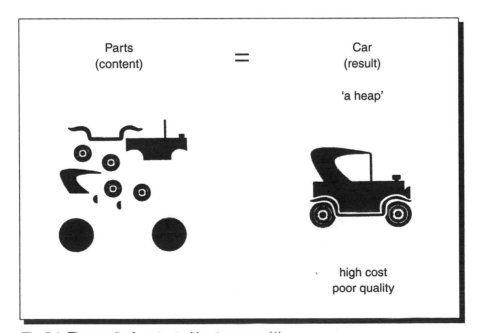

Parts (content) = Car (result)

'a heap'

high cost
poor quality

Fig. 3.1 The result of content without process (1)

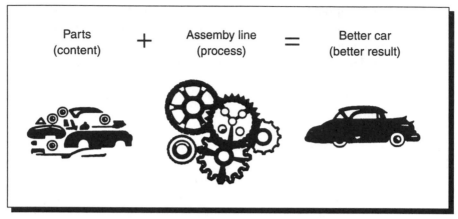

Parts
(content) + Assemby line
(process) = Better car
(better result)

Fig. 3.2 *The result of content plus process (1)*

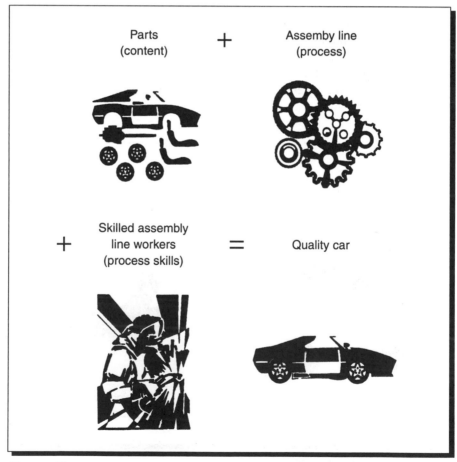

Parts
(content) + Assemby line
(process)

+ Skilled assembly
line workers
(process skills) = Quality car

Fig. 3.3 *The result of content plus process plus process skills (1)*

> **Quality Results = Content + Process + Process Skills**

Fig. 3.4 The quality results equation

content and process throughout the organization in order to continuously improve the quality of its results. They make the effort to interact with customers to unearth new or hidden problems and to invent new products and procedures to solve them.

PROCESS, NOT JUST CONTENT

Workers motivated by opportunity to spread creative wings

Another example of managing process and content comes from Japanese suggestion systems. Measured by numbers alone, these systems are impressive, yielding an average of eight implemented suggestions per employee per month. But their main purpose bears little relation to the content of the suggestions. Instead, the main purpose of these suggestion systems is to institute a process of continual problem finding, problem solving and solution implementation.

These organizations have learned that a continuous creativity process fosters motivated, committed people who enjoy finding flaws in the way they do their jobs. To these employees, the flaws are 'golden eggs,' or opportunities for creative improvement and innovation. Not only do these companies obtain an automatic, continuous flow of new products and better processes through creativity, but they also gain higher motivation and commitment, and team interaction. The results: higher quality, lower cost, and greater output of products and services.

The key to the systems is that, by deliberately mainstreaming innovation as a process, the organizations simply allow the desired quality results to fall into place. By contrast, most organizations focus only on content. The latter introduce employee suggestion systems with only one purpose in mind: obtaining immediate cost savings and new products. Small wonder that North American organizations receive no more than two suggestions per person per year.

These world-class Japanese organizations understand that in order to generate a quality result, they have to focus on the process required to deliver that result. They don't need to see evidence of bottom-line benefits springing directly from every suggestion. In most cases, their suggestion ideas are relatively small in scope and only minimally affect corporate results. But if people engage in a process of continually generating new ideas—and build their skills in this process—many small- and large-scale ideas will be implemented in the long run. And engaging in this creative process produces motivated, satisfied team players who work harder on keeping quality up and costs down.

For these Japanese systems, the 'value' of an individual suggestion is not the point. If it were, the Japanese would be managing content alone. In North America, most suggestion systems are justified only if the amount of money saved by an idea outweighs the amount of administration time consumed by the system in implementing it. This is an example of managing content only, not process. The result: only a few 'big' ideas get implemented, as employees learn that all that counts is the content of the idea. The process of generating fresh ideas dries up.

'BURNING THE FURNITURE'

Company forced to re-hire layoffs as higher-priced consultants

Another example of focusing only on content is the annual corporate ritual called 'burning the furniture.' In many organizations, this ritual occurs as year-end approaches. Managers realize that, unless they take drastic measures, they will fall short of their profit projections. To make up the gap, they 'burn the furniture.' They shut down all expenditures—on training, customer service, business development. They install answering machines to replace their receptionists. They load up their customers, moving January's business forward into December. Even if they 'make their numbers,' they have done so at the expense of quality results. Customers voice their irritation, employees feel stressed out, suppliers grumble about unpaid bills, and the managers themselves are unhappy. Their superiors are also unhappy: everyone knows that a price has been paid to make the numbers. The process of good management has been sacrificed again. The frenzied immersion in content has left them behind in next year's race to make plan.

Come January, new 'furniture' must be bought: laid-off employees must be re-hired and new employees trained, replacement customers must be found, and damaged relations with remaining customers must be repaired. This effort costs money and takes time. The reason that so many organizations find themselves having to 'burn the furniture' is that they fail to emphasize management of process throughout the year. As more time passes without attention to process, the organization begins to sense that 'the heat is on.' It becomes more and more difficult for people to focus on process when they are getting behind in their content.

Managing process *and* content in a meeting

Perhaps the simplest way I can explain how process and content can be managed together to achieve quality results is to explain how a meeting should be run. In facilitating a meeting, I begin by explaining that we will be using the eight-step Simplex process to guide us through the meeting toward an action plan. I educate the group on how meeting process differs from meeting content, and the process skills needed to make the meeting process work. I ask the group to define the difference between the words 'process' and 'content.' Somebody usually volunteers the idea that content is *what* you're doing and process is *how* you're doing it. I explain that the success of our meeting will hinge almost entirely on our skills in separating its process from its content (Figures 3-5, 3-6, 3-7).

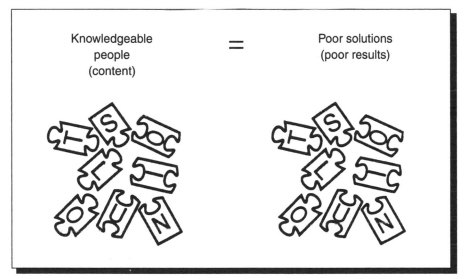

Fig. 3.5 The result of content without process (2)

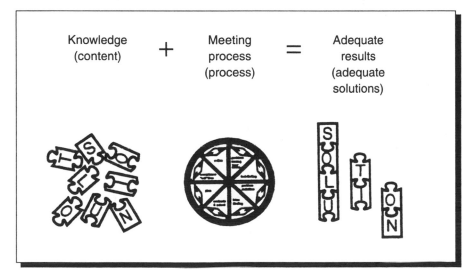

Fig. 3.6 The result of content plus process (2)

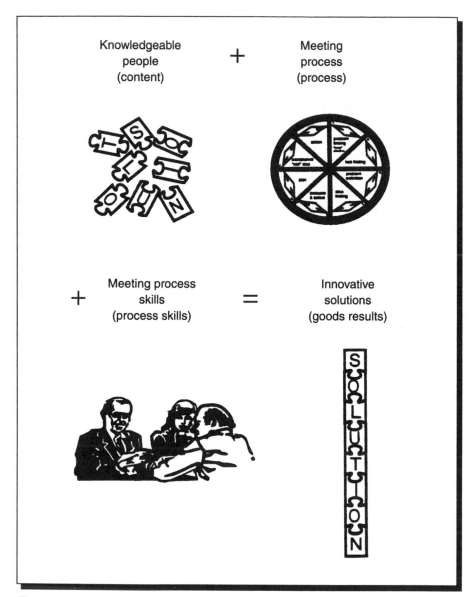

Fig. 3.7 The result of content plus process plus process skills (2)

To illustrate the idea of process versus content, I ask the group to experiment. I define a problem and ask the group members to write down possible solutions. Then I ask for a volunteer to share one solution. As soon as he does so, I begin to think of reasons that the idea will not work and express them out loud: 'But wouldn't that be pretty expensive?'; 'It sounds awfully theoretical, doesn't it?'; 'It sounds like a good idea, but...'; 'I think we tried that idea five years ago, but it didn't work.' The group's reaction is usually dead silence. I explain that my objections were an example of inability to separate process from content.

The point of this experiment is to introduce three process skills: deferral of judgment, active divergence and active convergence. Active divergence enables you to generate options. Active convergence enables you to evaluate options. Deferral of judgment permits you to separate these opposing skills. When everybody uses these skills together, the meeting flows more smoothly.

In my experiment, I could have encouraged the group to build upon the first solution offered. I might have asked them to withhold judgment until a wide variety of options had surfaced. Then I could have encouraged the group to converge upon the best option available. In doing so, I would have displayed an ability to manage the process of problem solving. Instead, I deliberately interrupted, superimposing convergence on divergence. Engrossed in content, I immediately leapt to pointing out the flaws in the potential solution, instead of deferring judgment and continuing the process of divergence. Not only did my inattention to process management shut down the flow of thinking, but it also caused hard feelings that would come back to haunt us later in the meeting. The person I shut down would likely await an opportunity to shut me down in return.

I then explain to the group that my fundamental role during the meeting will be to help them separate process from content. They must do so not only within each of the eight steps of the Simplex process, but also from one step to the next. Group members must avoid skipping in and out of different steps at random. Thus, a fourth process skill called vertical deferral of judgment helps all the participants to work through the Simplex process steps simultaneously (Figure 3-8). Vertical deferral of judgment means avoiding individuals' urge to leapfrog over different steps of the Simplex process. For example, many people lack the patience to fact find, preferring to jump straight to a solution before the problem is well defined. Others jump even further, and want to plan and take action immediately. I explain to the group that my job as facilitator is to ensure that the members move through the process one step at a time, and diverge and converge together within each step.

- Deferral of judgment
- Active divergence
- Active convergence

- Vertical deferral of judgment

Fig. 3.8 The fourth critical process skill

You can apply this Simplex process and process skills to any 'content.' It's a way of helping you think your way through any situation. In a meeting, for example, the process helps the group think its way through the meeting topic by calibrating or synchronizing the participants' thinking. When you recognize the difference between process and content, you realize that every participant brings to the meeting different ways of thinking, problem solving, and interacting with people, and that they themselves are often unaware of these differences. By leading the group through a common process, you avoid a clash of individual processes and prevent the chaos that dooms many meetings.

THE 'BIG SECRET'

Thus, the 'big secret' of this book is the ability to separate process from content—not just in a four-hour meeting but 24 hours a day, in all your dealings with people and in all the problems you are trying to solve. This permits you to learn how to mainstream innovation, the process of finding important corporate problems and getting them solved. By taking the lead in this process, you will deliver quality results for yourself and your organization.

An effective process is often invisible to an onlooker. Think of the major leaguer who makes baseball look easy, or the actor who makes the audience forget that he's only acting. Their years of practice have given them high process skills. Few people will truly understand the process-content dichotomy just through reading about it. You'll still find yourself too eager to jump into content without considering process. As with most things, what you need to do is practise, practise, practise. As you improve, it will become less noticeable to others that you are even using a process.

In the next chapter, we'll discuss the Simplex process in greater detail. Briefly, the process includes the following eight steps:

1 Deliberately seek out problems worth solving (for example, important customer problems).
2 Obtain facts about those problems.
3 Use the facts to define your most important challenges.
4 Think up potential solutions to meet those challenges.
5 Evaluate and select the most promising solutions.
6 Make a plan to implement these solutions (for example, create a new procedure).
7 Gain acceptance of the solution among colleagues.
8 Take action to implement the solution.

A half century ago, few organizations had formal research and development departments. They lacked formal processes for developing new products. Instead, products were developed almost by accident. A salesman might bump into a customer or supplier who expressed a need or an idea. The salesman might casually mention it to someone in the plant, and a new product might result. With the introduction of new technology after the Second World War, organizations began to realize that this haphazard approach to new products (or what they do) would leave them behind. They took steps to mainstream innovation for their products (or content) by creating formal research and development departments.

Decades later, organizations are finding that a haphazard approach to new processes (how they do things) will similarly leave them behind. This time, however, they can't afford to dump continuous process improvement onto a single department in the way that they left new products to the product development department. Instead, they must make continuous process improvement part of everyone's job. The organization must make employees at all levels and in all departments (including owners and stockholders) understand that *how* they get results is as important as *what* particular results they are pursuing.

This book is about managing process—thinking about *how* you are doing things and about ways to continually improve the how. It offers a technology called the Simplex creative problem solving process that will allow you to manage process in your job and in your organization. As a generic change management process, Simplex is the key to innovation and continuous improvement. I hope to help you understand the concept of process, particularly the Simplex process, and the process skills that drive it.

4

SIMPLEX: A PROCESS FOR MAKING INNOVATION A WAY OF LIFE

Short-term gain, long-term pain

Harry was on a roll now. 'Let me tell you more about this instant payoff thing,' he said. 'We've got 15 divisions, each with a general manager. Every one of them is under pressure to make the monthly profit plan. If the market suddenly goes soft and somebody's sales fall 10 or 20 per cent, then the manager has a big problem, because his fixed overhead isn't going away. The way our company works, the manager knows he's going to be evaluated solely on meeting his monthly plan.'

'So what does he do?' I asked.

'Well, we all know there are all kinds of things that affect your bottom line. Some you can do something about, some you can't control. But instead of taking a good look at all the factors that might affect his business and coming up with ideas to smooth out his profits over the long run, the manager jumps into short-term actions. Easy to understand, I guess. After all, he can't be seen to be doing nothing about the situation. You've got to act, right? Do what you can to preserve short-term profits. So they all do the same old thing.'

'Let me guess,' I said. 'Layoffs.'

'Right. First thing he does, he lays off about 25 people. Then he goes back to his plant and realises that he really can't operate with 25 fewer people. So next month he re-hires 15 of them on a contract basis. Of course, because they're on contract, he's actually paying them more now. Not only that, he fails to get all of his best people back because they're the ones who got good jobs somewhere else. So now he's operating at only about 70 per cent efficiency. The truth of the matter is that the cost of labour is just a tiny component of the whole profit picture. Because he didn't fix the real problem, he's actually less profitable in the months to come.'

⇨

I smiled, nodded. 'Strange, isn't it? And yet not so strange. After all, it's the easy way out.'

'It never ceases to amaze me,' Harry said. 'They get rid of people just to be seen to be doing something now.'

'Seems to me that what you need is a process that keeps people from jumping into immediate action on the wrong problem,' I said. 'You see this sort of thing so often. People jump from what I call a fuzzy situation right into action, when they should be taking the time to fact-find and define problems first. They should leave the part about creating solutions and taking action until they've nailed down the real problem.'

Harry shook his head. 'What do you mean—fuzzy situation, fact-find, define problems?'

'You actually said the same things but with different words earlier when you talked about all the factors affecting the bottom line. It's all part of a process for solving problems creatively.' ■

Summary of learnings

✦ *Contrary to the misconception that creativity and problem solving are different things, creativity is actually a problem solving process.*

✦ *Simplex is an innovation process that harnesses creativity. It consists of deliberately finding and solving valuable problems, and implementing workable solutions that yield changes in the form of new and better products, services and procedures.*

✦ *Most people work with only a limited and unconnected set of problem solving tools. By contrast, Simplex is a 'complete' process of creative problem solving with three stages (finding problems, solving problems, implementing solutions) and eight discrete steps. The process provides a framework for using various tools.*

✦ *Simplex is represented as a wheel to reflect the circular, perennial nature of problem solving. Its eight steps include problem finding, fact finding, problem defining, idea finding, evaluating and selecting, action planning, gaining acceptance, and taking action. The 'ninth' step is actually the first step of the next rotation of the wheel.*

In the following chapters, we'll describe a process for mainstreaming innovation and dramatically improving your personal performance. Simplex is a creative process of finding and solving important problems and implementing the solutions. In later chapters, we'll look at the skills you need in order to effectively use this process. First let's look at the process itself.

PROBLEM SOLVING: A CREATIVE PROCESS

You may find it odd to talk about creativity and problem solving in the same breath. For most people, problem solving is a distasteful task that they have to do when something goes wrong. By contrast, most people think of creativity as a pleasant 'task' that results in something new. Yet creativity is actually a problem solving process. Creativity begins when you're inspired to tackle a challenge. It evolves into your breakthrough idea for meeting the challenge. And it ends when you implement your idea.

Think of the many problems that challenge you and your organization every day. You find them in your competition, in government regulation, in interest group pressures, in new technologies, and in your customers' encounters with these same hurdles. Some of these problems are obvious. Others are more difficult to perceive. If you could tackle and uncover more problems and find better solutions, innovation would result in new or better products, services and procedures. Simplex is an innovation process that you can use daily to harness your creativity. It's a process of deliberately and continuously finding and solving valuable problems and implementing workable solutions that result in real changes.

Just as most of us work with a limited view of problem solving, we also use a restricted set of tools to handle problems. You've probably picked up various tools along the way—things like listing pros and cons to decide between alternatives, brainstorming solutions to a problem, and analyzing statistical data. Such techniques are all useful in helping to solve problems. But they are only pieces of a process. Gathering and analyzing statistical data, for example, is an excellent way to find facts to help define problems. But it leaves you short of developing a solution. Brainstorming is a wonderful technique for developing solution ideas once you've defined a problem. But it leaves you short of action and often yields off-target ideas. Listing pros and cons of various solutions is only useful if you have already created alternatives, and it still leaves you short of ways to implement them.

By contrast, Simplex is a *complete* process of creative problem solving. This process consists of three stages: finding problems; developing creative solutions; and implementing your solutions. Each stage requires creativity of a different kind, and all three stages are necessary to allow creativity to work. We divide the stages into eight separate steps that make up sections of a wheel, as in Figure 4-1.

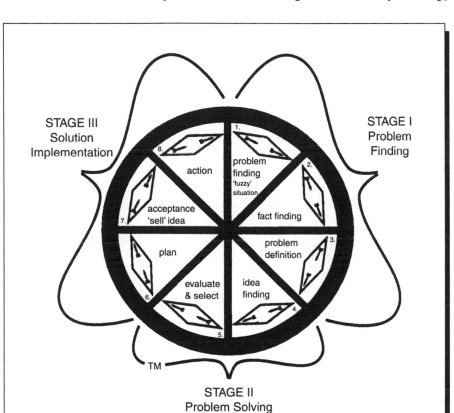

Fig. 4.1 The Simplex wheel: a complete process of creative problem solving

We use a wheel to emphasize the circular nature of problems. Think of how often you've implemented a solution only to have to amend it later. Even when solutions are perfect, they automatically create new problems. The microwave oven, for example, was a wonderful solution to the problem of speeding up food preparation. But consider the problems it created in turn. It required new kinds of cookware and compatible food products. It took up space in kitchens already filled with appliances. And it posed new safety hazards. For making microwave ovens or anything else, problem solving is a never-ending creative process.

EIGHT STEPS TO SOLVING PROBLEMS

Before learning the eight steps of the process in detail, let's take a quick look at what each of them means.

Step 1

Problem finding means sensing, anticipating and seeking out problems, changes, trends, needs and opportunities for improvement, inside and outside the organization. A skilled problem finder takes the initiative and welcomes change and imperfection as a chance to improve and compete. With an attitude of 'constructive discontent' and with little direction, this individual seeks out problems rather than simply reacting to them. He or she is comfortable with 'fuzzy' situations.

Step 2

Fact finding involves gathering information about a fuzzy situation without prematurely judging its relevance. A skilled fact finder avoids unwarranted assumptions, examines a situation from a wide variety of viewpoints, listens to and accepts others' versions of the facts, extends effort to dig out hidden information, and shows no reluctance to ask simple questions. Establishing what is not known is as vital as determining what is known or thought to be known. Only later does he or she worry about choosing the most relevant facts.

Step 3

Problem defining means composing clear, insightful challenges from a few key facts. These challenges reveal directions for solutions. An individual skilled in defining problems can create unusual ways to view them. He or she can broaden the problem's scope by asking why it needs to be solved (the intent) and narrow its scope by asking what stands in the way of solving it (the stumbling block). This individual creates optional ways of formulating the problem until a superior angle has been developed.

Step 4

Idea finding means creating a variety of ways to solve a defined problem. A skilled idea finder is never content with a single good idea but continues to hunt for more. He is able to build on and complete fragments of other ideas. Seemingly radical, even 'impossible,' ideas can be turned into more unusual but workable solutions. A few of the more promising ideas are selected for evaluation and further development into possible solutions.

Step 5

Evaluating and selecting involves converting selected ideas into practical solutions. An individual skilled in evaluation and selection considers plenty of criteria in order to take an unbiased look at the ideas. He or she avoids leaping to conclusions based on a single criterion or on unrelated hidden motives. Interesting but flawed solutions are creatively improved, then re-evaluated.

Step 6

Action planning means creating specific action steps that will lead to successful implementation of a solution. An individual skilled in action planning can see the end result in a specific, concrete way that motivates people to act on the plan.

Step 7

Gaining acceptance means understanding that even the best ideas and plans can be scuttled by resistance to change. Someone skilled in gaining acceptance creates ways to show people how a particular solution benefits them, and how possible problems with the solution can be minimized.

Step 8

Taking action means 'doing' the steps in the action plan, and continually revising and adapting the plan as things change in order to ensure that the solution is successfully implemented. An individual skilled in taking action avoids getting mired in unimportant details and minor roadblocks on the way to implementing the solution. He or she does not fear imperfect solutions, knowing that even perfect solutions can be revised and continuously improved (think of the microwave oven).

Because this change-making process is like a wheel, it actually has a ninth step: the first step of the next rotation. Each solution that you implement automatically changes things. It results in a new array of problems, trends and opportunities for improvement. Thus, we're back to Step 1. Now let's look at each of these eight steps in greater detail.

5

GETTING STARTED: PROBLEM FINDING AND FACT FINDING

'Why didn't you say so?'

The woman in the seat on my right looked up from her book and introduced herself as Alice. 'What you said about fact-finding really hit home,' she said to me. 'So many people waste so much time because they assume too much without even realizing it.'

She was interrupted by the flight attendant serving lunch. After he'd moved down the aisle, Alice proceeded to tell us a story.

'I've been the plant manager of a consumer packaged goods company for quite a while. One of our departments is kind of the training ground for new management hires, and there were two supervisors in there, both fairly inexperienced. They didn't spend a lot of time on the floor, mostly stuck to their cubicles and their numbers. The department had been putting out about 1,700 cases of product per shift. They had decided to try to find a way to get the average up to 2,100 cases. They did some brainstorming, came up with a few ideas, and finally settled on one. Then it was up to one of them, Ed, to go and sell the idea out on the packing line.

'Ed sweated over this for a couple of days, trying to think up ways to make the workers buy in. One day he struck up a conversation with the lead packer. "George," he said, "We've been kicking around some ideas for things you guys might do differently. We want to increase production to 2,100 cases." Before he could say anything else, George said, "You mean you'd like us to make 2,100 cases per shift instead of 1,700?" "That's right," Ed said. Then George said, "Why didn't you say so? We could have made 2,100 cases anytime you wanted. No sweat. I'll tell the others."'

'That's a great story, Alice,' I said. 'What's the main lesson?'

'To me it says you need to do a complete job of fact-finding before you plunge into anything,' she said. 'If these two supervisors had taken the time to talk over some of their goals and ideas with the people on the line, they wouldn't have wasted all that time working on a problem that didn't exist. The facts alone would have told them that all they needed to do was ask the packers for the higher production level. In fact, they solved a problem that had already been solved. That's what you mean by fact-finding, isn't it?'

'That's right,' I said. 'Usually there are all kinds of facts just sitting there waiting for someone to look at them. Often they're residing in the people around us, especially the people on the front lines. All you have to do is ask them. Not only that, but your story shows how important it is to follow a creative process, rather than just jump into solving a problem that you haven't even defined properly.' ■

Summary of learnings

✦ *Although the word 'problem' usually carries simplistic and negative connotations, problems are actually the beginning of the innovation process.*

✦ *Problem finding is taking the initiative to discover problems to solve instead of waiting to react to problems that discover you. Creative individuals set themselves goals and challenges simply for the stimulation of finding good problems to solve.*

✦ *Problem finding can be developed as a skill, using prompter questions for both the organization and the individual.*

✦ *The bridge between finding a problem and clearly defining it is fact finding. Seven fact finding strategies help to remove the 'fuzziness' from a problem: divergently seeking possibly relevant facts; using several viewpoints; being aware of unconscious assumptions; avoiding a negative attitude toward 'problems'; sharing information; having the courage to say what you think; and looking for the truth rather than ways to boost your ego.*

✦ *A number of useful questions help to uncover important facts about a problem. These facts go beyond information you generate from conventional techniques such as quality control histograms, process flow charts and market research questionnaires. The specific technique you use is less important than the process you follow in learning what you can about the fuzzy situation.*

✈ *Answers to these questions should be simple but precise in order to ensure effective fact finding and, hence, an insightful problem definition.*

✈ *Avoid the use of judgment while gathering facts. Then evaluate the facts in order to select the few that provide new insights.*

————————————

W e said earlier that effective individuals, groups and organizations are adaptable. They anticipate problems and opportunities and develop timely solutions. They continually seek out ways to improve their business. They search for changing circumstances that they can turn to advantage. Rather than wait for change, they make change. This is where the Simplex creative problem solving process starts.

STEP 1: Problem finding

A key point here is the meaning of the word 'problem.' Think of the negative words we normally associate with it: crisis, disaster, barrier, bottleneck, trouble, deviation, fear. Our negative perceptions cause us to avoid problems rather than seek them out, or at least to procrastinate in handling them. A negative view of a problem causes us to do a poor job in the next step of the process, fact finding. We will seek only the facts that support our preconceived negative view, leading to inadequate and off-target problem defining, the third step in the process. We're like the residents of Dogpatch in the Li'l Abner comic strip, who were always frightened off by the imminent arrival of Joe Btfsplk, the character who lived under a perpetual dark cloud.

Now let's expand our horizons. Let's think of some positive words associated with 'problems': challenge, goal, objective, opportunity, desire, wish. With imagination, skill and open-mindedness, we can often turn apparent negatives into opportunities for improvement. We must keep an open mind toward 'fuzzy situations' as the first inklings of barely sensed problems and opportunities. Remaining neutral about 'problems' leaves us room to define them in creative, challenging and productive ways.

Positive or negative, these words can all represent the same thing—new situations that you can turn to advantage. Written in Chinese, the word 'crisis' actually consists of two symbols: danger and opportunity. This symbol underscores the idea that there are positives and negatives in any 'problem' (Figures 5-1, 5-2).

LITTLE QUESTIONS THAT CHANGE THE WORLD

You can't solve a problem—or invent a phonograph—without finding a problem first

Some years ago, a Life Magazine cover story told the tale of Edwin Land's invention of the Polaroid camera. Having snapped the last exposure on his film, he suggested to his three-year-old daughter that they take the film for processing so they could see the pictures in about a week's time. Her response was, 'Why do I have to wait a week to see my picture?' Like a flash bulb going off in

Over countless years, the Chinese language has evolved in such a way that the written representation of the word 'crisis' is a synthesis of the symbols for danger and opportunity. This highlights the idea that there are positive and negative aspects in any situation. If we think of problems as fuzzy situations filled with opportunities, we will be more likely to anticipate and seek them out. This cannot help but improve our work and personal lives. We would also do well to remember this Chinese proverb:

> If one does not begin
> with a right attitude,
> there is little hope
> for a right ending.

Fig. 5.1 The Chinese symbol for 'crisis'

his mind, her simple question sparked a challenge that had never occurred to him: 'How might I make a camera that yields instantaneous pictures?' Within about an hour, he had formulated several solutions. And within about four years, he had commercialized a product that has changed our lives. Looking back, the then-chairman of Polaroid said the most important part of the process was not finding the solution itself—the camera—but finding the problem—how to get instantaneous pictures. The moral of the story, in Land's words: 'If you can define a problem, it can be solved.'

Think of Thomas Edison's invention of the phonograph in 1878. Until then, the world had revolved perfectly well without this device. People weren't walking around in distress without it. For whatever reason, Edison took it upon himself to tackle the problem, 'How might I record the human voice?' After sensing the opportunity, it didn't take him long to come up with the solution: a waxed disk. Imagine his own surprise when his first solution actually worked. Observers believe the real creativity in this invention was not the discovery of the solution but the discovery of the problem.

DANGER

OPPORTUNITY

Fig. 5.2 The two parts of the Chinese 'crisis' symbol

Land and Edison demonstrated problem finding skills—the ability to initiate problems to solve instead of waiting for problems to be handed to them. How to get your employees to follow their examples?

Creative individuals often set themselves goals and challenges simply for the stimulation of finding problems to solve. This is the idea behind participatory management—involving people in finding problems to solve for both personal and organizational improvement. Instead of waiting for the boss to explain what to do, employees suggest opportunities for improvement, selling them as new projects or techniques.

Attitudes and motivation are key parts of the creative problem solving process. You can't solve a problem until you find it—and finding problems requires motivation and a can-do attitude. Motivating workers to delight in discovering problems and possible improvements, to be 'constructively discontented' with the status quo, to look for 'golden eggs,' is important in training people to use their inborn creativity.

YOU CAN BE A BETTER PROBLEM FINDER

You can develop your ability to sense problems and to seek out opportunities just as you can hone any other skill. Many organizations have found the following prompter questions useful tools for triggering the process of finding problems. Can you add any more specific questions for your organization or yourself?

First, let's look at the present.

Organizational problem finding: Sensing the present

- What are your customers' major gripes and difficulties?
- What opportunities are your customers missing?
- What potential customers could you help if you only knew them better?
- What small problems for your department or organization could grow into big ones?
- What barriers impede communications within your organization?
- How could you improve quality?
- What are your most difficult people problems?
- What goals do you fail to attain year after year?
- What is likely to cause your next crisis?
- What issues do you think people are afraid to bring up?
- What makes it hard to plan?
- What problems experienced by other organizations do you want to avoid?
- What competitors' ideas could your organization adapt?

Now let's look at the future.

Organizational problem finding: Anticipating the future

- What changes, issues, problems and opportunities do you visualize three years down the road?
- As your organization's information needs increase, what new problems and issues will arise?

- Who might feel threatened by the idea of sharing information within your organization?
- What training do people need to meet challenges two years from now?
- What information would simplify your job?
- What customer needs will increase in the next three years? five years? 10 years?
- What will be your customers' biggest challenges over the next three years? five years? 10 years?
- What would you most like to see happen in the next three years?
- What new pressures might you encounter from your customers? the community? politicians? the media?
- What might cause your valued employees to leave?

Now let's look at your personal life.

Personal problem finding

- What existing risks and uncertainties do you face?
- What risks and uncertainties might you face in the future?
- What changes do you feel you need to make?
- With whom do you want to get along better?
- What would make you happy or proud?
- What makes you worry?
- What takes too much time?
- What has bothered you recently?
- What would you like to know more about?
- What goals have been lying fallow?

You must develop the habit of continuously asking yourself these questions. The best time to ask them is probably when things seem to be going perfectly well. What will distinguish you and your organization from the rest is your ability to continuously innovate and your refusal to be satisfied with the status quo.

SCIENTISTS IN SALES?

Company's 'sell , then create' approach ensures that researchers keep customers in mind

At Japan's electronics giant, Toshiba, I discovered that most engineers and scientists beginning their careers in research and development actually start working in the sales department. This apparently backward approach is designed to teach them the process of problem finding. If these people will spend their working lives creating products to solve customers' problems, then what better start than by learning first-hand about their customers, their needs, their habits and their problems—both visible and hidden? This approach is hardly backward. Rather, it's really the beginning of the process of creative problem solving.

LOOKING FOR GOLDEN EGGS

Seeking problems creates opportunities at this firm

At Nippondenso, a major auto parts supplier, employees are trained and encouraged from day one to find problems, to be discontented with their jobs. Employees write down their 'discontents' and post them for co-workers to read. At Nippondenso and many other Japanese companies, this is actually the start of the creative process called the employee suggestion system. What's important is that the entire suggestion system hinges on problem finding.

STEP 2: Fact Finding

Finding good problems to solve means more than anticipating and sensing opportunities for improvement. Beyond finding your opportunity, you have to uncover and soak up as much information about it as you can. This step is called fact finding.

'On your toes' and with your mind wide open, you must gather unbiased, comprehensive data about your fuzzy situation instead of making the fatal mistake of leaping to solutions. There's a big difference between a fuzzy situation and a well-defined problem. The bridge between the two is called fact finding.

SEVEN STRATEGIES FOR FINDING FACTS

Deferring judgment on the final definition or formulation of the problem, you must exercise seven fundamental fact finding process strategies, as outlined below (Figure 5-3).

Search divergently for possibly relevant facts

Deferring judgment and logic, consider any information that might relate to your fuzzy situation. It's not enough to say, 'I know the facts, let's get on with it.' Push beyond the obvious to get as many bits and pieces of knowledge about the situation as you can. Ask questions, including whatever comes to mind. Assume that whatever you think of is automatically relevant.

Think of the Saturn rocket that launched Apollo missions to the moon during the 1960s. Soon after the rocket left the ground, its first stage dropped

1 Divergently search for possibly relevant facts.
2 Use several viewpoints.
3 Beware assumptions.
4 Avoid a negative attitude toward problems.
5 Share information.
6 Say what you think.
7 Look for the truth, not just ways to boost your ego.

Fig. 5.3 Key fact finding behaviors

off. The second stage took over to lift the rocket higher before falling off in turn. The third stage then propelled the landing craft on a course to its final destination. Becoming aware of a new opportunity or problem is like the first rocket stage. It's enough to get you started, but it's only the beginning. The problem as you first perceive it may not at all resemble the problem as you finally perceive it. Searching for facts about the new opportunity or problem is the second rocket stage, the bridge between the two perceptions. Only by opening your mind to as many potentially relevant facts as possible can you ensure that you will improve, expand and enrich your final perception. (Recall the hot wax story from the preceding chapter.) Ask yourself what other facts might be considered. In what other ways could you view the situation? Who else might have a useful but different perspective?

Use several viewpoints

Each of us sees 'the facts' in a situation through our own biases, filters and acquired knowledge. Group problem solving brings together a variety of viewpoints. Group members will likely provoke each other to seek additional facts and to broaden their view of a problem. How to put yourself in someone else's shoes? Perhaps move around the room to 'view' the problem from a different perspective. Collar someone to share your problem. If you have been viewing the problem at a computer terminal, get out of your chair and visit the shop floor or the customer's location to experience the problem first-hand. Any way you can view a situation from other viewpoints is beneficial.

Beware unconscious assumptions

Failing to recognize unconscious assumptions often hinders fact finding. Assuming we know the nature of a particular problem, we may screen out apparently unrelated facts or take wrong information as fact. Remember from the hot wax story how assumptions can cause delays and waste talent during fact finding.

IS THAT *REALLY* A FACT?

Young engineer turns up 'new' information; offers way to get rail efficiency back on track

Another story vividly illustrates the problem with assumptions. For his first assignment with a railroad company, a recent engineering graduate was asked to find ways to increase efficiency on a major rail service carrying automobiles across the United States. The automobiles were stacked two-high on each of the railroad cars. The engineer's first idea was to stack them three-high, increasing efficiency by half. Suggesting this idea to several senior colleagues, he learned that it was hardly a novel one. But he was told that it was an impractical suggestion: numerous overpasses on the railroad system were so low that the company couldn't stack the cars three-high.

The engineer had two choices. He could simply accept this information and drop the idea, or he could do more fact finding. Rather than assume that the overpasses were too low, he viewed the responses themselves as a fact: 'Several people say that many of our overpasses are too low.' Investigating the company's specification manuals, he found that, among the thousands of overpasses throughout the system, only two were too low for three-high stacking. Armed with this new fact, he defined his problem as: 'How might we stack the cars three-high, and make the two low overpasses compatible?' What had appeared insurmountable facts turned out to be mostly assumptions. The real fact was that the company had to overcome only minor roadblocks in order to realize a great gain.

Avoid a negative attitude toward 'problems'

If you automatically consider a problem a negative thing, then not only does your attitude lower your motivation to tackle it, but it also confines your fact finding. You start looking only for negative facts. Without a complete picture of the facts—negative and positive—your subsequent problem definition will be off the mark (again, recall the hot wax story). No matter how formidable your initial perception of the problem, adopting a 'can-do' attitude helps you open your mind to consider more information and viewpoints. The result might be a new viewpoint, direction or definition that yields novel solutions.

Share information

In order to increase creativity and innovation, individuals and organizations must encourage information-sharing. You can't find and solve problems without the necessary information about your organization and about your place in it. Lack of trust hinders fact finding. People avoid asking questions or volunteering information for fear of getting their wrists slapped or having that information used against them. Lack of trust can even cause people to share misleading facts. They may purposely give their bosses incorrect information, or information twisted to look more positive than it really is. Managers screened from the facts cannot take appropriate action until it's too late. Misdirected fact finding leads to erroneous problem definitions. Good solutions and action plans might be developed, but for the wrong reasons.

Say what you think

If you offer information and ideas only to fit what you think the rest of the group wants to hear, you rob the group of your unique viewpoint. The person who sees things differently from the others is sometimes the one who sees them most clearly. However, the idea of seeing things differently makes some people uncomfortable. Many people second-guess themselves and believe that, if no one else sees the problem as they do, then they must somehow be wrong. In order to define problems accurately, you must overcome this discomfort and encourage everyone's open-minded input.

Look for the truth, not just ways to boost your ego

Work on determining 'what's right,' not 'who's right.' Less preoccupied with defending egos, people can more easily venture different points of view and different facts.

SIX FACT FINDING QUESTIONS

To carry out these seven thinking process strategies, ask the following questions to help uncover important facts about a fuzzy situation (Figure 5-4). Supplement these questions by asking the five W's (who, what, where, when, why) or any other questions that come to mind.

---

1 What do you know, or think you know, about this fuzzy situation?
2 What do you not know about this fuzzy situation (but you'd like to know)?
3 Why is this a problem for you?
4 What have you already thought of or tried?
5 If this problem were to be resolved, what would you have that you don't have now?
6 What might you be assuming that you don't have to assume?

Fig. 5.4 Fact finding questions

What do you know, or think you know, about this fuzzy situation?

Because they hold preconceived ideas about the nature of a problem, people often downplay what they actually know. They may hesitate to offer facts if they're less than 100 per cent sure of them. In fact, you often know more than you think you do. It's important to include anything you think might be relevant.

What do you not know about this fuzzy situation?

This question often produces even more revealing information than the first one, and encourages thinking in new ways. What you don't know about a particular situation can be the most pertinent fact. In our hot wax story, not knowing how well the competitive product worked led to the discovery that the problem was not how to avoid infringing on the carnauba wax patent, but how to come up with a different formula that really worked.

Why is this a problem, especially for you?

Why is this situation important to you personally? What's stopping you from resolving it? The first question aims at your motives for solving the problem and tries to pin down ownership of the problem. You cannot solve problems without some personal connection. The second question helps you understand the problem on a concrete, gut level rather than in the abstract.

What solutions have you already considered or tried?

This question aims to quickly provide as much background information as possible about the problem's current status. You're not interested in starting from scratch, as if the problem had never existed. Untried solutions may be important starting points. Your problem definition might be: 'How might I quickly implement one of these solutions in order to experiment with it?' or 'How might I get my colleagues' support in talking my boss into trying this solution?'

If this problem were resolved, what would be different?

What do you lack that you hope a solution will give you? In answering this fact finding question, be extremely specific. Merely saying, 'I want a solution to my problem,' gets you nowhere, as you have not yet defined the problem. Answering this question with a clear, simple fact helps define the problem. Only then can you identify what steps would be helpful. If you're having difficulty answering this question, try to visualize a successful resolution to the problem, then visualize the steps you would have had to undertake to resolve it. In your mind's eye, what actions did you have to take? What occurred? Who was involved?

What might you be assuming perhaps unnecessarily?

Even without realizing it, people often restrict their thinking by making unwarranted assumptions. Assuming, for example, that your boss won't go for a particular idea, you don't bother sharing it. In fact, he or she might welcome the idea, or even be thinking along similar lines. Because things have been done a certain way in an organization for a long time, people assume that they cannot be changed and don't bother to suggest new ideas. Only by deliberately confronting yourself with this question can you uncover these hidden barriers in your thinking.

There's nothing magical about these six questions. They simply work well and lead to many additional questions. Your organization probably already uses many fact finding techniques, including quality control histograms, process flow charts and market research questionnaires, to name a few. Use these six questions to go beyond the information generated from these techniques and to weave that information into your creative process for mainstreaming innovation. The specific techniques you use are less important than the process you follow in getting as much unbiased information as you can about the fuzzy situation.

For each of these six fact finding questions, state your answers in simple, complete sentences. For example, suppose the fuzzy situation were 'high customer complaints' and the fact finding question were 'What do you know or think you know about this situation?' Simply saying 'turnover' would be a far less useful answer than saying: 'We have so many salespeople leaving the company that we lack experienced people who understand our customers' problems.' Precision in your use of language permits an effective fact finding process, leading to an insightful problem definition.

Furthermore, it's important to convert assumptions into more accurate statements of fact. The statement, 'Mr. Jones does not believe in participative management,' is not actually a fact but simply someone's assumption. You can turn it into a more accurate statement of fact by stating, 'Mr. Jones told me three times last month that he thinks participative management won't work here.' Any reply to any fact finding question should be stated as a fact, even if the reply is simply an opinion, perception or belief.

Avoid using judgment while divergently gathering facts, for two reasons. First, you don't want to begin with a premature assumption about what facts are important or not. Second, you don't want to cut off people at the knees by making them worry about whether or not their 'fact' is worth uttering because they can't decide whether it's an opinion, perception or belief. What's important is to stimulate a flow of information. You'll have plenty of time later for sifting through and picking out the most relevant facts. For example, arguing over whether or not an organization's morale is truly low is a waste of time. Far better to simply state, 'Most of us *perceive* that morale is low,' or, even better, 'Most of us perceive that morale has taken a downturn since we reorganized our division nine months ago.' The latter are clear statements of fact about people's perceptions. A subsequent problem definition might become: 'How might we find out how many other people in our department share this perception about morale?'

In evaluating the facts you've obtained, the idea is to select the few that provide new insights. Sometimes such insights come from 'old' facts that had been neglected or considered too simplistic. Sometimes they come from entirely new facts. Good judgment is important at this early stage in the creative process: unwarranted assumptions or unimportant or irrelevant facts will lead to poor problem definition and, eventually, off-target solutions.

As always, two or more heads are better than one in selecting key facts. Particularly during teamwork, whoever is responsible for implementing a solution must have the opportunity to take part in selecting the key facts in order to ensure not only accuracy but commitment. Team members must be carefully selected at the beginning of a project to ensure that they generate and select only the most relevant facts. Having the most relevant facts in hand provides the foundation for the next step of the process, problem definition.

Don't underestimate the importance of fact finding. It's more difficult than you might think. Effective fact finding can be illustrated by the use of ambiguous pictures. Practise your fact finding skills by uncovering as many different things (at least five) as you can in Figure 5-5.

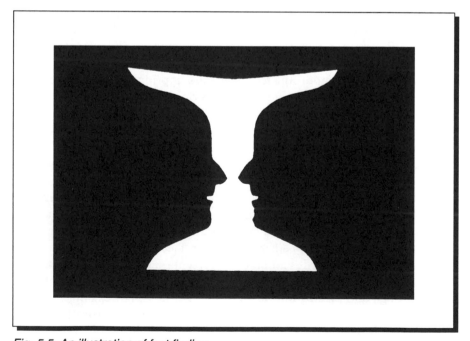

Fig. 5.5 An illustration of fact finding

Perhaps you've already 'seen' this picture before. But have you really seen the whole picture? Perhaps you see a white vase, or the black silhouettes of two people face to face. These are only a small part of this picture. What else do you see? Try to see at least three more things. Look at parts of the picture, top, bottom, left, right. Transpose black and white. Turn it upside down. Do you see any new things, any new facts? Do you see Smokey the Bear? Alfred Hitchcock and his brother? the whale's tail? the Texas longhorn steer? the keyhole? the seal? the sombrero? the coat hanger? the two people pouting? the two cars parked back to back, bumper to bumper (Figure 5-6)?

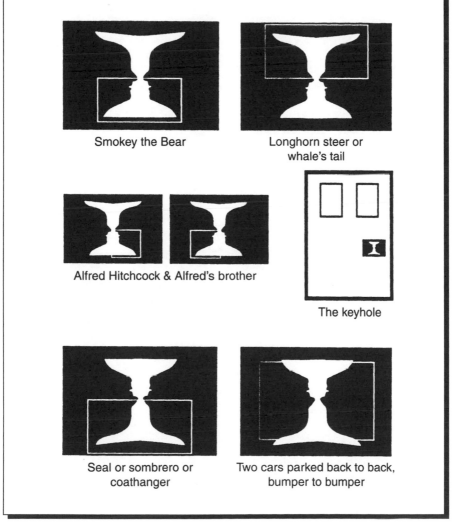

Smokey the Bear

Longhorn steer or whale's tail

Alfred Hitchcock & Alfred's brother

The keyhole

Seal or sombrero or coathanger

Two cars parked back to back, bumper to bumper

Fig. 5.6 Fact finding extended

Many people find these new facts after they've received training in fact finding skills. You will get an opportunity to practise your own fact finding process skills in a subsequent chapter. For now, let me leave you with two thoughts: fact finding is a vital part of the creative process; and most of us need to develop our skills in the fact finding process rather than take them for granted.

6

IF YOU DEFINE IT, THE SOLUTIONS WILL COME

Great product, no market

Alice said, 'You know, that reminds me of another story that happened in our company, not in my plant but at head office.'

'What was that?' Harry asked.

'Well, it turns out that we were trying to break into a new market. Until then, we'd been doing retail, grocery stores, department stores. We thought we saw a market on the institutional side, hospitals, schools, that kind of thing. So, figuring that we could repeat our successes in retail, we stocked the new division with people who could apply what had worked for them on the other side.'

'Sounds like a sensible thing to do,' I said.

'On the surface, yes. But here's what happened. What's worked for us in retail is to make a superior product, promote its advantages like the dickens, and then watch the customers pour in. So our marketing and product development people started by trying to make a superior product for the new division. They spent two years making a cleaning product for hospitals, one that would disinfect at the same time. You see, while our competitors' products did a good job of disinfecting walls and floors, none of them cleaned very well. It turned out to be a major technical challenge to put together disinfecting and cleaning ingredients in one product. Head office thought it would be a major coup to do it.'

'So were they successful?' I asked.

'You bet they were. Two years later they had patented a superior cleaning product that killed germs just as well as the competitors'. Of course it cost more. But we figured that hospitals would believe the dual benefits justified the extra cost. Guess what happened? Our sales force never sold a gallon, not one. It turned out that the hospital managers couldn't have cared less about improved cleaning.

They felt their cleaning was already good enough. The only things they cared about were cost, disinfecting power and good service from the salesperson. After about a year of trying, we gave up.'

'So a team of researchers and marketers wasted two years coming up with a great solution to the wrong problem?' Harry said.

'Exactly. They didn't take the time upfront to do good fact finding. If they had, they would have discovered that cost and service were the keys to cracking the market. So we should have defined our problem as how to improve cost and service for hospitals rather than how to improve cleaning for hospitals.'

'That's another great story,' I said. 'It illustrates the importance of what I call the problem definition step in the creative process. Besides defining the problem accurately, you've got to define it in words that motivate you to solve it. How might we improve cost and service for hospitals? How might we improve cleaning for hospitals? It's so important to make sure you're asking the right questions before you start worrying about finding the right answers.' ■

Summary of learnings

✈ *Problem defining is the hinge between fact finding and solution finding.*

✈ *Creativity is required to identify the most fruitful challenges or problem definitions from the key facts.*

✈ *Frame problem definitions as challenges. The phrase 'How might we?' is probably the most important question in the creative problem solving process. It is a way around the roadblocks posed by the phrase 'We can't because' (or variations).*

✈ *The 'why-what's stopping' analysis helps you map out problem definitions. The method involves a three-step process: asking 'why' (or 'what's stopping') of a challenge; phrasing the answer in a simple, complete sentence; and creating a new challenge based on the answer. Asking these questions repeatedly further broadens or narrows the problem's scope.*

✈ *'Mapping' the results of the 'why-what's stopping' analysis yields a hierarchy of interrelated challenges. The hierarchy is limited in size: at some point, you have to decide that the problem definition is sufficiently complete and then proceed toward solutions.*

✈ *The Simplex process helps you (and even requires you) to redefine problems before coming up with solutions. You become innovative in defining problems as well as solving them.*

✈ *The 'why-what's stopping' analysis is a way to involve people throughout the organization in defining problems, to link strategic goals with operations, and to help people understand how their function fits into the bigger corporate picture.*

As Albert Einstein once said, the most important scientific advances come not so much from thinking up solutions as from formulating problems in new ways or seeing them from different angles. Once you develop the formulation or angle, finding the solution becomes merely an exercise in mathematics or experimentation. Just as fact finding is the hinge between the fuzzy situation and a well-defined problem, so problem defining is the hinge between fact finding and solutions.

STEP 3: Problem definition

In the third step of the Simplex creative problem solving process, problem definition, you use the key facts you have selected to generate creative definitions of your problem. These represent new directions or challenges for you to consider. Rarely will you find a single 'correct' problem. Most problems map out into a set of related but different and useful challenges. What's important now is to use your creative skills to identify your most fruitful challenges.

'HOW MIGHT WE?'

One of the most important skills in this step is to frame problem definitions as challenges. The phrase, 'How might we?', is perhaps the most powerful in the

entire creative problem solving process. Every fact that you consider should be converted into a positively stated challenge that begins with this phrase. Most people and organizations use facts as roadblocks by saying, 'We can't because...' To distinguish yourself—to find important problems, solve them, and implement the solutions—you must learn to replace this phrase with, 'How might we?' This is the key to making valuable change and mainstreaming innovation in your organization and your life.

'WE CAN'T BECAUSE . . .'

'Negative thinking' number-one killer of good ideas, says study

The roadblock of, 'We can't because...', shows up in many forms, including the following (Figure 6-1):

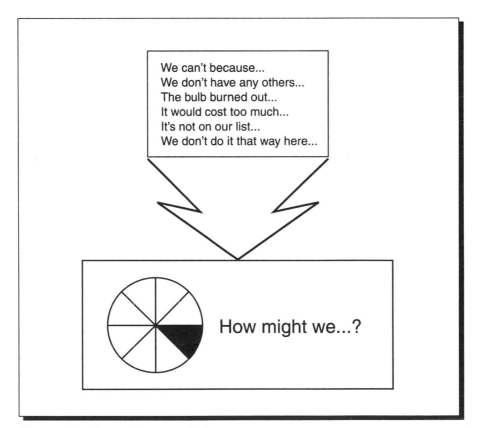

Fig. 6.1 Framing problems as challenges

'We don't have any others'

During one seminar I led, the participants' name tags kept falling off. I pointed this out to the co-ordinator, but her response was, 'They always fall off, but we don't have any others because the bookstore doesn't carry any other kinds.' Apparently, this had been going on for years. The co-ordinator had limited herself to the task of buying name tags at the bookstore. Her real challenge should have been worded as: 'How might I find name tags that adhere properly?', or, 'How might I find another way to ensure that participants can be readily identified by name?'

'The bulb burned out'

Before conducting my first overseas seminar, I had arranged with my hosts to hold a dress rehearsal upon my arrival. They had agreed to obtain the necessary audio-visual equipment, including a movie projector to preview a training film. During the rehearsal, however, one of the hosts said he hadn't brought the projector. 'It doesn't work,' he said. 'The bulb burned out.'

In our creative process, the fact that the bulb had burned out should hardly have been a roadblock. Instead, it should have been the fact that began the process, giving rise to such creative challenges as: 'How might we get another projector?'; 'How might we find another bulb?'; 'How might we find a way to preview the film without the projector?' The key is to turn the fact into a problem definition stated in the form of a 'How might we?' challenge.

'It would cost too much'

How often have you heard someone suggest an idea only to have another participant kill it by saying, 'It would cost too much'? Your skill in the creative process should immediately turn this killer phrase into a positive opportunity to improve the idea and reduce the anxiety it caused. For example, you might state the following challenges: 'How might we minimize the cost for the same result?'; 'How might we reduce the cost?'; 'How might we find a simpler but cheaper alternative?'; 'How might we gain acceptance for this idea despite its high cost?' Good ideas should not end with a killer phrase. Rather, the killer phrase should be only the start of a good idea. Automatically translating negative objections into positive problem definitions keeps the creative process working.

'It's not on our list'

Trying to increase sales, managers of an aluminum company decided to make a three-day blitz in each sales region to find as many potential customers as possible. Salespeople were asked to prepare ahead of time a list of potential customers. For each region, a trainee from headquarters would accompany the two local salespeople to gain experience.

While driving from one company on the list to another, one regional team happened to pass a large manufacturing plant with an enormous supply of aluminum scattered all over its premises. The driver continued past the plant toward the next customer on the list. When the trainee asked why they hadn't stopped to see such an obvious candidate, the driver's response was, 'We could have, but it's not on our list.'

Let's analyze what happened. The team's real challenge had been, 'How might we call on as many aluminum consumers in the region over the next three days as possible?' By the time the team had hit the road, the challenge had become distorted to, 'How might we visit as many of the aluminum consumers *on our list* as we can over the next three days?' Developed merely as a procedural aid to help the group meet the original challenge, the list itself had become the challenge.

Organizations create rules and procedures in order to achieve higher goals and improve customer service. Unfortunately, many employees believe that following rules and procedures is an end in itself rather than a means to an end. These salespeople, for example, believed that following the directive to create a list of potential customers, and to stick to the list, was more important than the directive's intent: finding new customers. Sometimes employees even view customers as roadblocks in their devotion to 'the rules.' No organization needs employees who are content to tell customers: 'We can't because...'; 'There's no reason why, it's just our policy'; 'The rules say we can't.' Instead, organizations need people to use the creative process to say: 'How might I use our rules to help our customers? How might I go beyond our prescribed procedures to help my customer get what he needs?' This is the kind of thinking that makes customers want to come back again and again.

'We don't do it that way here'

I had rented a condominium for a week's vacation. The units were normally rented from Saturday to Saturday. On the Friday before I was to check out, I asked the desk clerk whether I could pay to stay one extra day to Sunday. The reply was brief and to the point: 'Sorry, we don't do it that way here. We only rent from Saturday to Saturday.' I already knew that the condominium complex was half-empty, so space was available. For the clerk, however, the only important fact was that the company's policy was to rent its units from Saturday to Saturday. She failed to see two additional facts: a customer was willing to pay for an extra day's rental, and space was available.

Recognizing both additional facts could have led her to a host of creative challenges: 'How might I dig up a unit for one more day?'; 'How might I quickly find out whether any incoming guests will arrive later than anticipated?'; 'How might I find alternative lodging for this customer?'; 'How might I make this customer feel we really care for him?' 'How might I best help this customer and make him want to come back again?' The company's rental procedure had not been designed to prevent her from helping a customer obtain extra accommodation. Yet, in her mind, the creative process had ended with a roadblock—a company procedure. That company procedure should have been a springboard to begin the creative process, not to end it.

THE 'WHY-WHAT'S STOPPING' ANALYSIS

In order to better use the creative process, you must be able to broaden your point of view. Coming up with insightful problem definition challenges as above helps you do this. Another way is to map out challenges using the 'why-what's stopping' analysis. This analysis often provides the greatest surprises and discoveries about how a problem is formulated.

Using the 'why-what's stopping' analysis effectively depends on your skill in asking two simple questions—'why?' and 'what's stopping me?'—and in employing a simple three-step process, as follows (Figure 6-2):

- Ask the question 'why' (or 'what's stopping') of the perceived challenge.
- State a specific answer to the question in a simple, complete sentence.
- Based on the answer, create a new challenge.

Asking the question 'why' of a challenge, and then restating the answer into a new challenge, broadens your problem definition. For instance, suppose you're trying to help your teenage son think his way through a problem without solving it for him (Figure 6-3). If your son perceives his challenge as, 'How might I get tickets to the concert?', you ask him, 'Why do you want to get tickets to the concert?' (in other words, 'What is the intent?'). His answer might be, 'I want a date with Sue.' You then help him turn that answer into a broader challenge, 'How might I get a date with Sue?' There are many more solutions to this broader challenge than there are to the narrower challenge, 'How might I get tickets to a concert?'

Similarly, asking your son the question, 'What's stopping you from getting tickets to the concert?', helps him to narrow his challenge. Perhaps his answer

---

1 Ask the complete question: 'Why ...?' or 'What's stopping ...?'
2 Answer in a complete, simple sentence.
3 Restate the answer to create a new 'How might ...?'

Fig. 6.2 The 'why – what's stopping' analysis (1)

is, 'The tickets have been sold out for weeks.' You then help him turn that answer into a more focused challenge, such as, 'How might I find someone selling two tickets?' While there are fewer solutions to, 'How might I find someone who is selling two tickets?', than to 'How might I get tickets to the concert?', perhaps this narrowed focus is exactly what he needs to come up with a solution. (Note that asking the question 'why?' of this more narrow challenge leads back to the original challenge, 'How might I get tickets to the concert?' Hence the upward-pointing arrow in Figure 6-3 that links these two challenges.)

Of course, this example is an oversimplification. For one thing, there is usually more than one answer to either question, 'why' or 'what's stopping me.' Asking the questions repeatedly ('why *else*?', 'what *else* is stopping?') further broadens and narrows the problem's scope. Each answer leads to at least one more fresh challenge that offers new insights. Furthermore, any of your subsequent challenges can become launching pads for repeating the three-step 'why-what's stopping' analysis. When you have discovered sufficient new insights, it's time to select the most intriguing of the challenges for the next step, finding ideas for solutions to the selected challenges.

As you map out the results of the 'why-what's stopping' analysis, write each new challenge that you discover either above ('why') or below ('what's stop-

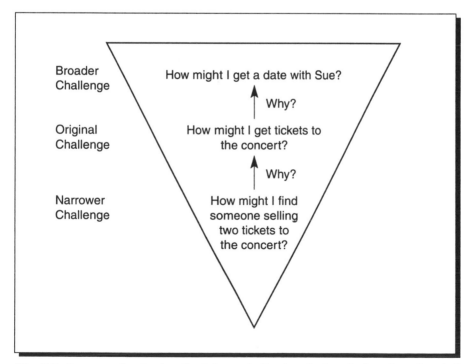

Fig. 6.3 *An example of using the 'why—what's stopping' analysis to broaden and narrow a challenge*

ping') the previous one. What results is a hierarchy of challenges. Indicate the relationships between successive challenges by drawing upward-pointing arrows toward the top of the hierarchy. Place the challenges resulting from the 'else' questions side by side.

Now let's look at how the 'why-what's stopping' analysis sorts out challenges of varying scope into a larger hierarchy. In this example, we'll ignore the 'else' question so that we can focus only on the idea of a hierarchy. (It's an adaptation of a story in 'Creative Action Guidebook,' written by Sid Parnes, Ruth Noller and Angelo Biondi.)

MORE THAN JUST A LEAK

The 'why-what's stopping' analysis: From repairing a leak to fixing a company

In a small chemical plant, a leaking metal float that had gradually lost its buoyancy had finally brought production to an abrupt halt. The plant's handyperson could hear water sloshing inside the float but couldn't detect the leak.

Considering these facts, if you were the handyperson using the creative process you would readily think of several challenges, such as: 'How might I find the leak?'; 'How might I make the leak more visible?'; 'How might I restore buoyancy?'; 'How might I restore production?' Now how do you apply the 'why-what's stopping' analysis in order to arrange these and other challenges in a simple but useful hierarchy?

Suppose you arbitrarily start with the challenge, 'How might I find the leak?' Begin your three-step process by asking, 'Why would I want to find the leak?' The answer might be, 'I'd like to repair the float.' This answer leads to a broader challenge that sits higher in the hierarchy, 'How might I repair the float?'

Suppose you decide to continue asking the 'why' question. Asking, 'Why would I want to repair the float?', might yield the answer, 'We have lost buoyancy.' This leads to the even broader challenge situated even higher in the hierarchy, 'How might I restore buoyancy?' Asking 'why' each time broadens the problem's scope. For example, there are more ways to restore buoyancy than there are ways to repair the float. Similarly, there are more ways to repair the float than there are ways to find the leak. Stated another way, while repairing the leak is one way to restore buoyancy, you might restore buoyancy without necessarily repairing the leak.

If you decide to continue asking the 'why' question, you will discover new, broader challenges, such as, 'How might I get the machine running?', and even broader, 'How might I get production going?' If at any point you decide to ask the 'what's stopping' question instead, you will discover narrower challenges.

For example, asking, 'What's stopping me from finding the leak?', could lead to, 'The leak is so small that I can't see it.' This could lead to a more focused challenge, 'How might I make the leak more visible?' The hierarchy resulting to this point is shown in Figure 6-4.

If you were to continue asking 'why' beyond the top of the hierarchy in Figure 6-4, you would enter the domain of the plant's management rather than that of the handyperson. However, the process continues to lead you to broader, more strategic challenges, like ever-larger waves from a stone dropped into a pond. Figure 6-5 shows nested hierarchies that illustrate how the company's strategic goals are linked to the day-to-day operations.

You could build the same hierarchical map in any number of ways. For example, suppose you start with a more lofty goal such as, 'How might I keep myself and my employees in long-term jobs?' You could then ask the 'what's stopping' question successively to create the same hierarchy, this time from the top down. Eventually you would reach the challenge, 'What's stopping me from making the leak more visible?', or even more narrow challenges.

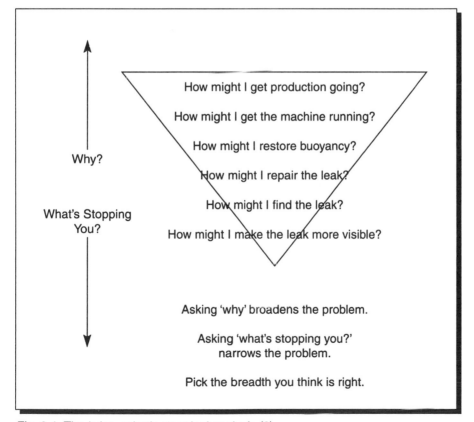

Fig. 6.4 The 'why—what's stopping' analysis (2)

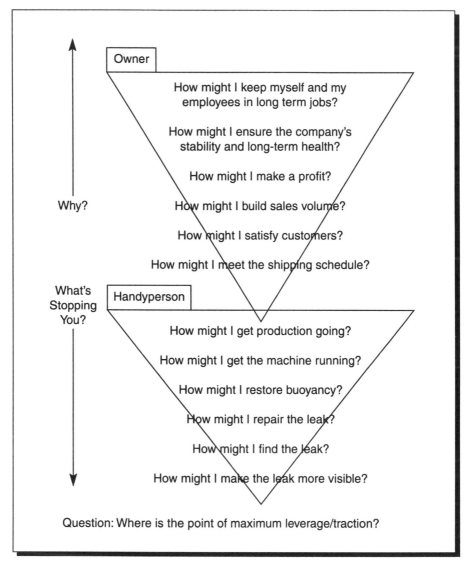

Fig. 6.5 The 'why—what's stopping' analysis—strategic perspective

As you'll see in later chapters, the 'why-what's stopping' analysis is a critical tool for strategic planning. Using the analysis, you can precisely link strategic company goals and objectives with all of the company's day-to-day actions and programs into one hierarchical map. The map itself is continuously updated and can be created by involving virtually everyone in the organization.

Organizations often have difficulty with their strategic planning process. Many individuals look at it as a make-work project, something to be done and put on the shelf until someone asks for a presentation on it. Rarely is it used for its main purpose of guiding daily activities, And it seems that everyone has their own set of terms and definitions: what is a mission statement? how does it differ from purpose or vision? what's the difference between a goal and an objective? is a goal broader than an objective or vice versa? where does policy fit in? what's the difference between a program and a tactic? is a strategy something that puts a goal into play or is it broader than that? So half the time is spent debating these terminology issues.

It doesn't matter what you call these things. What is important is that you develop a hierarchical map of challenges in which the higher you go the more you are talking about the 'why' of what you're doing, and the lower you go the more you are talking about 'what' you are going to do and 'how' you are going to accomplish it. This hierarchical map becomes the strategic plan itself. If you are unsure of what your mission is, the 'why-what's stopping' process will lead you to it. If you are unsure about how to achieve your goals, the process will lead you to very specific tactics lower in your map that you will need to execute. What is also important is that the strategic plan that results become a living, breathing road map that everyone can understand and own. It is also a road map to be revised continuously as actions are taken and events unfold.

MY PROBLEM IS OUR PROBLEM

Employees fit themselves into bigger corporate picture

Here's an example of how a strategic plan was developed by a major oil company. A team of managers met for a day and were given some training in the Simplex creative problem solving process, particularly fact finding and problem defining, including the 'why-what's stopping' analysis. After doing some fact finding together, the members were urged to put aside preconceived notions about what was meant by words like mission, goals or objectives. Then they were asked to put aside their judgment and free-wheel in order to generate as many challenges as they could that might be important for the company to resolve. From a lengthy list, they identified a small number that they agreed were the most critical challenges.

A facilitator wrote these challenges on index cards and stuck them on a large white sheet of paper on the wall. The team could then move challenges from one place to another and reword a challenge or even discard one challenge and make another. The team members clustered in a semi-circle facing the sheet in order to involve everyone as fully as possible in this mapping process.The team placed these most critical challenges in a hierarchical map using the 'why-what's stopping' process (Figure 6-6). Then the members began to identify additional challenges by asking why various critical challenges should be resolved (what would be the intent or benefit?) and what was stopping them from resolving various critical challenges. Each answer became a new challenge; all the challenges were stated in 'How might we?' form and placed either above or below the previous challenge in the map. Beside these new challenges or beside the original challenges, the team placed yet further challenges that it identified by asking 'why else?' and 'what else is stopping us?' of any challenge.

As this process continued, the team found that the challenges began to fall naturally into five separate levels in the hierarchy. The facilitator asked the team to label each level in their own terms, such as 'mission,' 'vision,' 'strategy,' 'goal,' etc. The group decided to label the top challenge in the map as their vision: 'How might we increase customer value?' The next four levels were labeled mission, objectives, strategies and programs. The group agreed that the word 'programs' incorporated processes, projects, products, tactics and actions. This approach meant the group didn't have to bother arguing over definitions for these terms. The members assigned 'definitions' that made sense to them, and were able to focus on what critical challenges the company had to meet.

More important, the action-oriented tactical programs at the bottom of the hierarchy were now clearly linked to the more broad, strategically oriented challenges at the top—something that many organizations find difficult to do. In the latter organizations, the top and bottom levels are often divorced: people at the top set out the important goals and objectives, but people at lower levels take actions that might not even lead to those goals and objectives.

If groups of employees at all the company's levels undertake similar exercises—creating their own strategic maps and plugging them into the 'corporate' map—then they acquire more ownership for their tasks. They better understand how what they do helps the company meet its overall strategic objectives. They can then make much more accurate or useful decisions about which of their own challenges to tackle, and can even create better challenges to address. This strategic mapping process also becomes an excellent tool for empowering people. Instead of simply being given standard solutions to implement without knowing why, employees now have to discover for themselves their own critical challenges and tailor their own innovative solutions to meet them.

This mapping process allows a company to compress a huge amount of knowledge into one page as in Figure 6-6. Each department can distribute to its employees a single-page copy of the 'corporate' map integrated with its own departmental map. This document then is easily reviewed and updated. Individuals can set goals for themselves—create their own maps—that are aligned with department goals and guide their daily activities accordingly. As an even more powerful alternative, any employee from the president down can display on his or her computer terminal the company's current strategic map and a particular department's map to see the most important challenges and how they link together, and easily revise maps.

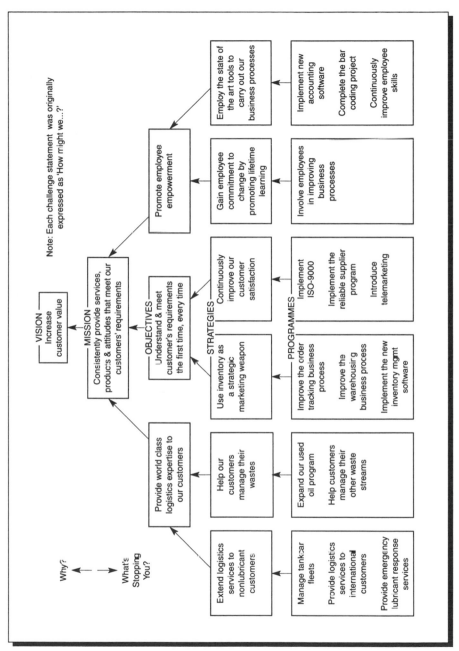

Fig. 6.6 Lubricants distribution division strategic plan as a hierarchy of challenges

FROM ONE THING TO ANOTHER

Engineer discovers right question; ignites energy conservation program

Let's look at another example. This time, using the 'what's stopping' question helped an industrial engineer who was trying to reduce the number of boilers providing energy to his plant's manufacturing processes (Figure 6-7). Having worked through fact finding, he had perceived his challenge as, 'How might I get the eight boilers reduced to four?'

Unable to meet this challenge on his own, he had asked a group of engineering colleagues for help. One of the group familiar with the 'why-what's stopping' analysis asked him, 'What's stopping you from getting the plant to use only four boilers rather than eight?' His first answer was, 'Nothing's stopping me; a similar plant in another region has already moved to four boilers from eight. Our plant could do the same.'

His questioner knew enough about the analysis to probe further. He rephrased his question to ask, 'If you already know how to do it, then what's stopping you from getting the plant to use only four boilers rather than eight?' After a great deal of thought and prompting from the rest of the group, the engineer said, 'You know, what's really stopping me is that the plant manager is

---

'Four Boilers from Eight'

***3. How might I reduce my plant's energy use?

  *1. How might I get the boilers reduced to four?

  **2. How might I get the plant manager to realize how important energy conservation is to attaining our goals, and how might I get the department managers to take the time to hear my proposal?

Legend

  * Starting point challenge as originally perceived.

  ** New challenge providing new insight created by asking 'what's stopping you?' repeatedly of the stakeholders to the original challenge.

  *** Additional challenge created by asking 'why?' of original challenge.

Fig. 6.7 An example of using the 'why—what's stopping' analysis

not interested in energy conservation, and the department managers are too busy to listen to my proposal.' His challenge was then restated into, 'How might I get the plant manager to realize how important energy conservation is to attaining our goals, and how might I get the department managers to take the time to hear my proposal?'

To complete the 'why-what's stopping' analysis, he was asked, 'Why do you want to use only four boilers rather than eight?' His answer was, 'Four boilers use less energy than eight.' The problem was then restated as, 'How might I reduce my plant's energy use?' Contemplating what was preventing him from using only four boilers gave the engineer a flash of insight. The key was not that he lacked the technical know-how, but that his manager was not interested in energy conservation and that the department managers were too busy. Getting the managers' attention and convincing them turned out to be his key challenge. In this example, the owner of the problem obtained a new insight, a far better way to state his problem. This often results from repeated use of the 'why-what's stopping' questioning process. The new challenges you create, whether broader or narrower, are often better. This isn't always the case— sometimes the original challenge turns out to be the best of all. But this analysis helps you to consider other viewpoints, more broad and more narrow, before you decide.

KEEP THE 'WHY-WHAT'S STOPPING' ANALYSIS SIMPLE

During the three-step 'why-what's stopping' analysis, keep your answers to these two key questions simple, specific and complete. Complicated or vague or incomplete answers will lead to ambiguously stated challenges. Rather than successively broadening or narrowing a challenge, you may find yourself simply going around in circles.

For example, when you reply that morale is low in response to the question, 'What's stopping us from decreasing our product defects?', you've provided an incomplete and vague response. If you really mean that people are not paying much attention to quality, then the challenge that results from this much more specific answer is, 'How might we get our employees to pay more attention to product quality?' (more clear and complete than 'How might we improve morale?'). Similarly, when you reply that morale is low in response to the question, 'Why would we want to reduce product defects?', perhaps what you really meant was, 'Employees would feel better about their work.' Then, the challenge would be, 'How might we help employees feel better about their work?' Keeping the answers simple, specific and complete gives you a logical hierarchy of more meaningful challenge statements, preventing you from going around in circles.

Is there a limit to the size of the problem definition map created by the 'why-what's stopping' analysis? The map's size is limited by three factors. At some point, broadening the problem further only makes it more esoteric ('How might I obtain happiness and bliss in life?') and impossible to answer concisely. Going in the other direction, you can continually narrow the problem into smaller and smaller chunks until the only thing that's stopping you is actually implementing an obvious solution. The third limitation is that you can spend only a finite amount of time on any particular problem. At some point, you have to decide that you've made your problem definition sufficiently complete and proceed toward solutions.

Once you have selected a problem definition, creating specific solutions is easy. It's your use of creativity in defining the problem or in looking at it from new angles that gives you the edge. Too often, people rush into developing solutions without taking enough care to develop an effective problem definition.

Perhaps the single most powerful part of the entire Simplex process is its emphasis on redefining problems before coming up with solutions. In many organizations, this is the step that most worries those people who value stability and control. Most of us have been taught to believe that problems come to us already well-defined, and that all we need do is come up with solutions. The Simplex process requires you to re-examine your preconceived beliefs and assumptions, to become an innovator in defining problems as well as in solving them. Not only must you respond to problems defined by your boss, for example, but you must offer problems and opportunities that you have defined on your own. You must also be able to redefine stated company goals, objectives and problem definitions in more useful ways, and sell your new definition to others.

As a manager, even if you already have a 'pet' solution in mind, you might still encourage employees to redefine the problem in their own ways. In doing so, you run the risk that the selected problem definition and solution will differ from your preconceived notions. But this is a great way to build employee commitment to resolving problems. When you give people a chance to take part in formulating a problem, they develop a sense of ownership for its successful solution. And when employees get a chance to practise their skills in defining problems, rather than simply implementing someone else's solutions, they are more likely to look ahead for themselves, anticipate problems, and expect the unexpected. They 'handle' problems before they occur. They become more and more valuable to the organization because they begin asking the right questions and stating problems in exciting and insightful ways, rather than waiting to be told what to do and how to do it.

Besides involving people in this way, the 'why-what's stopping' analysis has many other applications. As mentioned above, it is a strategic planning tool that links strategic goals with operations and helps employees understand how their work fits into the company's big picture. And it helps research and development groups identify which objectives to pursue.

7

MORE—AND MORE CREATIVE—SOLUTIONS

'Of all the hare-brained ideas. . .'

'You know,' said Harry. 'It's not just in defining problems incorrectly that people go astray. A lot of people in our company have trouble coming up with new and different solutions even when they know exactly what the problem is.'

'Why do you think that is?' I asked.

'Well, they seem boxed in,' he said. 'Seems they can only come up with the same old solutions again and again.'

'What have you tried to get them out of the box?'

'Well, we tried brainstorming for years but it didn't work.'

On my right. Alice leaned forward and pulled a mock grimace. 'Oh boy, brainstorming.'

Harry nodded and went on. 'No matter how much we emphasized following a few simple rules, people just couldn't take the process seriously. They were really embarrassed to throw out wild ideas like you're supposed to. In fact, most people would only mention ideas that they were sure no one else would ridicule. Whenever anybody did venture an even slightly unusual idea, others would snicker, make faces. Even if they didn't say anything critical, their body language made it pretty clear what they thought. It was just a game for them.'

'So what happened?' I said.

'After a while, all we got were the tried and true ideas that everybody already knew. And we eventually gave up on brainstorming.'

'Sounds to me like we're back to the question of process again,' I said. 'You tried a technique that was supposed to give you creative solutions. But because people felt awkward about using the technique and even about coming up with creative ideas, they didn't use it properly.

It's another example of giving too little emphasis to following a process and too much emphasis to getting good content. If people would try harder at mastering the process of brainstorming, they would get better ideas. But by short-circuiting the process, all they get are duds or recycled solutions.' ■

Summary of learnings

✦ *Idea finding is the hinge between defining a problem and solving it.*

✦ *Rather than seize immediately on a preliminary solution, you generate as many potential solutions as possible.*

✦ *Four excellent but simple techniques for generating ideas include brainstorming, blitzing, forcing relationships, and deliberately building radical ideas.*

✦ *Brainstorming involves following four rules: do not criticize ideas; go for quantity of ideas; hitchhike on ideas; and practise freewheeling.*

✦ *Follow four useful guidelines in selecting solutions for subsequent evaluation. Pick ideas that are so concrete and easily understood that the next step is obvious. Make sure the solution is focused on the problem as you've defined it.*

✦ *The idea evaluation step helps you to form a solution around which to develop an implementation plan.*

✦ *Proper evaluation requires selection of appropriate criteria for judging possible solutions. Two useful methods for evaluating ideas are the criteria grid method and the paired comparison analysis.*

In the fourth step of the Simplex creative problem solving process—idea finding—we move from discovering problems to discovering solutions. During the first three steps, we emphasized the importance of asking useful questions rather than simply giving useful answers. The goal: to come up with useful problem definitions. Now it's time to develop imaginative solutions. The idea finding step is the hinge between a creative problem definition and selecting a solid solution.

STEP 4: IDEA FINDING

Imagine an archery target. In the Simplex process of creative problem solving, the problem definition or challenge that you have selected from step three becomes the target's bull's-eye. The better defined the target, the easier it is to hit the mark. The process of idea finding means creating potential solutions and hurling them toward that bull's-eye. How to fashion your arrows?

If you have done a good job during the first three steps of the Simplex process, your targeted problem definition will probably be so well stated that one or two good solutions will leap out at you. In fact, you may find it difficult to resist simply grabbing one of these solutions and 'running with it.'

However, as in each of the previous three steps, you must fight the temptation and instead generate as many potential solutions as you can without judging them. The more potential solutions you generate for a challenge, the more likely you are to find a superior solution. And it is much more efficient not to stop to analyze each idea as it is generated. Only a small fraction of the ideas will actually be worth further consideration anyway. It's in the next step of the process, idea evaluation and selection, that you will select a small number of ideas for further scrutiny.

FOUR IDEAS FOR GENERATING IDEAS

There are many specific techniques for generating ideas. Most are based on these principles of deferring judgment and extending effort to create many ideas before selecting from among them. They also require specific process skills to make them work, process skills that we'll examine in detail later. For now, let's look at four excellent idea generation techniques that you can use immediately: brainstorming, blitzing, forcing connections, and deliberately building radical ideas (Figure 7-1).

Brainstorming

One of the earliest, and still the most effective, techniques for generating solutions is called brainstorming. You can do brainstorming alone or in a group. In either case, you come up with ideas for meeting your targeted problem definition challenge while following these four important rules:

● Do not criticize any idea.
● Go for quantity of ideas (quantity breeds quality, so the more ideas the better).

- Brainstorming
- Blitzing
- Forcing connections
- Deliberately building radical ideas

Fig. 7.1 Four techniques for generating ideas

- Hitchhike—or piggyback one idea onto another—as much as you can.
- Freewheel as much as possible (the wilder the idea the better—it is easier to tame a wild idea than to enliven a dull one).

It is inefficient to stop to criticize ideas as they are uttered, as it slows the flow. Such criticism also prevents people from creating novel ideas, and they become reluctant to let their imaginations blossom. Remember that the point here is to find new approaches.

Statistically speaking, you're more likely to find a good idea from a long list than from a short one. And as more ideas are expressed, the opportunity to build additional ideas through hitchhiking increases. By piggybacking ideas onto one another, any idea or idea fragment becomes a building block for yet another. Don't waste time pondering what you dislike about an idea. Instead, select promising fragments and use your imagination and experience to build on them.

Some people find it difficult to accept or practise freewheeling. For many, it seems a waste of time to offer obviously silly, irrelevant or wild ideas. But freewheeling helps people to break from their accustomed thought patterns, to see problems from new angles, and to provide leads to other solutions. It's a technique that many people must experience before they'll believe in it.

Suppose you've defined a problem as, 'How might our salespeople better attract attention from potential buyers?' A freewheeling idea might be to have each salesperson take along an elephant (yes, a real one) on sales calls. While this is hardly a practical idea, it would almost certainly attract customers' attention. Now by visualizing the idea, you might find intriguing fragments to build on. Picturing the elephant's trunk, you might suggest that the salesperson take along a travel trunk filled with contest prizes or product samples. Thinking of the elephant's call, you might suggest they take a trumpet to herald their arrival or an audiocassette with music and a monologue about their products. Building practicality into a radical thought often gives you feasible yet novel ideas and stimulates more imaginative ideas.

Blitzing

The second technique for generating possible solutions, called blitzing, means 'blowing up' an idea into many, more specific, ideas. Here, you focus on a single idea that suggests a broader theme. For example, a team working on the challenge, 'How might we improve our potato chip bags?', might have come up with the suggestion, 'to make them more useful when empty.' In order to blitz this theme, the team creates a new problem definition: 'How might we make our potato chip bags more useful when empty?' Brainstorming this new challenge leads to more specific ideas, like modifying the bags to be used as trash bags for the car.

Forcing connections

A third idea generation technique, forcing connections, requires you to use your imagination to force a fit between seemingly unrelated ideas or objects. For example, a product development engineer's challenge might be, 'What new household products might we introduce?' You could make two lists. One could be a list of objects you might find in a room of the house. The second could be a list of objects from somewhere else, say, the contents of your work desk. If you chose one object from each list at random, you might end up with a skylight and a pair of scissors. You could ask yourself, 'How might I improve a pair of scissors by making them more like a skylight?' Ideas for solutions might include, 'put miniature lights on the scissors so you can use them in low light,' or, 'equip the scissors with a magnifying glass for visually impaired people.' You have forced a connection between two apparently unrelated things.

'Deliberately building radical ideas'

A fourth idea generation technique I call 'deliberately building radical ideas.' Here you select a preposterous idea from a list of possibilities and blitz it, focusing only on its good aspects. For the problem definition, 'How might we generate publicity for our sports team?', a group might select the seemingly wild idea of using a cobra as a mascot. Blitzing could lead to finding mascots from among other creatures that are less lethal but just as provocative. Or the group might use the cobra figuratively to jazz up the team's uniform and promotional material.

Using these kinds of techniques deliberately helps you to generate a surprising number of innovative yet practical ideas worth pursuing. But often the real problem is that people are reluctant to move toward action. New ideas by nature cause discomfort. They require change of habit and, usually, hard work to make them succeed. When a team develops a promising new product, for example, it often decides to wait for field testing experience even when it's not needed. Waiting for field testing is actually a ploy to put off the risk of going to market. Managers may even hope to be transferred or promoted before having to make the decision, leaving the risk to someone else. Instead, you must take calculated risks and accept that you can never be entirely sure of any decision.

How many solution ideas are worth a closer look in the next step of the process? Remember that the goal of the Simplex process is to help you implement at least one good idea. It's better to accomplish one good thing than to accomplish nothing because you have too many good ideas to choose from. If none of your selected ideas survives the subsequent evaluation step, then you can always return to the previous step to generate more. A good rule of thumb is to select five solution ideas to take to the subsequent evaluation step. Here are four useful guidelines for this selection process (Figure 7-2):

- **Concrete**
  Able to visualize what this idea will 'look' like when completed.

- **Easy to understand**
  An innocent bystander should be able to read the idea and know what it means.

- **Targeted on solving your 'How might' challenge**
  Remember, you are trying to solve the challenge(s) converged upon in Step 3, Problem Definition.

- **An easy next step is obvious.**

Fig. 7.2 Criteria for converging on best ideas

- Pick concrete ideas. You should be able to visualize what the idea will look like when completed.
- Pick ideas that are easy to understand. An uninitiated bystander should be able to understand your idea.
- Make sure the selected ideas are on-target. They should address the selected problem definition challenge, rather than other related challenges.
- Pick ideas for which an easy next step is obvious.

Following these four guidelines helps you avoid ideas that appear noble but that are too esoteric and vague. If your challenge is, 'How might I reduce tension in our department?', for example, one idea might be, 'Be more friendly.' This is nowhere near as useful an idea as, 'Shake hands with the first 15 people I meet each morning.' The first one is a nice philosophy but not specific enough. The latter is much more likely to lead to actions that you can implement, the ultimate goal of the Simplex process.

STEP 5: EVALUATE AND SELECT

Recall the story in an earlier chapter of how an idea for a telescoping trash bag container was killed by lack of imagination. Just as it takes an open mind to effectively develop new ideas, so it takes an open mind to effectively evaluate new ideas. Once you've selected a small number of ideas in step four, your next step in the Simplex creative problem solving process is to evaluate those ideas. You want to choose at least one idea as a useful solution for which you can develop a practical implementation plan.

This evaluation process can be relatively simple or relatively complex, for a number of reasons. Determining which of three people is heaviest, for example, requires nothing more complicated than comparing readings on a set of scales. A more challenging task is to evaluate, say, the best person for a job or the best third baseman in the league. It's more difficult to make these decisions when you lack a single, simple yardstick or scale to measure the relative worth of the choices. You have to use more than a single criterion in choosing.

Think about buying the right car from among a few models. You wouldn't base your decision on only one criterion. While price may or may not be important to you, so might gas mileage, roominess, style, color. Your final choice will be based on several of these yardsticks. Selecting the appropriate 'yardsticks' or criteria themselves is an important and often tough job.

Similarly, you can't often evaluate possible solutions to a challenge by using only one criterion. It would be a mistake to evaluate an idea based on cost alone, for example, and simply ignore other criteria such as customers, long-term profits and changeover times on the assembly line.

Choosing the right criteria can be equally complicated whether you're evaluating options alone or as part of a group. When you are making your evaluation on your own, it is sometimes too easy to leap based on one obvious criterion. When you belong to a team making the evaluation, it can be difficult to agree on which criteria to use. What's important to one person might be less important to another.

Your first step in evaluation is to create a list of potential criteria for measuring your selected ideas. As you do so, suspend judgment and logic and extend effort. You'll find that some of the best criteria will come to you further down your list. Only after creating this list should you exercise judgment to select the most important few criteria, perhaps through discussions with other people. In any case, taking the time to develop and select useful, comprehensive criteria is a must. Just as in the idea finding step, it's hard to say just how many criteria are the right number. Having too many can be as counterproductive as having too few. No matter the number of criteria you use, the idea is to carefully and open-mindedly examine each of your selected potential solutions.

Sometimes this evaluation process does not even lead directly to the implementation phase. Instead, it often points you in new directions. For example, team members might suddenly decide to try modifying an idea that they like but that falls short against a particular criterion. This spontaneous surge of idea building can lead to a much different and better idea.

Once you have selected the appropriate criteria, you can then apply them to your selected possible solutions from step four. As in the other steps of the Simplex process, what specific technique you use to evaluate ideas is less important than the process itself. Two useful techniques for evaluating ideas are the criteria grid method and paired comparison analysis.

CRITERIA OF CHOICE: THE CRITERIA GRID METHOD

The criteria grid method helps you to judge your selected possible solutions against each of a few selected criteria. Let's use the car purchase example from above to illustrate this method. Suppose you have narrowed your list to four car models and three criteria: initial cost, gas mileage, and access to service (Figure 7-3). List the four models vertically on the left and the three criteria horizontally across the top of the grid.

Now you will evaluate each of the four models against each criterion in turn. Start by evaluating all four models for their initial cost. Then evaluate all four for gas mileage. Then evaluate all four for access to service. Keep in mind that you are not *ranking* the models against one another. The point of this exercise

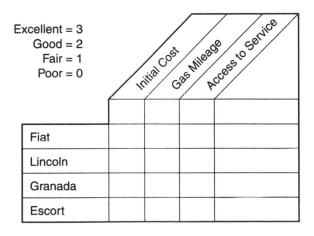

The criteria grid is an organized approach to prioritizing or selecting the best one of several 'top contender' ideas for solutions.

1 Generate a list of possible criteria; select the key criteria. Word them carefully.
2 Select an arbitrary scale (e.g., 0-3.) Fill in chart.
3 Proceed down with one criterion, not across the criteria.
4 Examine possible weighing opportunities after filling in the chart.

The chart does *not* tell you what choice to make. It helps you understand why you select an alternative.

Excellent = 3
Good = 2
Fair = 1
Poor = 0

	Initial Cost	Gas Mileage	Access to Service
Fiat			
Lincoln			
Granada			
Escort			

Fig. 7.3 Evaluation of car options using criteria grid method

is not to pick the best of a bad lot or, conversely, to discard several good options. Perhaps none of the models will turn out to be suitable, all of them will be suitable, or only some will be suitable. That's something you will determine later during your selection decision. For now, your goal is simply to understand the worth of each model option.

That's why it's important to *rate* each model separately from the other models against each criterion in turn. Furthermore, make your ratings against each criterion separately from the other criteria. Don't evaluate a single model, or a single idea, against all the criteria at once. By rating each idea in turn against one criterion at a time, you avoid the 'halo error.' This occurs when a rating against one criterion biases your evaluation on subsequent criteria.

All you have to do now is choose an arbitrary scale to make your ratings. You might use a four-point scale of letters, say, E for excellent, G for good, F for fair, and P for poor. Or use numerals, such as 3 for excellent, 2 for good, 1 for fair, and 0 for poor. It doesn't matter whether you use letters or numerals. Nor does it matter how much latitude your scale has. As a rule of thumb, a four-point numerical scale is easy to understand and provides a handy picture, such as that in Figure 7-4.

After you have filled in the grid, you might want to weight the criteria if you think they carry significantly different importance or impact. (Avoid weighting until after you've graded the ideas. If you try to weight the criteria before evaluation, you may be tempted to base your decisions on weights rather than simply on the criteria themselves.)

	Initial Cost	Gas Mileage	Access to Service	
Excellent = 3 Good = 2 Fair = 1 Poor = 0	1X	2x	2X	Total
Fiat	3	3(6)	1(2)	7(11)
Lincoln	1	1(2)	3(6)	5(9)
Granada	2	2(4)	3(6)	7(12)
Escort	3	3(6)	3(6)	9(15)

Fig. 7.4 Ratings of car options using criteria grid method

Be careful, especially if you use numerical ratings, not to get carried away with the numbers. The criteria grid method is not designed as a purely analytical procedure. It is difficult to account for all the relevant criteria. And you can't possibly have all the knowledge at your fingertips to accurately rate each option or to weight each criterion. While this method permits you to apply judgment and logic to the options, its main purpose is to help you understand the strengths and deficiencies of each idea. Because the method generates lots of discussion within a group, it ensures a more complete understanding of the options and a better consensus on what to do next.

BLENDED CRITERIA: PAIRED COMPARISON ANALYSIS

The second evaluation method, paired comparison analysis (PCA), forces you to blend all the criteria together, rather than separate them as in the criteria grid method. PCA is a method of evaluating several options by a head-to-head comparison of all pairs of options taken in turn. In each head-to-head evaluation, you consider two questions: Which of these two options is the best or most important? How much better or more important is it? Let's use this method in another example to evaluate the relative importance of several pressing problems.

Suppose you're a company manager pondering five trends that affect your business: increasing foreign competition (A), growing economic uncertainty (B), rapidly changing technology (C), rapidly changing consumer tastes (D), and a growing shortage of skilled employees (E). You are trying to decide in which order to address these trends. Using PCA, you place the trends both vertically and horizontally on a grid, as in Figure 7-5.

You begin the analysis by comparing A on the vertical axis with B on the horizontal axis. Suppose you feel that growing economic uncertainty (B) is a more important trend than increasing foreign competition (A). If so, you place a B in the A-B box. Next, you must judge whether the difference in importance is only slight (1), moderate (2) or great (3). If you decide slight, you mark the number 1 beside the letter B in the same box (B-1).

Your second comparison is between B on the vertical axis and C on the horizontal axis. Deciding that growing economic uncertainty (B) is a much more important trend than rapidly changing technology (C), you mark B-3 in this box. Next, you compare C on the vertical axis with D on the horizontal axis, then D on the vertical axis with E on the horizontal axis, and so on. In effect, you are descending the 'stairs' formed by the shaded boxes.

When you have reached the foot of the stairs, you return to the top, and descend the second set of stairs, comparing A-C, B-D and C-E. Don't forget to place a number beside each letter to reflect each trend's relative impor-

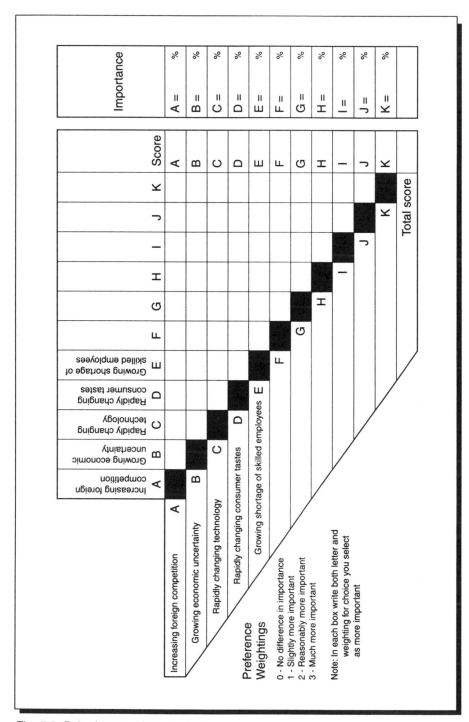

Fig. 7.5 Paired comparison analysis

tance. If you truly believe that two options are equally important, use a zero. However, do your best to avoid zeros. The whole idea of PCA is to differentiate between options.

On the third descent, you compare A-D and B-E. The final descent consists of only one comparison, A-E. 'Going down the stairs' is a simple way to avoid making comparisons of one option repeatedly, such as comparing A with B, C, D and E in succession. It's a way of mixing up the choices so that none is favored. The idea is to make as unbiased a comparison as possible for each pair of options.

After you've made all the descents, score the results by adding the numbers beside each letter, no matter where in the grid it appears. Then mark the five totals under the Score heading. Thus, your scores in this example are 7 for A, 9 for B, 3 for C, 1 for D, and 0 for E, totaling 20.

Your final step is to calculate the weight that you have assigned to represent the importance of each of the five trends. Divide the score for each of the five options by the total score of 20, then multiply the result by 100 to obtain a percentage figure. Thus, the relative importance of increasing foreign competition (A) is 7/20 x 100 = 35 percent. The relative importance of growing economic uncertainty (B) is 45 percent, the relative importance of rapidly changing technology (C) is 15 percent, the relative importance of rapidly changing consumer tastes (D) is 5 percent, and the relative importance of a growing shortage of skilled employees (E) is zero. Thus, not only have you ordered the options according to their priority, but you have assigned weights to their relative importance. You believe, for example, that growing economic uncertainty (B) is the most important trend of the five, and is about three times as important as rapidly changing technology (C). Under PCA, the option judged least important frequently earns a weight of zero. This does not mean that the option is unimportant, but only that it's the least important of the group (Figure 7-6).

Paired comparison analysis in team decision-making is a powerful method of promoting give-and-take and consensus-building. Group members discover that they have different ideas about which criteria are important. They also find that their teammates have different values and knowledge that, taken together, help everyone better understand the options. The more skilled the members are in listening open-mindedly to each other, and in valuing each others' knowledge and points of view, the better their understanding of the options and the better their evaluation.

With a technique like the criteria grid method or PCA, you can evaluate the solution options you created during the first four steps of the Simplex process. To proceed toward implementation, you now must select at least one solution that you believe will make a valuable change in your procedures or products. If none of your solutions appears good enough, you must move back in the process to create better solutions for fresh consideration. In doing so, you might have to go all the way back around the wheel to problem defini-

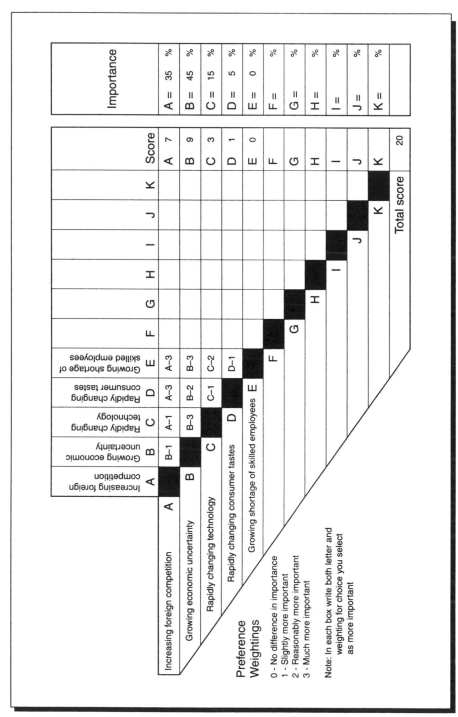

Fig. 7.6 Paired comparison analysis

tion to create more insightful challenges, or even back to fact finding to uncover new information.

Remember that the solution or combination of solutions that you pick may not have scored highest on a numerical scale. The solution you consider the most valuable might have received a lower score not because it's a poor one but because it will be the one most difficult to gain acceptance for and the most time-consuming to implement. If you believe your solution is worth a lot of hard work to sell and implement, then you may well select it over a higher-scoring option. Whatever your decision, what lies ahead is the implementation phase of the creative problem solving process. You must creatively plan for implementing your change, for gaining acceptance of the change, and for taking action to make the change permanent.

8

PUTTING CREATIVE
SOLUTIONS TO WORK

All talk, no action

I could tell Harry was mulling over yet more stories. He waited until the attendant had cleared away the lunch trays, then turned to me again.

'In the last place I worked,' he said, 'we were really into all the buzz-words. TQM. Intrapreneuring. Managing by walking around. You name it. But that's all they were to us. Words. We never actually did TQM or any of the others. It was as if one group somewhere in the company was busy thinking up all these programs, and the rest of us were just as busy carrying on as we'd done all along.'

'For example?' Alice said.

'Well, one of our big buzzwords was actually a motto,' he said. He held his hands out in front of him as if he was framing a sign. 'We will be a customer-driven organization. That was our motto. It was supposed to mean that everybody would do whatever it took to make sure a customer was satisfied. Sounded good, but in fact nobody changed the way they worked to pull together for the customer. Everybody just looked after their own functional area and did what-ever was expected of them. At the end of the day, if they'd made all their phone calls, gone through all the motions, then they figured they were finished. Even if a customer was waiting for something that evening, and it required more than one person to pull things together to deliver it, then it just sat there till the next day. You couldn't pin responsibility on any one individual because each of them had done what their narrow functions required of them.'

'So it wasn't like one unified team working toward one focused goal,' I said.

⇨

'Right,' Harry said. 'We had no process to ensure that everyone's work would be integrated to deliver a quality result to the customer. Instead we were all just going through the motions. We believed in the motto but we really didn't do anything differently to achieve it.'

'In other words, the motto was a great idea but nobody really looked at how it would be implemented or worried about taking action on it.'

'That's right,' Harry said. 'It was another great idea that went nowhere. A lot of people called it just another program.' ■

Summary of learnings

✦ *Implementing the new solution is as important as finding a problem, defining it and solving it. Successfully implementing a solution requires creating a plan of action, gaining acceptance for it, and actually carrying it out.*

✦ *A number of psychological roadblocks often impede action, including fear of failure, fear of the unknown, fear of imperfection, and inability to say no to other things.*

✦ *Creative action planning requires you to motivate others to act. To do so, list the potential roadblocks and ways around them. Then clearly specify the first few steps you will take.*

✦ *Gaining the acceptance, support or approval of key people requires reducing the anxiety they may feel about making any changes you suggest. To do so, present your ideas in simple terms to ensure understanding, prepare responses to potential fears or objections, and show others how your solutions will help to solve their own problems.*

✦ *Taking action to implement your solution is the final but crucial step. Techniques that will help you to take this step include: writing down the worst that can happen, sharing your plan with others, closure, the 'pepperoni principle,' reverse prioritizing, setting deadlines, sharing deadline commitments, promising yourself rewards for meeting deadlines, and the 'broccoli first' principle.*

In the previous steps of the Simplex process, we progressed from uncovering problems to selecting a solution. A third and equally important part of the process is implementing the solution. Successful implementation includes three steps. You need to create a plan of specific actions you will take to implement the solution, and to gain acceptance for the solution. And you need to take the plunge to carry out the specific actions in your plan.

STEP 6: ACTION PLANNING

Let's take a moment to understand the psychology behind what you are about to do. In effect, you are about to create change. Pushing yourself or someone else to change is one of the most discomforting things we can do. You'll have to practise a bit of amateur psychology on yourself and on whomever your change will affect. It's one thing to have a good solution. But it's an entirely different thing to encourage yourself and others to make the changes needed to turn the new solution into standard practice. That's why we give as much weight to the steps involved in implementing the new solution as we do to discovering and formulating the new problem, and to creating the new solution.

In order to understand the importance of steps six and seven in the process (action planning and gaining acceptance), consider the psychology behind step eight, taking action. Taking action on a new idea means heading into unfamiliar territory. Discomfort is natural. Think of how you felt before you plunged off a diving board for the first time. In the same way, it's easy to back away from taking the plunge to implement a new solution. It's always easier to think about doing it later. You need to use your ingenuity to overcome the urge to procrastinate.

PSYCHOLOGICAL ROADBLOCKS TO ACTION

Let's look more closely at several psychological roadblocks that impede action, as outlined below (Figure 8-1).

Fear of failure

Because failure is rewarded with punishment in many organizations, many people make it their primary career goal to avoid failure at any cost. Rather than expose problems or attempt anything novel, they hide problems. If their performance is judged on attaining specific goals, they set those goals as low as possible. Unsure that they can deliver results in time, they refuse to commit themselves to timetables. Working in interfunctional teams, they hesitate to do

1 We don't convert ideas into simple, specific, realistic action plans.
2 We fear the unknown.
3 We fear our solution might fail.
4 We fear our solution isn't perfect.
5 We can't say no to other things.
6 Figuring we need a home run every time, we don't even go up to bat.
7 We avoid tasks we don't like.

Fig. 8.1 Psychological roadblocks that impede action

their part until others have already done theirs. They disown new opportunities or problems that don't fall clearly within their jurisdiction. While people busy themselves with narrow departmental issues, many vital problems affecting the entire organization simply fall between the cracks.

Our upbringing and education equate failure with being wrong. We soon learn that taking risks is not a good idea. Better to act only when you're certain of being correct. Yet in a changing world, you can never be certain of being right. A failure to try is actually a failure to learn.

A major problem for North American businesses is indecision and reluctance on the part of middle and senior managers to adopt new product and technology ideas. Who wants to be identified with a decision that might fail? Because few members of the management 'team' actually operate together as a cohesive unit, they fail to agree as a group on taking a risk. Their subordinates view them as indecisive, uninterested in innovation, and committed only to short-term results. Small wonder that frustration results.

Fear of the unknown

Implementing a new solution is like walking on unfamiliar ground. Without being able to read the terrain, it's impossible to predict where you'll end up. And the new solution will bring its own set of new problems or opportunities in the form of new fuzzy situations. Hence it's more comforting to stick with the routine.

Fear of imperfection

Too much of our education is based on choosing the right answers to questions. Under this system, a flawed or imperfect solution must be wrong. People prefer to wait until the perfect solution occurs, an unrealistic hope.

We can't say no to other things

For many people, it's easier to keep busy with routine, familiar tasks than to tackle anything new. This is particularly true if the 'new' carries a risk of failure or imperfection that might harm their esteem, career or wallet. It's this thinking that leads many people to focus on the simplest items on their to-do lists in order to gain a quick sense of accomplishment. In fact, the to-do items that involve implementing new solutions and entering unknown territory are usually so time-consuming and so risky that they're left undone. In organizations with so-called matrix teams working on long-term projects, members start missing team meetings in favor of carrying out 'vital' short-term tasks within their departments. After all, how can you ignore today's pressing matter in order to devote time to the team's mission of tomorrow?

For example, many research and development departments regard ideas submitted from outside the department as disruptions to their own routines. Its employees already have their hands full with their own projects and deadlines—developing new and improved products and processes, conducting market tests, obtaining government approval for new products, helping support other departments. Doing well on these projects and deadlines is what counts in their performance appraisals. They are reluctant to take time away from these established routines to explore an untried idea. Instead, the simplest response is often to come up with a reason to reject the idea outright.

Few organizations provide the incentive to build on such ideas. They actually penalize individuals who take too much time from their allotted projects. For these organizations, if anyone has the time to explore new ideas, it's a sign that the department must be slack and inefficient.

The importance of creating a specific action plan

Procrastination needs no elaborate explanation. Suffice to say that most of us encounter it all too frequently. One reason that we put things off is that we fail to translate our ideas into simple, specific action plans. Without detailed action steps, an abstract idea for a solution remains just that. How often have you left a problem solving meeting feeling unsure about what you were supposed to accomplish? What's missing is a clear plan showing exactly who was supposed to do what, when, where and how. The more specific, clearly understood, easily visualized, and realistic yet challenging the plan, the more motivated and committed people are to accomplishing it.

This is the sixth step in the Simplex process—creatively planning action. In this step, the individual or group must provide motivation and commitment to act by developing a clear, creative implementation plan, a 'road map to success.' An action plan like the one in Figure 8-2 helps to build commitment to action through the closure principle. Once you've started something, you want to see it through to attain a sense of completion.

Problem statement: ————————————————————————

Idea selected: ————————————————————————

	What will be done	How will it be done	By whom	When	Where
1					
2					
3					
4					
5					
6					
7					
8					

Fig. 8.2 Action plan

So how do you create this action plan?

As in all the previous steps in our process, you first suspend judgment and extend effort to create a list of difficulties that you might encounter in implementing your new solution. Use prompter questions like those in Figure 8-3 to help you uncover these difficulties.

Based on this list—still deferring judgment and extending effort—you must generate a list of answers to the following prompter question: 'What specific steps might I take to get the ball rolling on this solution?' (Figure 8-4). Make your answers as simple, specific and action-oriented as possible. Start each one with a verb. Avoid philosophizing.

As in all previous steps, your next task is to select the most important step to take. Write this step on Figure 8-2 under the heading 'what will be done.' Then write 'how it will be done' in the next column. In the third column, 'by whom,' place your own name. In the next two columns, 'when' and 'where,' put specific times and places where you will accomplish the 'what' and 'how.'

1 What new problems might this idea create?
2 Where might there arise some difficulties?
3 Who will this idea affect? Who will gain or benefit? Who might be concerned?
4 How should this idea be introduced?
5 When is the best time to introduce it?

Fig. 8.3 Prompter questions for anticipating difficulties in implementing a solution

Idea selected: _____

_____

Diverge: What specific steps might we in this group take to get the ball rolling?

Fig. 8.4 Action plan divergence

STEP 7: GAINING ACCEPTANCE

During your action planning, you probably identified people whose acceptance, support or approval you'll need in order to successfully implement your solution. In fact, you might have listed as one or more of your action steps the need to gain acceptance from one of these people. Why? There are a number of reasons.

When you ask someone to take a personal risk by approving or participating in your solution, you are asking them to venture into the unknown. You must figure out how to reduce their attendant discomfort, or you will not get their approval or the participation you need.

Even if your idea causes no discomfort, you will want to entice others to participate in making the change. When people feel they have taken part in making a change, they will help to make it work. If they feel excluded from the process, they are less likely to help and may even oppose its implementation. In organizations, this is called the 'not invented here' factor. If a new idea is associated exclusively with a single department, others may automatically reject it on principle.

Seeking approval or agreement on anything involves 'selling' people. You may resent having to 'sell' others on the merits of a seemingly valuable idea. In fact, better ideas are often harder to sell, because they usually mean greater change. Thus, you have to become an effective salesperson if you hope to implement creative ideas. In effective organizations, people develop their selling skills. For example, someone in marketing learns skills in convincing a product development colleague to help in recommending a new advertising strategy. A manufacturing vice-president develops skill in encouraging a sales colleague to improve production forecasting accuracy.

HOW TO SELL IDEAS

Here are some ideas on how to build your skills in this step of the creative process (Figure 8-5). One of the major skills is reducing the discomfort that new ideas bring.

Present your idea in simple terms to ensure it's understood. If I have difficulty grasping your idea, I'm immediately on the defensive. The less I understand it, the more I will fear it. If you make the idea simple, I immediately feel more confident and fear the idea less. I also trust you more, knowing that you have done your homework and are comfortable with the idea yourself.

Anticipate the listener's possible objections and prepare your responses to them. Here the seller actually becomes coach and teacher. Anticipating objections increases the buyer's confidence in your ability to successfully implement your solution and helps him better understand the idea itself.

- Give others some control; be sensitive to the 'people' aspects of your change.
- Spread ownership of your idea.
- Give others credit at every opportunity.
- Show others that they have already used the concept.
- Leave something for the listener to change or improve.
- Involve others in fleshing out the implementation details.
- Don't make it easy for others to say no.
- Present your idea at a good time.
- Let your enthusiasm be contagious.
- Acknowledge your own misgivings.
- Ask your listeners to 'do', not just 'listen.'
- Use attractive visual aids.
- Appeal to all five of your listeners' senses.
- Ask for others' opinions.

Fig. 8.5 Reducing others' discomfort with new ideas

Ensure that the listener understands how the idea will benefit him or her. If I am a rational decision-maker, and if your proposal benefits me or my organization, then I would be illogical or foolish to oppose it. On the other hand, if your proposal benefits only you, then it is difficult for me to see why I should go to some trouble and risk to support it.

Even better, show the potential buyer how your idea helps solve his or her important problem. Use a planning instrument as in Figure 8-6. Your knowledge of the entire Simplex process will help you with this step. It's your job to walk the listener through the process—to realize that an opportunity for improvement exists, to get agreement that a useful challenge can be solved, to propose an idea, to discuss variations and agree on a final solution, and to make an action plan. Any objections merely become challenges for you to help the listener overcome. By using this planning instrument over and over again, you can improve your skills in gaining acceptance for your new ideas. Practise your use of the instrument by role-playing. Ask a colleague to serve as the guinea pig and give you advice on improving your presentation.

More ways to sell ideas

Here are some more points to consider when you're creating and presenting your selling plan.

Find a way to involve the listener and others affected by the change in implementing your idea. This gives them some control over what happens.

1 Selected idea: _____

_____

2 The listener is: _____

3 What problem of the listener will this idea help solve? _____

_____

4 What specifically do I want the listener to do?
I want the listener to: _____

_____

_____ on/by _____

5	Why should it be done? (List benefits)	Evidence? (How might each benefit be understood?)
A.		
B.		
C.		
D.		

6	What are the listener's possible concerns?	How might these concerns be overcome?
A.		
B.		
C.		
D.		

Fig. 8.6 Selling your idea

Remember that changes that seem small to you might appear big to others. For example, asking people in an open office arrangement to give up a few inches of space to accommodate an office reorganization might dredge up all kinds of unrelated grievances that have lain buried for years. To them, your idea threatens a loss of status, however unintentional. Show them that you're sensitive to the social implications of the change. Do your best to spread ownership of your idea. If someone else triggered the idea in your mind, even ever so slightly, make sure that you give him credit whenever you can. Try to show others that they have already used the 'new' concept themselves in other ways, perhaps without realizing it. Deliberately leave something to be changed or improved in your idea that might be added by the listener. Involve them in developing further details of how the change should be implemented. Rather than ask for a yes or no answer (which means running the risk of their saying no), give the listener the choice of two yeses: 'Should we start tomorrow or the day after?'

One way that people take the edge off of uncomfortable situations and lighten them up is by making their ideas attractive, perhaps by using humor. Make your presentation fun. Avoid proposing your new idea when people are not in the right frame of mind to accept it—late Friday afternoon, first thing Monday morning, 10 minutes before lunch. Let your enthusiasm for your idea be contagious. Acknowledge any misgivings that you might have had about treading into the unknown, then explain how you relieved your own anxiety by emphasizing your idea's advantages. Involve your listeners in doing something as you present your idea rather than allow them to just sit back and listen. Encouraging them to 'do' rather than 'listen' will help them better understand the idea. Use visual aids that are as attractive as possible or that require their assistance, or that involve listeners' senses besides the obvious one of sight. Let them touch, smell or taste a prototype. Let them hear what your product sounds like or what others have said about it. Ask for their opinions. Remember the adage: people don't resist change, they resist being changed.

STEP 8: TAKING ACTION

Taking action is a specific eighth step in the Simplex creative problem solving process. By now, you've discovered a great problem, uncovered intriguing new facts, formulated an insightful challenge, created an outstanding solution, made a foolproof action plan, and gained all the support you need. But unless you take the plunge, all your work until now will have been a waste of time. Creativity is as important here as anywhere else around the wheel.

If you find it hard to take action, you're hardly alone. Most of us have trouble encouraging ourselves to take necessary action, even when we know exactly what to do. We find it even more difficult when we are somewhat fuzzy about the necessary action. Having won acceptance and approval for your idea, you still have to go from putting the idea down on paper to putting it into play.

How to overcome your own fear of the unknown, fear of failure and fear of the imperfect? How to overcome your own procrastination? How to become not just an 'action thinker' but an 'action taker'?

If you learn to use the Simplex process, you'll find ways to solve this particular problem just as you solve any other kind of problem. Begin by determining your major personal roadblock to action. Come up with 10 or 15 specific ways to overcome it. For any particular solution you are trying to implement, think of ideas to help you propel yourself into action. Following is a list of specific techniques that might prompt you into action (Figure 8-7).

HOW TO PROMPT YOURSELF TO ACT

The first three techniques address three common fears that prevent action: fear of the unknown, fear of failure, and fear of an imperfect solution. One technique for conquering *fear of the unknown* I call 'writing down the worst that can happen.' The worst outcome is seldom so daunting when you see it on paper instead of simply rolling it over and over in your mind. Developing a strategy to cope with the worst-case scenario can help reduce this fear.

In order to overcome the *fear of failure*, why not share your plan with others? By doing so, you might obtain their ideas to improve your chance of success. This helps you to realize that your situation is hardly unique—others have failed and survived. This technique helps you develop a strategy to minimize problems associated with potential failure. You might even turn failure into opportunity. And it helps you realize that fear of failure is the price of taking a risk on the way to success.

1 Write down the worst thing that can happen.
2 Share your plan with others.
  Develop a strategy to minimize your discomfort and a way to turn failure to your advantage.
3 Ask yourself: 'If I wait, how much better will a later solution be?'
4 Use the closure principle.
5 Break big tasks down into smaller pieces.
6 Learn to 'reverse-prioritize' (Learn to say No.)
7 Set deadlines for yourself (in writing if possible).
8 Share your deadline commitments with others.
9 Promise yourself significant rewards on meeting deadlines.
10 Use the 'broccoli first' principle—do the part you hate the most first to get it out of the way.

Fig. 8.7 Ways to spur yourself to action

Think of Babe Ruth, considered by many as the greatest player in baseball history. Other batters with two strikes against them might have shortened up on the bat in order to reduce the risk of striking out. But Ruth swung just as hard as ever. As a result, he struck out more often than any other player. But he also hit far more home runs per time at bat (one in 11) than anyone else. Asked what he thought about when he struck out, he said, 'I think of home runs.' He saw more failure as the necessary price to pay for a bigger goal—more home runs. Failing on small goals is a way to achieve success with bigger goals.

What you'll probably find is that your solution will be neither a complete success nor a complete failure, but something in between. Consider it as a first pass on which you can build toward real success. You will likely need to adapt the solution and your plan more than once, as your actions involve people, things and events in unpredictable ways.

The third fear is that *your solution might be less than perfect*. And haven't we all been taught that if a solution is imperfect, it must somehow be wrong? Think of school exams of the true-false, multiple-choice variety with either right or wrong answers. Carrying this mindset over to our work, we often look for the flaw in a solution rather than looking at the solution as a whole. In order to overcome this fear, simply ask yourself, 'If I wait, will a better solution present itself?' You will probably realize that no amount of time will bring you the perfect solution. In fact, if you wait much longer, your opportunity for making valuable change may be lost.

The fourth technique uses the psychological phenomenon called *closure*. We have a natural desire for closure, for hearing the second shoe drop, for completing what we've begun. For example, you invoke the closure principle when you write your daily to-do list. If by the end of the day, you have not checked off several of the items as complete, you will lack a sense of accomplishment or closure. This knowledge propels you into action. Many writers use the principle in order to 'break the ice' of a blank screen on their word processor. They get themselves started by simply typing in nonsense. Having begun to fill the screen, they feel compelled to continue writing until something valuable begins to emerge. Similarly, you can employ closure in implementing your action plan by starting somewhere, no matter how insignificant the step. (Don't confuse this technique with procrastination, the trick of diving into the easiest items on your to-do list in order to put off your truly important tasks.)

The fifth technique works on the same principle. People are often unable to begin a particular step in an action plan because they view the plan as a single, large task that is too big to handle. Try the '*pepperoni principle*': visualize the giant task as a lot of smaller pieces to be bitten off a slice at a time. Even delegate a few smaller tasks in order to build momentum. In trying to get your mind around larger tasks, make closure work for you. Deliberately set aside a large enough block of time to start and complete the task without interruption. Perhaps collar someone whose job it is to get you out on time with a finished product.

The sixth technique is called 'reverse prioritizing.' Think of this technique as starting at the bottom of your priority list. Decide what items are relatively unimportant, and refuse to do them. Instead, get started on the action steps that will lead to real improvement. This single skill will take you further toward distinguishing yourself in your organization than almost any other skill that we'll discuss in this book. People often avoid committing themselves to act on important matters by purposely tying themselves up in more trivial activities. In his book *Up the Organization*, Robert Townsend, former highly successful president of Avis, kept the following question posted on the wall before his desk: 'Is what I'm doing or about to do getting us closer to our objectives?' This reminder continually saved him from countless worthless trips, meetings and lunches. It helped him to 'reverse prioritize,' triggering him to act only on important matters.

Two other techniques—*setting deadlines for yourself in writing,* and *sharing your deadline commitments with others*—combine the principles of closure, and setting goals and visualizing success in meeting them. The latter principle is described by Maxwell Maltz in his book *Psychocybernetics*: when we clearly visualize success in accomplishing a specific task, we automatically trigger a mechanism hidden within ourselves that moves us toward that success. Spelling out your deadlines makes them more clear, turns them into tangible, visible goals, and starts closure working. Telling others about your deadlines further builds closure, as you have committed not only to yourself but to others.

Another technique, *promising yourself rewards on meeting deadlines*, employs modern motivational and behavior modification theory. The idea here is that rewarding a particular behavior is a way to stimulate its occurrence. For example, promising to treat yourself to lunch at a nice restaurant if you meet an action plan deadline will trigger the action.

You have probably known the last technique, '*broccoli first*,' since childhood. It is one that your mother might have used to encourage you to eat everything set before you. Once you got through the broccoli, everything else tasted better. Similarly, accomplishing the most unpleasant task first may make the others seem easier. In making innovative changes, early action steps are often such unpleasant tasks. This is to be expected. But after you get through these steps, you begin to see your innovative solution take shape. The excitement you experience makes the early discomfort worthwhile.

Having come up with ways to trigger you into moving from thinking about action to taking action, you now must take steps to achieve completion. You must diligently involve yourself in bird-dogging (ensuring that others are getting their action steps done), clearing roadblocks and adapting your plan as the solution unfolds. Always remember that no one wants your plan to succeed as much as you do. Others can easily be drawn away by competing priorities. Persistence is important here. Recall Thomas Edison's quote: 'Genius is 1 per cent inspiration, 99 per cent perspiration.' As the final step in the process of creative problem solving, this is the one that most requires your hands-on attention in order to avoid dropping the ball. Accomplishing this eighth step is like playing a football game with only seconds on the clock and the goal line only a yard away. While everyone on the field knows the play, it's still up to one ball carrier to make it happen.

In the preceding chapters, we discussed a circular creative process called Simplex designed to mainstream innovation and help you to dramatically improve your personal performance. When you use the process, you work your way through all eight steps to deliberately find and solve important problems and implement the solutions. The valuable changes you accomplish point you to new opportunities for further improvement and innovation, launching you on your next cycle around the wheel. In the chapters ahead, we will introduce the process skills you must develop in order to make this creative process succeed.

9

THREE PROCESS SKILLS FOR MAKING INNOVATION A WAY OF LIFE

Making a bad decision worse

Alice said, 'You know, Harry, your story about going through the motions reminds me of what's going on at our place right now. We've got two plants in two different regions, both making the same products. That used to be okay when we were running flat out, but these days it just means overcapacity. We don't really need two plants.'

Harry said, 'So the company's trying to decide which plant to close, right?'

'Exactly. But what bothers me is the way head office is going about it. See, we've got a motto of our own that the human resources people came up with. We are supposed to be a data-driven organization.'

'What does that mean?' I asked.

'It's supposed to mean that we make decisions based on accurate facts, without bias. We let the facts speak for themselves and tell us what to do. But in this case we're doing exactly the opposite.'

'I'll bet they're closing the wrong one,' said Harry.

'Precisely. The plant they're going to close is the one with lower costs, higher quality, a more loyal workforce. But you see, senior management got sandbagged when they bought the other plant three years ago. It was only after they'd bought it that they found out it had all kinds of problems. Poor quality. Lousy union–management relations. High costs. But they can hardly shut it down now. If they did, you can just imagine what the shareholders would have to say about it.'

'So just to save face, they're going to make a bad decision worse instead of making the right decision,' I said.

'That's it. Not very creative, was it? I mean, it's one thing to create options. But isn't part of being creative the ability to make good choices from among the options? Just think: if Edison had only been able to generate ideas but couldn't evaluate them properly, he wouldn't have come up with anywhere near the number of successful inventions that he did.'

'I couldn't agree more,' I said. 'The creative process means you need skills not just in generating options but also in converging on the good ones. Above all, you need to be able to keep an open mind instead of simply prejudging options.' ∎

Summary of learnings

✦ *Whether it's a simple process like brainstorming or a more complex one like total quality management, process skills are needed to properly execute the process.*

✦ *Three process skills required to implement any process are deferral of judgment, active divergence and active convergence. They are especially critical in implementing the Simplex process to mainstream innovation. The three skills help to make each of the eight steps of the Simplex process work.*

We discussed earlier how important it is to separate content from process. We also outlined the circular process of Simplex creative problem solving that you can use to distinguish yourself in your organization and dramatically improve your performance. Now let's take the discussion a step further. Here we'll outline the specific skills you need in order to use the process to full advantage. If half the battle is in understanding the difference between managing process and managing content, then the other half is in developing these necessary process skills.

QUALITY RESULTS = CONTENT + PROCESS + PROCESS SKILLS

Remember our equation that summarizes these distinctions (Figure 9-1). Few organizations truly understand this equation. Concerned only with content, and unaware of the power of both process and process skills, they end up with inferior results. Let's look at three examples.

Quality Results = Content + Process + Process Skills

Fig. 9.1 The quality results equation

IT'S NOT JUST *WHAT* YOU DO, BUT *HOW*

Buying a training program won't change the way you do things

Suppose an organization wants to improve its inventory management in order to reduce costs (*the desired quality result*). It spends $2.5 million on computer hardware and software (*the content*) designed to improve inventory control. However, it allots only about $20,000 to developing and documenting a new inventory control system (*the process*) within which the equipment will function. And while it may train individuals to use the equipment, it provides no training in the skills needed to execute the new process (*process skills*). By rights, the organization should set aside more money and resources to establish the process and the process skills, not just the content. Without enough attention to process and process skills, the equipment will remain underused or only haphazardly used by people still working under the previous process.

A second related example may hit closer to home. How many people have rushed out to buy personal computers, only to leave them sitting unused on their desks? What they have failed to consider are the new processes by which they plan to use the equipment (*the content*). Suppose you're looking for a more efficient way to mail information to customers (*the process*) from your home-based business. If you plan to spend several thousand dollars on a new PC, isn't it worth spending the necessary amount for a computer expert to design your process and provide the necessary training (*process skills*)? Having invested in all three elements—content, process and process skills—you're ready to reap your quality results: more efficient mail-outs.

A third example comes from total quality management (TQM), a concept many organizations have tried to adopt (Figure 9-2). Many of these companies have done nothing more than provide seminars and books that explain the concept to employees. In other words, they have invested in nothing more than content. Their employees often return to their jobs with an understanding of the TQM philosophy and a few standard tools like flowcharting and fishboning. But, finding no change in their jobs (*the process*), they soon revert to doing the same old things in the same old ways. But total quality management itself embodies a process, not just content. TQM is really a process of continually finding customers' problems and changing internal processes to solve them. Unless the organization establishes this continuous innovation process

Results	Content	Process	Process Skills
Unsuccessful TQM program	TQM philosophy and standard quality tools	Everyone returns to work without any change in their jobs. Their jobs do not include a change-making process of finding and solving customer problems.	Everyone returns to work without any new skills in the change-making process.
Successful TQM program	TQM philosophy and standard quality tools	Everyone's job includes the process of finding and solving customer problems.	Everyone has creative skills in finding and solving customer problems.

Fig. 9.2 How lack of process skills renders TQM programs unsuccessful

throughout its ranks, and unless people receive training in the skills they need to execute the process, the organization will see no improvement in its results.

It's one thing for a company to *say* that it believes, for example, in the TQM philosophy of putting quality ahead of profits. It's another thing to establish performance appraisal and reward systems that actually encourage employees to work toward long-term rather than short-term gains. Unless the organization makes these kinds of investments to improve its internal processes, the money it spends on TQM's content will be wasted.

Having bought only the content, these organizations have come only partway. They have failed to mainstream TQM as a process. They have failed to invest the necessary time and effort to change organizational processes that will make total quality management 'stick' in daily practice. And they have failed to invest in giving their managers training in the necessary skills to support the process. So people assume that TQM is something 'extra,' something above and beyond their regular jobs.

Developing your process skills

Managing process is one important part of instituting TQM. Developing the process skills you need to manage process is another. Part of TQM's content, for example, is customer service. Just talking about the importance of customer service will accomplish nothing. Installing a process that motivates employees to improve customer service is a good start. This process might include a schedule of regular meetings designed to allow employees to learn about and prioritize their top customers' problems. The meetings would also help employees to come up with new procedures that solve these problems, perhaps through new or improved processes or even new products or services.

But if the team members lack skill in executing this process, then the team will accomplish little more. The process skills needed in this case include teamwork skills in problem finding, problem solving and solution implementation. The group needs these process skills for conducting effective fact finding and fact sharing, for focusing on solving problems rather than simply protecting turf, for leading problem solving teams, and for helping customers and suppliers join in to solve problems. Senior managers also require process skills in this case: establishing and executing performance appraisal and reward systems that encourage team members to carry out the process; providing training that helps team members develop their own process skills.

Let's take another example that differentiates between process and process skills. This time, we'll look at the skills needed by the group mentioned above during a brainstorming session (Figure 9-3).

Recall that brainstorming is a specific technique in idea finding, the fourth step of the Simplex process. Here, a group generates potential solutions to a specific challenge using four rules: no criticism, go for quantity, hitchhike, and

Results	Content	Process	Process Skills
Solutions which are unimaginative and not new	People knowledgeable about a problem	Brainstorming	• Poor • Lots of killer phrases • Radical ideas ridiculed • Few ideas ventured, low quantity • Lots of prejudging • People inhibited
New imaginative solutions	People knowledgeable about a problem	Brainstorming	• Good • No killer phrases • Lots of ideas ventured, high quantity • Lots of radical, wild ideas • Lots of hitchhiking and piggybacking on each other's ideas

Fig. 9.3 How lack of process skills renders brainstorming sessions unsuccessful

freewheel. Most people are familiar with this process, including these four rules. But few have the needed skills to successfully execute the process. Among these skills are the following:

- Avoid making negative judgments on fledgling ideas;
- Welcome other points of view as a chance to strengthen a solution rather than as a threat to your ego;
- Show an open mind to new ideas and approaches;
- Be willing to choose an unusual solution;

- Think up many novel, or even wild, ideas and options without fear of ridicule;
- Extend effort to generate yet more new ideas;
- Develop and use unbiased criteria for selecting from among the ideas.

Few brainstorming groups actually behave in this way. Instead, the group generates few ideas, and most ideas that do come out are logical, safe and hardly novel. Most people feel they must explain and justify each of their ideas. Few wild ideas are ventured. The few that do come out are usually greeted by laughter or a patronizing attitude ('I know you meant that as a wild idea, but you know we'd get into a lot of trouble if we adopted it'). Rarely does the group attempt to build upon the wild ideas in order to create more practical ideas. Most members feel they have to judge each idea's value, believing that they are saving the group time.

Take a look at the 'killer phrases' in Figure 9-4 common to many organizations. Are any familiar? You've probably encountered them yourself. They are a

```
 1  A good idea, but ...
 2  Against company policy.
 3  All right in theory.
 4  Be practical.
 5  Costs too much.
 6  Don't start anything yet.
 7  It needs more study.
 8  It's not budgeted.
 9  It's not good enough.
10  It's not part of your job.
11  Let's make a survey first.
12  Let's sit on it for a while.
13  That's not our problem.
14  The boss won't go for it.
15  The old timers won't use it.
16  Too hard to administer.
17  We have been doing it this way for a long time and  it works.
18  Why hasn't someone suggested it before if it's such a good idea?
19  Ahead of the times.
20  Let's discuss it.
21  Let's form a committee.
22  We've never done it that way before.
23  Who else has tried it?
```

Fig. 9.4 Killer phrases

sure sign that your team members fail to understand the difference between knowing the theory behind a process and developing the process skills they need in order to make the process work. We'll discuss killer phrases in greater detail in the next chapter.

In fact, the process skills required in this brainstorming example are the key to making any process work. We can classify these process skills into three categories: deferral of judgment skills, active divergence skills, and active convergence skills. These three process skills are *the* critical skills for implementing the Simplex process of creative problem solving and for mainstreaming innovation. In each of the eight steps of the process, you must exercise skills in deferring judgment, actively diverging and actively converging. You must also exercise these skills *between* each of the eight steps. Let's take a closer look at these process skills, and understand how they make each step in the Simplex process work.

10

THE THREE PROCESS SKILLS: DIVERGING, CONVERGING AND DEFERRING JUDGMENT

If you get yelled at everytime . . .

'You know', I said, 'all this talk about brainstorming and creating and evaluating options reminds me of somebody I knew, the executive vice-president of a big company. He really believed in innovation. But he thought he could save a lot of people a whole lot of time by cutting to the chase, pointing out flaws in people's ideas just so they could dispense with them and move on. Trouble was, he only ended up embarrassing people in front of others. It got to the point that nobody ventured any new ideas because they didn't like being yelled at.'

'Ah yes,' said Harry, nodding his head. 'The tyrant.'

'Yes, but a benevolent tyrant. This guy honestly believed he was helping people. In his way, he was trying to train them to come up with practical ideas and stay on track. He thought the louder he yelled at them, the faster they would learn to create better ideas and make better decisions. But, in fact, what happened was that people just clammed up. Many of his best employees were actually leaving the company rather than live in fear and be frustrated.'

'Were you able to help him?' Alice asked.

'I tried all kinds of things. I pointed out that people could be more creative in a relaxed, supportive environment, one where they didn't feel they were walking around with a sword over their heads. And I suggested using creative process skills, especially during teamwork. Skills like active divergence, thinking up all kinds of options. Then active convergence, using good judgment to select the best options. And then deferral of judgment, to keep the two apart. I hear that my benevolent tyrant has made some progress. At least he's able to recognize when he starts to fall into his old ways. Time will tell, I guess.' ∎

Summary of learnings

✦ *Within each step of Simplex, you use divergent thinking to generate options and information, then use convergent thinking to judge, evaluate and analyze the options and information. The quality of your final solution depends on your skill in executing both kinds of thinking within each step, and in separating the two.*

✦ *Most formal learning conditions us to emphasize convergent thinking to the virtual exclusion of divergent thinking.*

✦ *The key to balancing divergent and convergent thinking—and thus improving your creativity—is developing the third process skill of deferral of judgment.*

✦ *We find it difficult to separate the skills of divergent and convergent thinking, even though these are separate functions of the brain along with two others— absorbing knowledge and retaining knowledge in memory.*

✦ *Killer phrases, which impede the entire creative process, are an example of attempts to diverge and converge at the same time.*

✦ *Separating divergent and convergent thinking through the process skill of deferral of judgment allows our minds to work most creatively. Learning to defer judgment allows you to execute the two-step process of ideation-evaluation. Ideation is roughly synonymous with divergent thinking; evaluation is roughly synonymous with convergent thinking.*

✦ *You can learn to execute this ideation-evaluation process by following guidelines for ideation and for evaluation.*

✦ *Effective ideation requires you to deliberately assume different points of view.*

Divergent thinking is the kind of thinking you use when you're generating options or information in each step of the Simplex process without pausing to judge or analyze them. The term reflects the idea of radiating outward in many directions from a single point. But you need to do more than simply come up with a lot of options or a lot of information. Eventually, you have to select one or a few options or pieces of information to take toward an implemented solution. Selecting options or particular bits of information in each step requires convergent thinking, using your ability to judge, evaluate and analyze. The quality of the result of your creative work depends on your skills in executing both divergent and convergent thinking.

DIVERGENCE AND CONVERGENCE: THE TWO-SIDED THINKING PROCESS

Let's ponder this two-sided thinking process a bit further. If you defer judgment and logic, and concentrate only on generating options within any step of Simplex, you will end up with even more options. But if you judge each option as it occurs to you, and point out its flaws along the way, will you come up with as long or as interesting a list? Probably not. For this reason, logic and judgment are taboo during divergent thinking. Only during later convergent thinking do they come into play.

In order to effectively find and solve important problems and implement good solutions, you need skills in both divergent thinking and convergent thinking—and skills in separating the two. Each step in the Simplex process incorporates this two-sided method—the freedom of divergent thinking tempered later with the discipline of convergent thinking (Figure 10-1).

Recall an earlier chapter in which we divided real-world problems into two kinds: analytical, or those with one correct answer, and creative, or those with many correct answers. It's usually easier to find the first workable answer than to think divergently for richer solutions. That's why we become conditioned to emphasize convergent thinking almost entirely over divergent thinking.

Think about the learning process, at school, at home or at work. Most of our formal education emphasizes training on the converging side of this two-sided thinking process. We usually need to look for the one correct answer to a question. Think of your high school exams in physics, chemistry and mathematics. Didn't the questions have one correct answer? How about history and geography? Weren't there a lot of true/false and multiple-choice questions requiring a single correct answer? Even for an English exam, in which you might have expected to enjoy some latitude, you knew deep down that it was safer to regurgitate the teacher's preferred analysis of a poem or story rather than chance something different. Your teachers probably would rather have encouraged you to think divergently, as this would have led to richer answers. But they were likely constrained by too little time and too large classes.

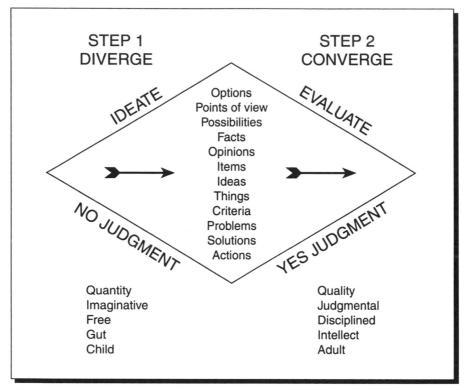

Fig. 10.1 The ideation-evaluation process

If we want to use the creative process, we need to exercise a two-sided approach that balances divergent and convergent thinking. Because we fail to nurture the former, our inborn creative capacity begins to ebb early. By the time we become adults, most of us use only about 10 per cent of our creative potential. Our task, then, is to learn to balance the process skills of convergent and divergent thinking.

BETWEEN DIVERGENCE AND CONVERGENCE: DEFERRAL OF JUDGMENT

A key to learning this balance is to develop the third vital process skill—deferral of judgment (Figure 10-2). In his book *Applied Imagination*, Alex Osborn, the father of brainstorming and founder of the Creative Education Foundation in Buffalo, New York, underscores the importance of this process skill. He tells of a successful business leader who was asked one question again and again throughout his career: 'How do you spend your day?' His reply was just as straightforward: 'I have one job to do. I try to keep closed minds open.' What

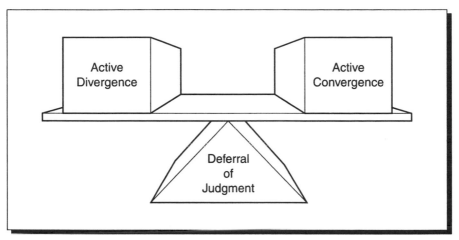

Fig. 10.2 Balancing the process skills of active divergence and active convergence using the process skill of deferral of judgment

he was talking about is the process skill of deferral of judgment. He knew that it was impossible for people to think divergently if they were unable to defer convergent thinking. Only by coaching them to improve this process skill could he help them tap into their imaginations. In order to improve your creativity, you have to work at keeping your own mind open by developing your process skill of deferral of judgment.

Why is it so hard to develop this process skill? Why do we jumble the two essential process skills of divergent thinking and convergent thinking? Strangely enough, according to the 'Structure of Intellect' model developed by University of Southern California psychologist J.P. Guilford, our brain functions can be simplified and easily divided into four separate operations (Figure 10-3). (Guilford actually identified five operations, but for our purposes, we can condense them into four.) These distinct functions are absorbing knowledge; retaining knowledge; diverging, or using imagination to generate options and new knowledge; and converging, or analyzing and judging. Despite the fact that these are distinct operations, few of us can separate them in practice.

1 Absorb – understanding; knowledge.
2 Retain – memory.
3 Diverge – imagination.
4 Converge – judgment; logic.

Fig. 10.3 The four functions of the brain

Recall that we said in the previous chapter that fledgling ideas and options floated during brainstorming sessions are often shot down by killer phrases even before they get airborne. Our use of these killer phrases extends far beyond simple brainstorming. Beyond idea finding alone, they trip us up throughout the entire creative process. What exactly is a killer phrase?

KILLER PHRASES

A killer phrase is a verbal or visual expression that shuts down a train of thought. It might be a judgment of a fledgling solution, perhaps not intended as negative but perceived that way by others. It can be analysis or logic inserted in the wrong place, like prematurely dissecting a fact offered during divergent fact finding. Killer phrases might reflect the user's lack of understanding of an option or piece of information. Or they might reflect a biased viewpoint that favors a predetermined outcome. Whatever its source and however it shows up, a killer phrase makes people apprehensive and reluctant to offer further thoughts, thus 'killing' the creative process. What a waste of potential.

Suppose instead that we were highly skilled in deferring judgment and in freely sharing our thoughts with each other. Unfortunately, because we lack this process skill, we unwittingly use the same killer phrases continually. How many times a day do we say, for example, either to ourselves or to others, 'That's a good idea, but...'? Whenever we do this, we interrupt a train of thought and often cause hard feelings at the same time. We seesaw back and forth between constructing new thoughts and tearing them apart.

This particular killer phrase is a classic example of our attempt to diverge and converge at the same time. We want to recognize the idea as a good one, but we also want to be 'helpful' by invoking judgment and logic to point out its flaw. Trying to use both process skills at the same time is like trying to open a door without realizing that someone on the other side is trying equally hard to close it. Both people's good intentions work at cross purposes, resulting in frustration, wasted energy, and no progress. Our minds work most creatively when we can separate the two operations. We separate them by using the process skill of deferral of judgment.

By learning to do so, we can execute the two-step process of ideation-evaluation. Ideation, meaning roughly the same thing as divergent thinking, involves aggressively generating ideas and options without applying judgment or logic. Evaluation is a process of applying judgment to select the most appropriate ideas or options. In the two-step process, you ideate first, evaluate second.

Perhaps you can see that using the process skill of deferral of judgment to separate the process skills of divergent thinking and convergent thinking is better than mixing the two together. But how do you do so? Here are seven extremely useful guidelines to help you develop your ideation ability (Figure

---

1 No evaluation or logical thinking permitted.
2 Relax your brain. Don't worry about being right.
3 Quantity of ideas is all-important.
4 Strive to maintain an uninterrupted stream of ideas.
5 Reach for radical, impossible ideas.
6 Think in pictures. Use all five senses.
7 Build on 'idea fragments.'

Fig. 10.4 Guidelines to effective ideation

10-4). These guidelines help you to exercise the process skills of deferral of judgment and active divergence, both essential for ideation.

TOWARD BETTER IDEATION

- No logic or judgment permitted. By definition, this is self-evident. As soon as you use judgment or logic, you're no longer ideating but evaluating.
- Don't worry about being right or wrong. Worrying about whether particular thoughts are right or wrong as you generate them is evaluation, not ideation. Relax. Research by Bulgarian psychologist Georgi Lozanov, for example, shows that a relaxed frame of mind dramatically improves learning and problem solving (the principle behind such techniques as meditation).
- Strive for quantity of ideas, not quality. Quality results from quantity. Don't worry about how good the idea is while you're ideating. Extend your effort to generate many options and additional information, no matter the quality. If you're too concerned about quality, you'll end up with fewer good ideas— not to mention the fact that you've slipped into evaluation.
- Think in a continuous, rapid stream. Consider each idea not as an end in itself but as a stepping stone to another idea.
- Welcome radical ideas. Anyone skilled in producing highly unusual, even seemingly impossible or impractical thoughts, will eventually come up with novel approaches. This skill is even more invaluable when you're working in a group. Radical ideas shed a completely different light on a problem. They stimulate others to build new ideas of their own in previously unseen directions.
- Think in pictures. Try to make each idea concrete. Visualize it in order to make it real. Use your senses to imagine seeing, hearing, touching, tasting, even smelling the idea.
- Build on idea fragments. Once visualized, the idea is easier to build upon. Ignore the parts of an idea that you dislike. Instead, build upon the parts you do like. Make it fun. Remember that the name of the game is quantity.

Guidelines are great, but we need to gain solid skills in ideation. 'Understanding' ideation is hardly the same thing as being able to do it well. In order to learn something new, you have to want to overcome old habits. Your first step in building ideation skills is to learn just how hard it will be to overcome your habit of prematurely converging. You need to learn to defer judgment and permit divergence to flourish.

Active divergence takes practice

Try this experiment. Clasp your hands together, intertwining your fingers in your usual manner. Look carefully to see which of the two you've placed higher than the other. Now unclasp them and reclasp them, this time reversing their order. Most people feel uncomfortable in the new position, and may even feel that they've somehow lost a finger in the process. What's caused the discomfort is having to break a habit. Learning the process skills of deferral of judgment and active divergence—the secrets to ideation—means you have to experience the same kind of discomfort in order to break the habit of prematurely converging.

Let's use a simple exercise to begin developing our new process skills. In the next 90 seconds, think of as many uses as you can for a leather belt (except for holding up a pair of pants). Jot them down if you like. In any case, try to use the above ideation guidelines to lengthen your list.

Having compiled your list, compare it with the following examples I've collected from others: sling, leash, carrying books, supporting a car muffler, matching a pair of shoes, necklace, watchband, bracelet, bottle opener, holding a door shut, yardstick, food, sharpening a razor, musical instrument, saving a drowning person, burning for heat, decoration, guinea pig fence, template, rope, shoelaces, book mark, holding a hot pot, door hinges, picking a lock, noise maker, straight edge, tapping out Morse code, and flashing a signal in the sunlight. You probably had more uses. Which of these examples did you not include on your list? Were there some examples that later seemed obvious? What prevented you from including them in your own list? Were your ideas somehow 'boxed in' by hidden assumptions? Some people limit themselves by considering the belt only in terms of its original use. Or they balk at including ideas that others might frown upon or scorn. Some ignore the belt buckle's uses. Others think it's against the 'rules' to consider the belt's uses if it's cut into smaller pieces. Did you purposely omit ideas that you felt weren't good enough, or were illogical or unfeasible?

How did you do? How good were your process skills of deferral of judgment and active divergence? Whenever you decided against recording a particular use for the belt, you were showing lack of skill in deferral of judgment. And whenever you felt like quitting—'I've already got two or three good uses, why bother thinking up more?'—you were showing lack of skill in active divergence.

For most people, this exercise points up their discomfort with these two process skills. But when confronted with the wide range of examples that other people have come up with, they also find themselves eager to improve. Assuming that you wish to improve, here are further exercises to improve your process skills of deferral of judgment and active divergence, and your ability to ideate.

VALUING AND CREATING DIFFERENT POINTS OF VIEW

There are always different ways of viewing any situation, all of them valid. In fact, deliberately taking different points of view is essential in effective divergence. For example, when fact finding about a selected fuzzy situation, it's vital not to stop with your first impression. Instead, you must dig for additional facts and perceptions, especially those that might be less visible.

Points of view: Exercise #1

Looking at a situation from a different angle usually reveals something new. Remember how our earlier exercise with the white vase and two black silhouettes unearthed many additional images. For another example, look at the picture in Figure 10-5. What do you see? A young woman? An old woman? Both? Neither? Other images (like the groundhog)? If you're having trouble picking out either the old woman or the young woman, keep trying. Show it to someone else for help. If you're still having trouble, look at the pictures in Figure 10-6. They may help. Once you've seen both images, practise shifting back and forth between them. Do you find it getting a little easier? Once you've picked out one or the other, it's often difficult to alter your point of view to see the alternative image, but practice helps. Such is the power of the first impression.

In fact, a common response to this picture is, 'I've seen this before.' Perhaps you have seen this picture before. Perhaps you have already stopped looking. But look again. What other images can you see? I mentioned the groundhog above. Can you find him? Perhaps it looks more like an iguana to you. If you need help, look at Figure 10-7. If the groundhog (or iguana) is now clearer to you, try your hand at finding additional images. Here are some others that people have found: eagle's head, drowning man or orchestra conductor, praying mantis, squirrel, baby seal, Florida in reverse, Bob Hope's profile. If you need help, look at Figure 10-8.

We call Figure 10-5 an ambiguous picture because there are many ways to 'see' it, or many different and correct points of view. In order to see the whole picture, we must realize that first impressions are less than complete. We must deliberately defer our judgment. We must look harder for new impressions. We

Fig. 10.5 Valuing different points of view

must actively diverge and try to see many other things. So it is with our work. If we deliberately examine our jobs, our products, our customers, and our problems from more than one point of view, we are often surprised by the number of new impressions we receive.

Not only is the power of the first impression strong, but so is the power of interpretation. Looking at Figure 10-5, you might first see the ear of the young woman. Someone else might first see the eye of the old woman. (Someone might even see a drowning man or orchestra conductor.) We tend to fix on a particular part of a picture, a fixation that helps determine how we view the

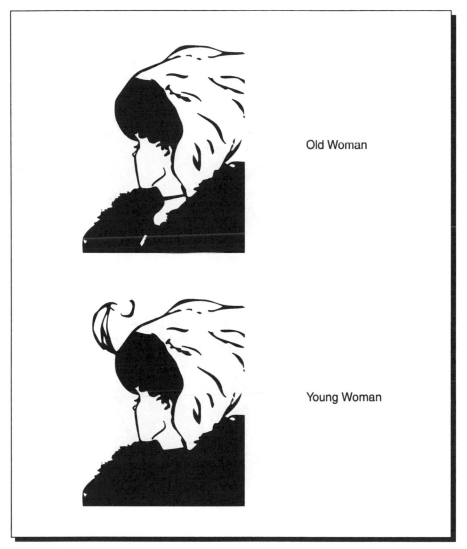

Old Woman

Young Woman

Fig. 10.6 Two ways to see a situation

entire picture. We're surprised to find that someone else saw something entirely different, even though we seemed to be focusing on the same detail.

'Seeing' is an active, not a passive, process. We tend to construct our picture of a situation in our own way, based on our past experience, without realizing that others are constructing their own pictures. Consider how witnesses to an accident can come up with different versions of the event based on their own perceptions. They were looking at the same thing but constructed different pictures. Similarly, at work, if we defer our judgment that our way is the only way of viewing a situation, we are more likely to seek out additional refreshing

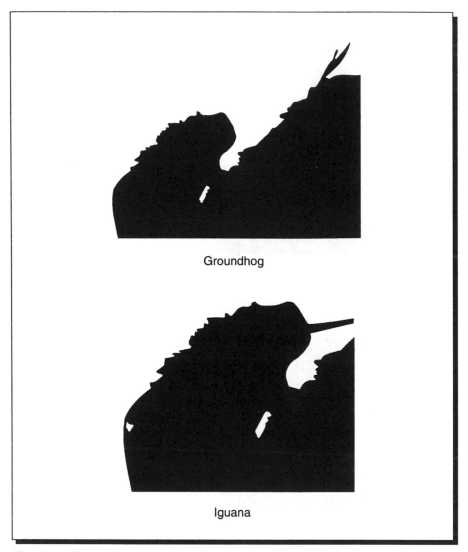

Fig. 10.7 More ways to see a situation

viewpoints, sometimes by involving others. This allows us to make continuous improvement and innovation in what we do and how we do it, for ourselves, our customers and our suppliers.

Points of view: Exercise #2

Let's try another exercise to help you take different points of view. Copy the symbol in Figure 10-9. Putting your judgment and logic aside, and revving up

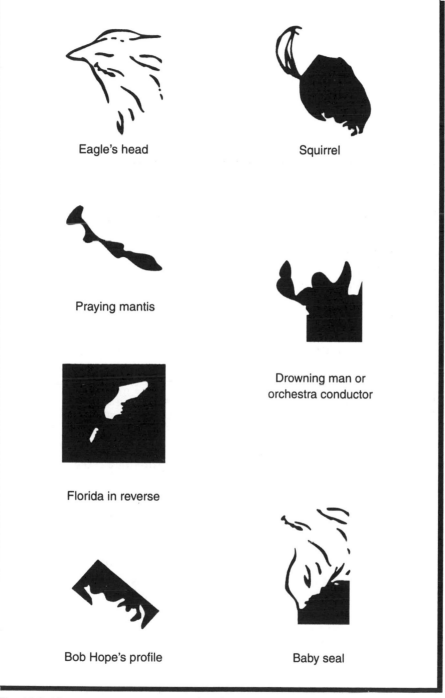

Fig. 10.8 Many more ways to see a situation

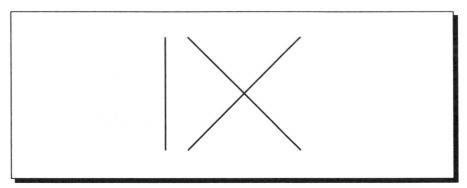

Fig. 10.9 A symbol

your imagination, use your process skills of deferral of judgment and active divergence to find at least three or four ways to add one line to make 6.

Remember that the point is to develop these two process skills. As you work on the challenge, worry less about the results you are getting and concentrate more on how you are getting them. In other words, focus on *process* and let the content fall into place. Deliberately take different points of view toward the symbol. Turn your paper upside down, sideways, backward. If you feel an urge to ask, 'What do you mean by a line?', or 'What do you mean by 6?', tell yourself, 'I am free to see this challenge in any way I like, without restrictions.' In fact, defining this challenge in multiple ways is the key to finding multiple solutions. You may find a way that no one else has uncovered. Your answers don't have to please anyone but yourself. If the answer works for you, it is correct.

How are you doing so far? Have you thought of at least one answer? Perhaps you have written an answer that you are only partially satisfied with. Don't discard it. Play around with it, or let it sit for a while and come back to it later. I have used this problem with thousands of people, who have come up with hundreds of answers that work. Don't forget, a secret of active divergence is to not stop with just one answer. Pat yourself on the back and try for yet another answer, and another, and another. Remember you are practising active divergence and deferral of judgment.

Compare your answers with some that other people have come up with. Some people draw a vertical stroke on the right, then visualize the X as four shorter lines that meet at the center (Figure 10-10). The result: six lines. As the figure illustrates, there are many possible variations on this theme; all are correct.

Others draw an S-shaped line before the symbol to spell the word 'six' (Figure 10-11). Too simple? This is one answer that children often get more quickly than most adults. Why? Adults often make needless assumptions, such as, 'It must be a straight line because all the other lines are straight,' or, 'It must be a Roman numeral.' You might remember being taught that the 'correct' definition was the shortest distance between two points, and, hence, ruled out anything but a straight line.

Fig. 10.10 Practising active divergence and deferral of judgment in many ways . . .

Perhaps you have other answers, or perhaps the above two have triggered fresh approaches. Did you try drawing a horizontal line through the center of the entire symbol as in Figure 10-12? In how many ways can you see an answer in this figure? Look at the portion above the line, which is the Roman numeral IV. While at first glance this appears incorrect, perhaps you haven't worked hard enough to change your point of view to make it correct. Turn the page upside down and look again. Do you see the Roman numeral VI above the line now?

Although our first glance at a solution may appear incorrect, you must consider it as a stepping stone to yet another solution. Recall the fourth ideation guideline: think in a stream, with each idea merely a stepping stone to another. The answer IV was not incorrect, but just a limited point of view. Seen upside-down as VI, your answer becomes correct. This illustrates the powerful

Fig. 10.11 Pracising active divergence and deferral of judgement in many ways . . .

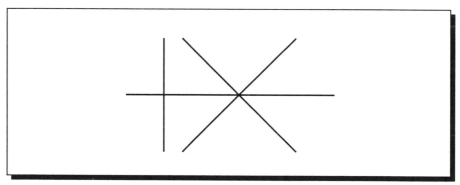

Fig. 10.12 Practising active divergence and deferral of judgment in many ways . . .

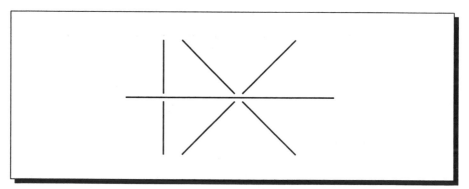

Fig. 10.13 Practising active divergence and deferral of judgment in many ways . . .

transformation principle of 'reverse,' which helps you see a problem backward. Using the reverse principle by deliberately putting yourself in someone else's shoes lets you see a problem from a completely different perspective.

Incidentally, some people find other routes to correct answers in Figure 10-12 above. Perhaps you did also. The horizontal line through the center actually cuts the symbol into two equal halves with three short lines above it and three below, making 6 (Figure 10-13).

How about placing a curved line shaped like the numeral 6 to the right of the symbol, as in Figure 10-14? Many people take this different point of view, thus seeing the X as the mathematical operation signifying multiplication.

Did you think of simply adding a loop to the bottom of the vertical line on the left (Figure 10-15)? This is another solution that many adults miss because it seems too simple. Children find it more quickly. To some adults, it feels strange to make a solution that doesn't use all the parts. In this case, the X was unnecessary. But remember no one said you had to use all the parts of the symbol.

How often do we impose similar constraints on ourselves in day-to-day problem solving? In high school, we always thought an answer was wrong if we didn't use all the information given in the question. In real-world problem solv-

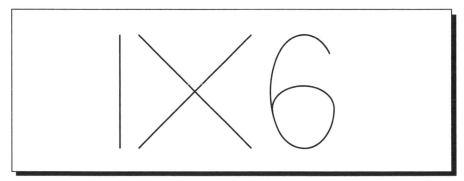

Fig. 10.14 Practising active divergence and deferral of judgment in many ways . . .

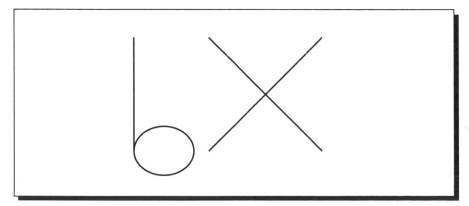

Fig. 10.15 Practising active divergence and deferral of judgment in many ways . . .

ing, you hardly ever have all the information you need. Sometimes you have too much data. Rarely does someone hand you the precise amount of information you need to assemble the correct answer. This example illustrates the transformation principle of 'omit.' Frequently, solutions are derived or improved by leaving something out.

Here's another example of this principle. Perhaps you drew a horizontal line through the center of the X to form an asterisk (Figure 10-16). Many people do so. In how many ways can you see 6? For example, can you see the six

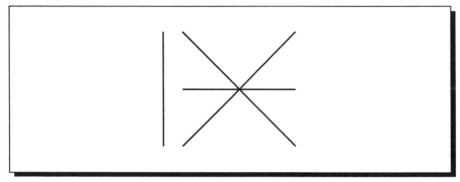

Fig. 10.16 Practising active divergence and deferral of judgment in many ways . . .

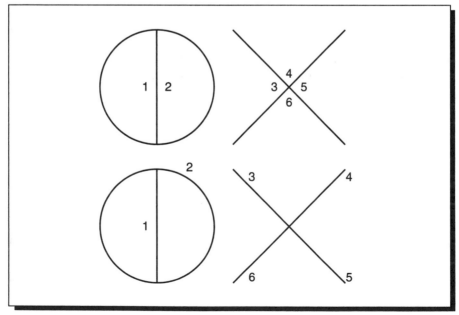

Fig. 10.17 Practising active divergence and deferral of judgment in many ways . . .

spaces or angles within the asterisk? Can you see six points equidistant from the center of the asterisk? Can you see six short equal lines radiating outward from the center? Did you block these solutions from your mind because you focused only on the lines, not the spaces? Or did you assume these answers were wrong because they omitted the vertical line? In every case, the vertical line of the symbol is unnecessary. Learning to use the transformation principle of 'omit' helps you remember that few problems come with just the right amount of information.

Try drawing a circular line around the vertical line. What do you see? Do you see six spaces or six lines as in Figure 10-17? Now draw a circular line around the vertical line without touching its bottom end. What do you see? Do you see a clock face showing six o'clock, as in Figure 10-18? Yet another point of view (especially for those raised with digital clocks).

Some people balance a line atop the vertical line to make a T, and then count the six angles in the entire symbol (Figure 10-19).

Other people build upon the theme of a mathematical operation. We saw above that the X could be a multiplication sign. Could it become something

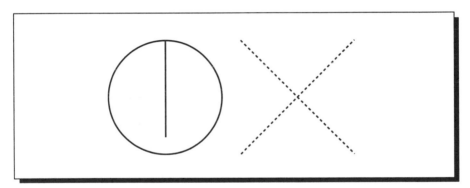

Fig. 10.18 Practising active divergence and deferral of judgment in many ways . . .

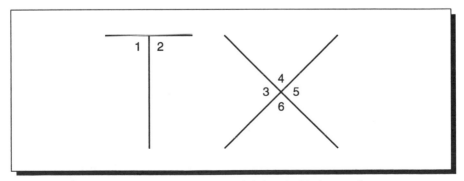

Fig. 10.19 Practising active divergence and deferral of judgment in many ways . . .

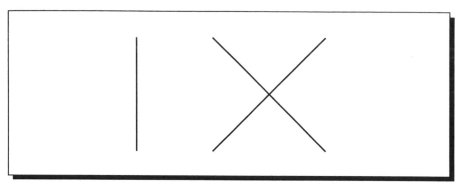

Fig. 10.20 Practising active divergence and deferral of judgment in many ways . . .

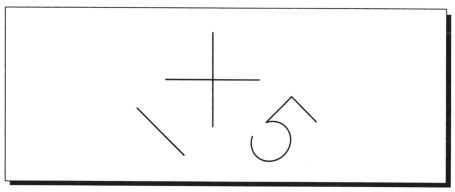

Fig. 10.21 Practising active divergence and deferral of judgment in many ways . . .

else if we took a different point of view or somehow transformed it? Another transformation principle is 'rotation.' Look again at the symbol in Figure 10-20. Try rotating it, not too far, but far enough to see the X in a new way. Perhaps you have discovered the answer in Figure 10-21, in which a new line shaped like the numeral 5 follows the new plus sign to make the sum 6. (Imagine our symbol written along the edge of a round table.) What changed? Did the problem change or did you change? Did you *transform* your point of view? When you develop your process skills of deferral of judgment and active divergence, you find such transformations easier to make.

Some people use the transformation principle of 'rearrange.' They take the symbol apart and re-arrange it in the shape of a digital 6 after adding one line (Figure 10-22).

Other people apply the 'omit' principle and adapt the 'SIX' solution above. Test yourself on this one if you haven't already come up with it. What if you omitted part of the S? Would you have a new way to solve the problem? Could you leave out the right side, the left side, the top, the bottom? Take different

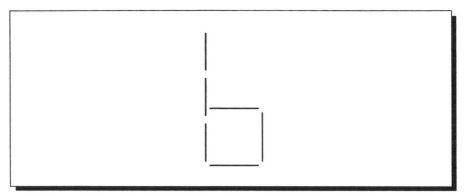

Fig. 10.22 Practising active divergence and deferral of judgment in many ways . . .

Fig. 10.23 Practising active divergence and deferral of judgment in many ways . . .

viewpoints, then look at the answer in Figure 10-23. Have you made a new word? No. Have you made the number 6? No. But have you made the *sound* of the number in a new way? Yes. What's the difference between the letter that begins the words 'cistern' and 'sister'? To a reader, they're entirely different. To a listener, there's no difference.

A few people have suggested another very different point of view. Looking at the symbol, they say, 'I see only one line.' When I ask them to explain what they mean, they say that they see the IX as one line on a page, like a line of poetry. They then tell me to add exactly the same line to the page below this first line, as in Figure 10-24. When I ask them how they have now made 6, they say that, by repeating the entire line, they have made six small lines, three in each of the two lines on the page. The viewpoint of the symbol being a line on a page, while very different, is of course entirely correct.

You may be uncomfortable with adopting such a different view. However, remember that others are entirely comfortable with it. In fact, some people think of this answer first. In order to improve your creativity, you have to over-

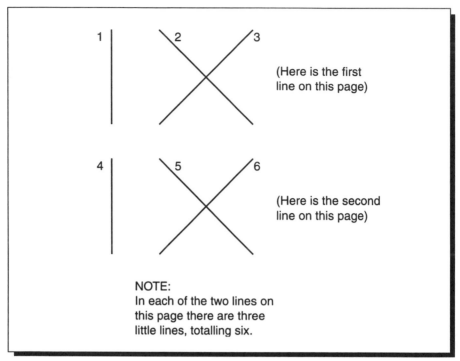

Fig. 10.24 Practising active divergence and deferral of judgment in many ways . . .

come this discomfort and develop your process skill of deferral of judgment. Consider your discomfort as a positive thing rather than negative. Whenever we learn a new skill, we experience some discomfort. Remember your first attempts to ride a bicycle. You probably fell off more than once until you mastered the new skill. In order to develop your process skill of active divergence, ask yourself what you like about this new uncomfortable solution. Ignoring what you dislike, deliberately extend effort to build upon the good points to create additional viewpoints.

For example, when people have built upon this theme of a line on a page using another transformation principle called 'fusion,' they have combined the notions of arithmetic operations and Roman numerals to create a new answer (Figure 10-25). Subtracting the Roman numeral III (the second line on the page) from the Roman numeral IX (the first line on the page) yields VI. Everyone sees some of these viewpoints more easily than others. This simply recognizes our individual differences. No matter what answers you feel are more or less appropriate, the point of this exercise is to build your acceptance and awareness of the wide number of ways to view a particular problem. Furthermore, why not turn these different ways to your advantage? Whenever you

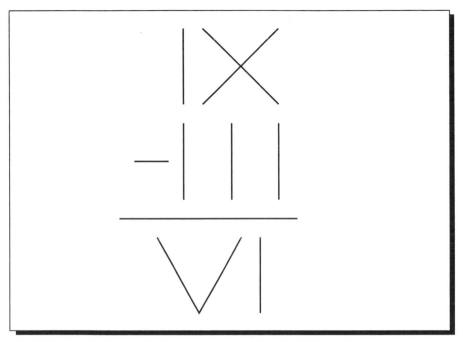

Fig. 10.25 Practising active divergence and deferral of judgment in many ways . . .

face a tough challenge, why not share it with someone to get a fresh perspective? This in itself is an example of using your process skills of deferring judgment and active divergence.

TOWARD BETTER EVALUATION

Just as the process skills of deferral of judgment and active divergence are the keys to finding diverse options through ideation, the process skill of active convergence is the key to evaluation. Remember that the quality of the result in any step in the creative process depends on how well you exercise both parts of the ideation-evaluation process. Just as during ideation you must avoid the tendency to slip into evaluation, the reverse is true. When you are evaluating, you must avoid slipping back into ideation. This tendency leads people to spin their wheels rather than progress toward action. Here are several guidelines to help you evaluate effectively (Figure 10-26):

- Exercise good judgment and logic.
- Go for quality of ideas, not quantity. It's better to have one good workable idea than five that aren't good enough, no matter how appealing.

- View differences of opinion as a help, not as a hindrance, in deciding. Seek out and actively listen to others' opinions to enrich your own.
- Focus on a good decision on its own merits. Trust your intuition, but don't let your ego get in the way.
- Express the options you are evaluating in clear, simple, specific terms. Make sure you fully understand them.
- Be sure you evaluate the options by the appropriate criteria. For example, is cost the only issue, or are there equally pressing criteria to consider? And ensure that your criteria are clear: is 'cost' specific enough or should you say 'capital cost,' 'operating cost,' or 'opportunity cost'?
- Don't rush to judgment just to get it over with. Remember that evaluation is equally important as ideation in the creative process. Think of at least five good things about an option before addressing any concerns (keep an open mind).
- Don't discard potentially good options prematurely just to get rid of them. Think of the pizza box mentioned in our earlier example, in which a team was only too eager to discard a novel solution. Recognize an option that deserves more work and return it to the ideation phase. Bring the improved idea back to evaluation only when it's ready.
- Avoid picking 'safe' options if your only reason for choosing them is to avoid the conflict or discomfort that would come with more novel and risky—but superior—options.
- Don't let preconceptions or hidden motives sway decisions.
- Be willing to discard all but the critical few good options and move on toward action. Don't wait for the perfect option to emerge.
- In a group, be willing to compromise and strive for consensus. Then move on decisively.

Remember, exercising skill in evaluation differs from just *talking* about guidelines for effective evaluation. For example, suppose you had to choose the best answer from among all the options generated to the 'IX problem.' How would you go about it? In order to get it over with quickly, would you just close your eyes and throw a dart at your list? Would you simply pick your first option just because you felt it must be best if it came first? If you thought of only one answer, would you stick with it, resenting the fact that you couldn't come up with any others? Would you limit your choices only to those that were mathematically logical? Would you reject those that made you uncomfortable? Would you pick the one you thought most other people would pick? Would you choose one that you thought was the most radical because you believed this was what was expected in a book about creativity? Make a quick choice right now, more or less off the top of your head, and make a note of it.

- Use good judgment and logic (avoid simply just going through the motions).
- View difference as constructive.
- Focus on good decisions, not preconceived notions.
- Keep your ego out.
- Strive for consensus; listen carefully to others.
- Don't back away (from uncomfortable, superior options).
- Don't wait for perfection; move good ideas forward.
- Don't discard potentially good options prematurely.
- Express your opinions clearly.
- Pick the right criteria so you see the whole picture.
- Quality is all-important.

Fig. 10.26 Guidelines for effective evaluation

Active convergence takes practice

Now let's try a different approach. Let's apply our process skills of deferral of judgment and active divergence. Put aside any preconceived notions of what's 'best.' Write down at least 10 different criteria by which you might make your evaluation. To do so, ask yourself the following questions, beginning with: 'Why might the author be asking me to make this choice?' Is the reason that I, the author, want to get a large sample of responses to answer some mysterious research question about creativity? Is it perhaps that your creativity is being tested? Or is it just that I want you to practise the process skill of active convergence? Now ask yourself another question, 'Who might want to know the best answer?', or, 'For whom am I making this evaluation?' Perhaps it's for a group of psychologists, a reporter, a children's book editor, or the president of a large company writing a speech on creativity.

Using these kinds of questions in order to keep your mind open, make your list of potential criteria. Here's a list of criteria that others have come up with: the most novel, the most mathematical, the most unusual, the most logical, the most artistic, the most childlike, the most likely to win a bet in a bar, the most creative, the most practical, the most exciting, the safest, the one most likely to appeal to the most people, the one most commonly picked, the most far-fetched, the most simple, the most complex, the most clever one, the best example of deferral of judgment, the best example of active divergence, the most controversial. If you thought of additional criteria, just add them to this list.

We've now completed the first half of the evaluation process. Keeping an open mind, we have generated a large number of optional criteria. Begin the second half of this process by making an unbiased selection of the best criteria. We would usually pick more than one criterion. Most decisions in the creative process require a blend of multiple viewpoints. With this in mind, reduce your list of criteria to a small number, say, four. Which would you pick? Would you weight them in different ways? Make sure your choices follow the evaluation guidelines above.

Using the criteria you have selected, what is your final best answer to the IX problem? Compare this answer to your original 'top of the head' choice. Is it different? If so, is it different because you took into account a wider range of criteria and made a more informed choice? If not, have you confirmed your first impression by taking into account this wider range of criteria? Either of these two possibilities is fine. They indicate that you have demonstrated process skill in evaluation. Hopefully, you did more than just go through the motions, only to return to your original choice.

Ultimately, your choice is the only one that counts. When it's your problem, you have the ultimate responsibility for the choice. There is no textbook answer. In order to generate a quality result, you must use a quality ideation process to generate good options and employ a quality evaluation process to make wise choices.

11

A FOURTH PROCESS SKILL: FOLLOW THE SIMPLEX PROCESS

Aren't you supposed to be the expert?

'You know,' said Harry, 'your story about the benevolent tyrant makes me think that the way people behave has a lot to do with their creativity. And you know something? It's not so much being born creative that counts but being able to develop skills that help you use the creativity you're born with.'

'I think that's true,' I said. 'And there's also a flip side to that. From what I've seen, a lot of the training we get through life—from our parents, our schools, society in general—teaches us behaviors that only prevent our using the creative process.'

'Oh, I could tell you some stories about that,' Harry said. 'I've talked to a lot of R&D managers. They usually hire engineers directly out of university—if they're hiring, that is. And you know what? One of the greatest shortcomings among their new hires is that they hardly ever venture out of their labs.'

'Why not?' Alice asked.

Harry shook his head. 'Seems that, having come all the way through university, they believe they're supposed to have all the answers. They spent their school years being pitted against their classmates, living in fear of failing and of ending up near the bottom of the class. They learned to be very competitive, but they also learned that not knowing the answer is a sign of weakness. They'd rather sit in their labs than visit the library or talk to other people to gather information about work problems. So they have a lot of trouble defining problems or identifying what customers need. And as a result, they often do a poor job of solving problems.'

I smiled. 'The way I define it, the creative process has to start with things like looking for new problems to solve, keeping an open mind, fact finding in every direction, trying to get a better handle on things.

⇨

That means admitting that you really don't know that much about the problem. If you're hung up on trying to fool everyone into believing that you're an expert, you'll never get out of your box. You'll never come across any new information. When you confess to your own ignorance, you start asking a lot of questions that you weren't even capable of asking before. That's a big part of being creative.' ■

Summary of learnings

✦ *Deferral of judgment, active divergence and active convergence are horizontal process skills that you use within each step of the Simplex process. A fourth process skill, vertical deferral of judgment, allows you to separate the eight steps of the process from one another.*

✦ *We all prefer different parts of the creative process. People with the generator style incline toward using the horizontal process skills in the first two steps of the Simplex process, problem finding and fact finding. Other people—conceptualizers, optimizers, implementers—prefer to use the horizontal process skills in subsequent steps.*

✦ *Vertical deferral of judgment helps you to progress systematically from one stage to the next around the Simplex wheel, instead of leapfrogging between stages or becoming bogged down in a particular stage.*

If you hope to successfully execute any of the eight steps in the Simplex creative problem solving process, you must develop and use within each step the three process skills of deferral of judgment, active divergence and active convergence. But even these process skills aren't enough. In order to separate the eight steps of the wheel from each other, you must develop and use a fourth process skill, vertical deferral of judgment.

VERTICAL DEFERRAL OF JUDGMENT

Imagine jumping, for example, directly to step four from step one. No matter how well you execute either step one or step four, you will only achieve poor overall results. Recall our hot wax example from an earlier chapter. After the team had found a good problem (step one), it had immediately jumped to searching for possible solutions (step four) to an assumed problem definition, 'How might we create a carnauba wax formula outside the competitor's patent?' The team skipped steps two and three, fact finding and problem definition. Recall also the green-striped bar example, in which the team failed to do steps one, two and three. The team members didn't actively search out and find the problem themselves but were forced into it; they didn't fact find or define the problem. Instead they began their process in step four, divergently searching for possible solutions to the assumed problem definition, 'How might we create a green-striped bar that people will like better than Irish Spring?'

In both cases, the teams were able to use the two-step ideation-evaluation process *within* one step of the Simplex process. But because they lacked skill in vertical deferral of judgment, they leapt prematurely to a later step of the Simplex process. Had they been able to defer judgment throughout Simplex, they would have moved from step one into step two, fact finding, and then step three, problem definition, ultimately discovering a much better challenge before entering step four. If you picture the three process skills of deferral of judgment, active divergence and active convergence *within* any step as *horizontal* skills, then the fourth process skill, *vertical* deferral of judgment, becomes the skill that allows you to *move stepwise* through Simplex (Figure 11-1).

Here are skills that will help you practise the process of vertical deferral of judgment:

- Know the difference between a fuzzy situation and a well-defined problem.
- Know the difference between defining and solving problems.
- Dig out pertinent facts before trying to define a problem.
- Turn premature critical evaluations into new 'how might we?' challenges.
- Understand that new solutions that don't work perfectly are not mistakes, but learnings and new facts that you can use as the basis for your next trip around the wheel.

- Realize that problem solving does not always yield immediate results.
- When asked for help on a problem, avoid immediately giving advice. Instead, stay in fact finding to help the person think their way through the problem.
- Recognize that team members in a meeting are likely in different steps of the Simplex process, and help them move through the process in sync.
- Avoid leaping to action immediately upon discovering a problem. Instead follow steps one *through* eight through the Simplex process rather than jumping from step one *to* eight. (Jumping from step one to step eight is like 'ready, fire, aim'; proceeding from step one *through* step eight is like 'ready, aim, fire.' In the former, you'll find yourself running back and forth and getting nowhere; in the latter, you'll find yourself creating on-target, workable solutions to well-defined problems.)

Each of us prefers different steps and stages of the Simplex creative problem solving process. Maybe you prefer the first two steps, problem finding and fact

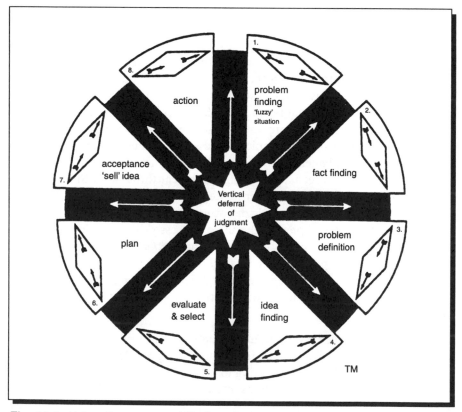

Fig. 11.1 *Using the process skill of vertical deferral of judgment to separate the eight steps of Simplex*

finding. You are more naturally inclined to be a generator, and prefer to use the three horizontal process skills within these two steps than within the other six. Someone else might incline toward being a conceptualizer, optimizer, or implementer. They prefer to use the three horizontal process skills within the latter six steps. It's these individual preferences that make the process skill of vertical deferral of judgment such a vital one. This is the process skill that prevents you from leapfrogging prematurely to your preferred stage. It ensures instead that you move systematically from stage to stage.

If you want to dramatically improve your performance, you must learn to use the Simplex process daily to mainstream innovation. And you must develop all four process skills to make the process work, both within and among its steps. Let's practise putting together the process skills and the process. We'll start by selecting a real fuzzy situation (the content) that matters to you, and then walk through all eight steps of Simplex. In other words, let's practise putting together the entire equation from earlier chapters: Quality results = Content + Process + Process skills. If you need help working your way through this exercise, refer to the example at the end of the chapter called 'I want to improve my poker game.'

SIMPLEX FROM START TO FINISH

STEP 1: PROBLEM FINDING

Remember that you start this step by sensing and anticipating 'problems.' Call these problems 'fuzzy situations' to emphasize that you shouldn't prematurely assume anything about them.

A. Diverge

Let's start by setting aside judgment. Use the prompter questions in Figure 11-2 to list fuzzy situations that you might like to address. Practise your process skill of active divergence to come up with more than 10 fuzzy situations.

Organizational problem finding: Sensing the present

1 What are your customers' major gripes and difficulties?
2 What opportunities are your customers missing?
3 What potential customers could you help if you only knew them better?
4 What small problems for your department or organization could grow into big ones?
5 What barriers impede communications within your organization?
6 How could you improve quality?
7 What are your most difficult people problems?
8 What goals do you fail to attain year after year?
9 What is likely to cause your next crisis?
10 What issues do you think people are afraid to bring up?
11 What makes it hard to plan?
12 What problems experienced by other organizations do you want to avoid?
13 What competitors' ideas could your organization adapt?

Organizational problem finding: Anticipating the future

1 What changes, issues, problems and opportunities do you visualize three years down the road?
2 As your organization's information needs increase, what new problems and issues will arise?
3 Who might feel threatened by the idea of sharing information within your organization?
4 What training do people need to meet challenges two years from now?
5 What information would simplify your job?
6 What customer needs will increase in the next three years? Five years? Ten years?
7 What will be your customers' biggest challenges over the next three years? Five years? Ten years?
8 What would you most like to see happen in the next three years?
9 What new pressures might you encounter from your customers? The community? Politicians? The media?
10 What might cause your valued employees to leave?

Fig. 11.2 Using prompter questions to develop fuzzy situations

Personal problem finding

1 What existing risks and uncertainties do you face?
2 What risks and uncertainties might you face in the future?
3 What changes do you feel you need to make?
4 With whom do you want to get along better?
5 What would make you happy or proud?
6 What makes you worry?
7 What takes too much time?
8 What has bothered you recently?
9 What would you like to know more about?
10 What goals have been lying fallow?

Fig. 11.2 cont. Using prompter questions to develop fuzzy situations

B. Converge

Now practise your process skill of active convergence. Select one problem that truly interests you and that you'd like to resolve soon. Since you're trying to develop your skill, make sure the problem you select is neither the most difficult you've ever faced nor the most trivial. Describe the problem in writing in 15 words or less. Don't include a lot of detail. And don't try to solve it right away—remember that your fuzzy situation is merely a starting point. Your brief description completes the first step of the Simplex process.

STEP 2: FACT FINDING

A. Diverge

Now diverge again. List as many simple, specific, clear answers as you can to each of the following six fact finding questions. Defer judgment: don't analyze your answers as you go, no matter how trivial or irrelevant they may appear. Try to capture complete thoughts in sentences.

1 What do you know, or think you know, about this fuzzy situation?

2 What do you not know but wish to know about the situation?

3 Why is this a problem, especially for you? Why can't you make it go away?

4 What solutions have you already tried or thought of trying?

5 If this problem were resolved, what would you have that you lack now? What specifically would be different?

6 What might you be assuming, perhaps unnecessarily?

B. Converge

Now converge again. Circle a few of the most intriguing facts on the above list. Look for things that stand out as particularly meaningful or important, and that perhaps surprise you. There's no special number to select, perhaps three or four.

STEP 3: PROBLEM DEFINITION

A. Initial divergence

Defining your problem is so important that you actually diverge and converge twice in this step. Keeping your eye on your key facts, and setting aside your judgment, list several optional problem definitions.

Phrase each problem definition as a challenge beginning with, 'How might I...?' (How might I find out how many employees have read our policy manual? How might I entice all employees to read our policy manual? How might I encourage all employees to teach each other the policy manual? How might I make our policy manual more interesting to read?) Write down at least seven such challenges.

'How might I ...
'How might I ...
'How might I ...
'How might I ...
'How might I ...
'How might I ...
'How might I ...
'How might I ...

B. Initial convergence

Now converge again. From your seven statements, select the one that you feel best represents your challenge at this point. Get ready to diverge a second time.

C. Final divergence

This time, you'll diverge using the 'why-what's stopping' analysis. To begin, write down your selected 'How might I?' challenge statement. Then ask yourself the question 'why?', that is, 'Why do I want to meet this challenge?' For example, if your stated challenge is, 'How might I find out how many employees have not read the policy manual?', then your why question might be, 'Why do I want to find out how many employees have not read the policy manual?' Next, answer your question in a simple, concise but complete sentence. In our example, perhaps an answer is, 'I would learn how many employees probably don't know our policies.' Write down your particular answer above your original challenge statement. (Keep in mind that these particular answers are only examples of countless other suitable possibilities.)

Now transform your answer into a new challenge. For example, the second statement above might be rewritten as 'How might I quickly convey the policy manual's contents to employees who have not read it?'

Write down this new challenge statement above the former one. (Again, this particular challenge is only one example of numerous possibilities.)

Now let's go the other way. Return to your original 'How might I?' challenge statement. Ask yourself the question, 'What's stopping me?', that is, 'What's stopping me from meeting this challenge?' In our example, the 'what's stopping' question might be, 'What's stopping me from finding out how many employees have not read the policy manual?' Perhaps the answer is, 'I fear that, if I ask each employee outright whether or not they've read the manual, they may not tell the truth.' Write down your particular answer below your original challenge statement.

Now, using your imagination, transform this answer into a new challenge, again beginning with the phrase 'How might I?' In our example, a new challenge might be, 'How might I put employees at ease when I ask them whether or not they've read the manual?' Write down this new challenge statement below the former one.

You could do a much more thorough analysis by asking 'Why else would I want to...?', or, 'What else is stopping me...?', several more times in both directions. And for each of the resultant challenges, you could repeat the why-what's stopping questioning to create even more challenges. The more time you spend on this analysis, or the more frequently you repeat these powerful questions, the better you will understand your problem.

D. Final convergence

Now it's time to make your final convergence in this step. From all of the challenge statements in your 'why-what's stopping' map, select the one that you feel best describes your problem. (Incidentally, there's nothing stopping you from selecting more than one challenge—except perhaps lack of time.) With your problem definition in hand, you're ready to move from the problem *finding* stage of the Simplex process to the problem *solving* stage.

STEP 4: IDEA FINDING

A. Diverge

Now it's time to diverge again. This time, you're searching for answers rather than for questions. Write down your selected 'How might I?' challenge statement.

'How might I ...

Lay aside your judgment. Brainstorm at least 10 potential solutions to meet this challenge.

Keep your ideas simple and concise. Begin each statement with a verb to emphasize action. Deliberately create radical ideas that you can build upon. Think of ideas that would probably cost you your job, land you in jail, or at least get you into trouble. Prompt further ideas by asking yourself questions like: What new ideas might a friend offer? What ideas might a competitor offer? What ideas might your mother suggest? What would your worst enemy suggest (then reverse it)? What if you were flying a mile high on the back of a large bird and could see yourself below? What solutions might you see from that vantage point that aren't obvious to you at ground level? What other points of view might you take to generate even more ideas? Perhaps you could double your list to 20.

B: Converge

Now let's converge on your ideas. Circle the four best bets. (There's nothing magical about the number four, of course, but you should attempt to whittle down your list to a manageable number for further evaluation.) Remember to choose ideas that are concrete, that are easy to understand, that point the way to an easy next step, and above all, that aim directly toward solving your chosen challenge.

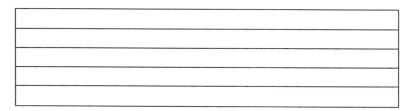

STEP 5: EVALUATE AND SELECT

A. Diverge

Now it's time to evaluate your list of potential solutions. Ideally, you want to select one good candidate, or a combination of several. You might even end up with a modified version of one of your original ideas.

To get started, set aside your judgment again. List at least 15 potential criteria that you might use in measuring the worth of these selected solution ideas. Remember that useful criteria must be specific, clear and simple. Extend your effort to think of a wide range of criteria; don't be too quick to home in. When you think you've finished, try to add five more potential criteria to your list.

```
┌─────────────────────────────────────────────────────┐
│                                                       │
├───────────────────────────────────────────────────── │
├───────────────────────────────────────────────────── │
├───────────────────────────────────────────────────── │
├───────────────────────────────────────────────────── │
├───────────────────────────────────────────────────── │
├───────────────────────────────────────────────────── │
├───────────────────────────────────────────────────── │
│                                                       │
└─────────────────────────────────────────────────────┘
```

B. Converge

Now it's time to converge. From your criteria list, circle four that you feel are most important. To refresh your memory about developing valuable criteria, refer back to the guidelines for effective evaluation in chapter 10. Make sure you know exactly what your selected criteria mean.

On the grid below, list your selected solution ideas vertically on the left, then list your selected criteria across the top. Using a simple numerical rating scale with 0 for poor, 1 for fair, 2 for good, and 3 for excellent, judge each solution in turn against the first criterion. Remember not to rank the solutions. Instead, rate each one individually. You may find all of your ideas are excellent or all are poor, or any conceivable combination. Then move on to your second criterion and repeat your evaluation procedure, and so on for the remaining criteria.

SELECTED CRITERIA

SELECTED IDEAS / / / / TOTALS

```
┌─────────────────┬───┬───┬───┬───┬─────┐
│                 │   │   │   │   │     │
├─────────────────┼───┼───┼───┼───┼─────┤
│                 │   │   │   │   │     │
├─────────────────┼───┼───┼───┼───┼─────┤
│                 │   │   │   │   │     │
├─────────────────┼───┼───┼───┼───┼─────┤
│                 │   │   │   │   │     │
├─────────────────┼───┼───┼───┼───┼─────┤
│                 │   │   │   │   │     │
├─────────────────┼───┼───┼───┼───┼─────┤
│                 │   │   │   │   │     │
└─────────────────┴───┴───┴───┴───┴─────┘
```

If you believe that some criteria are more important than others, you can weight them accordingly to reflect their differing effects. Suppose you believe that the criterion of cost is three times as important as another criterion, say, implementation time. Simply multiply each of the cost ratings by three. (You might not have to weight the criteria at all. Even if you do, remember that this is not intended to be a rigorous method. Its main intent is to help you carefully think through each of your ideas.)

If you wish, add up the ratings horizontally for each solution idea. These totals are useful guides to your final selection, but you're not committed to any particular idea at this point. One of your lower scoring solutions may be the right one if you believe in it strongly enough to do what it takes to overcome the hurdles suggested by its low rating. For example, suppose a very good idea rated very low for cost, and very low for ease of gaining acceptance because of its extreme novelty, but was a super idea on all other counts. You might pick it, realizing that it will take a lot of creativity, persistence and hard work on your part to overcome these barriers. On the other hand, you might find that none of your selections is good enough. If so, return to the beginning of step four to generate new solution ideas. Or you can backtrack even further. Perhaps you need a more imaginative problem definition. Perhaps you missed important facts. On the other hand, you might like two solution ideas equally: perhaps there's a way to combine them into a single solution.

Now write down your final selection below at the beginning of step 6 as your solution for action. Remember that you must know exactly what you mean by your solution. If there is any ambiguity in the solution, take the time to clarify it. Having reached a solution, you're ready to move into the next phase of the Simplex process, solution implementation.

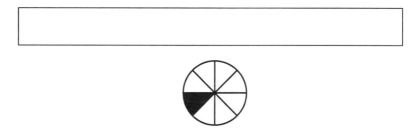

STEP 6: PLANNING ACTION

Selected solution:

Now let's continue our diverging/converging process into the implementation phase. Remember that your ultimate goal is to take action, creating a valuable change. You need to exercise just as much creativity in these last three steps as in the first five.

A. Diverge

Begin diverging again. Keeping an eye on your chosen solution, write down at least one answer to each of the following six questions:

1 What new problems might this idea create?

2 Where might you encounter difficulties with this idea?

3 Who might be negatively affected by this idea?

4 Who would benefit from this idea?

5 How might you introduce this idea?

6. When might be the best time to introduce this idea?

_____
_____
_____
_____

Now continue diverging. Imagine yourself alone in a movie theatre, watching yourself on the screen as you successfully implement your solution idea, creating a valuable change. What are you saying, hearing and doing? Who else is in the movie? What are they doing and saying? Where is the movie taking place? When? How do you feel as you watch? It's important to visualize yourself taking specific actions with specific results. Write down your answers to these questions.

_____
_____
_____
_____

Let's diverge further. Putting aside your judgment, quickly list at least 10 simple steps that you might take toward putting yourself into this movie scene. Don't worry about getting the steps in any 'correct' order. Include even unusual steps. Write down each thought as it occurs to you. Prompt yourself with questions like, Whom could I call? What could I buy? Where could I go? What would I need?

_____
_____
_____
_____
_____
_____
_____
_____
_____
_____

B. Converge

Now it's time to converge. From this list of possible actions, circle the one you believe you should do first. Make sure it starts with an action word and is simple, clear and specific. On the action plan below, write this action under the heading 'What will be done.' However, make sure you don't write it as number one, two or three. Write it as perhaps the third or fourth step so you leave space both above and below it on the action plan: you may discover earlier necessary actions as you build your action plan.

Now write your own name under the heading 'By Whom' for this first step. Then fill in the blank under the heading 'How it will be done.' This makes your action step more specific. For example, if your action step were to call a meeting, you would specify how you would call that meeting: by phone; by checking a list of meeting candidates with your boss; by delegating the task to someone else. Under the heading 'When,' write down a specific date and time for taking this action. Then under the heading 'Where,' write down the specific place in which you plan to take the action.

You'll likely think of further action steps that should be carried out either just before or just after your first step. In either case, repeat the procedure above. Perhaps you can nail down only a few action steps right now—subsequent actions might depend on how your first steps turn out. Leave room for exercising creativity as your action plan unfolds. Recall the famous adage: Plan your work and work your plan.

What Will Be Done	How Will It Be Done	By Whom	By When	Where

You now have a simple plan for implementing your chosen solution.

STEP 7: GAINING ACCEPTANCE

A. Diverge

It's quite likely that your action plan included getting support or approval from at least one other person. Whose approval might you need? Whose support might you need? Write one of the most important names below.

Continue diverging. Might your idea solve any of this person's problems? Pick one of the most important problems and write it down here.

Diverge again. Write down three benefits that this person would derive if your solution were implemented. Now converge. For each of the three benefits, write down at least one way in which you might illustrate or prove the benefit or in which you might clarify the benefit for this key person.

BENEFITS	CLARIFY THE BENEFITS

Now list at least three objections that you anticipate this key individual might raise to your solution. Remember that new ideas cause discomfort for all of us. Converge again. For each objection, write down at least one way in which you might show the person how it can be overcome or minimized.

OBJECTIONS	OVERCOMING THE OBJECTIONS

You can tailor similar plans for each individual you will have to sell. With each decision-maker, begin by establishing their particular problem that your idea will help to solve. Frame your presentation to reinforce the idea that you plan to help them solve an important problem. Make sure you have enough time to explain the solution's benefits and to answer objections.

STEP 8: TAKING ACTION

A. Diverge

Now apply the two-step diverging/converging thinking process one more time. Write down whatever you think might prevent you from taking the first step in your action plan. Circle the most important impediment, then list at least three ideas for overcoming it. Refer back to Figure 8-7, which provided ideas on overcoming these impediments and building personal commitment to action.

POTENTIAL IMPEDIMENTS	IDEAS FOR OVERCOMING THE IMPEDIMENTS

B. Converge

Set this book aside, and go and carry out one of these ideas for overcoming this impediment. Having removed it, now carry out this action step. Repeat this for each action step.

'I WANT TO IMPROVE MY POKER GAME'

If you haven't already taken a look at the following example, here's a sample of how the Simplex process works in practice. I call this example, 'I want to improve my poker game.' George had decided to apply the process to creatively solve a problem, after losing a fair amount of money for the first time at his weekly poker night. Here's how George walked his way through Simplex from start to finish.

STEP 1: PROBLEM FINDING

A. Diverge

1	Selecting vacation site.
2	One of the children falling behind in school.

3	Completing Master's degree.
4	Improving my poker game.
5	Anticipating inheritance from 99-year-old Uncle Bill.
6	Pressure from wife to purchase a larger home.

B. Converge

'I want to improve my poker game.'

STEP 2: FACT FINDING

A. Diverge

1 What do you know or think you know about this fuzzy situation?

1	We play once a month.
2	There are seven people in our poker club.
3	We rotate houses.
4	We play for about 4 1/2 hours.
5	We drink beer (about a six-pack each).
6	We play nickel, dime and quarter stakes.
7	Six of us are company employees.
8	Two of the others work for me.
9	We play dealer's choice (lots of strange games).
10	We play a three-raise limit up to a quarter for each raise.
11	Last night was the only time I ever lost money.

2 What do you not know but wish to know about the situation?

1	Was my losing luck- or skill-related?
2	If I told my wife, would she be upset about this?
3	Was anyone cheating?
4	Were the cards marked?
5	Would I have done better if I hadn't drunk as much?
6	Was this a one-time thing or will I lose frequently?

3 Why is this a problem especially for you? Why can't you make it go away?

1	I don't have enough spending money this month.
2	I feel like a loser.

4 What solutions have you already tried or thought of trying?

1	Revert to more conservative behavior.
2	Shake it off and wait for the next time.
3	Cut out my kids' allowance.
4	Take a little extra money out of my savings.

5 If this problem were resolved, what would you have that you lack now? What specifically would be different?

1	A plan to increase my winnings or cut my losses.
2	A way to win back the money I lost.
3	Regain my self-esteem.

6 What might you be assuming, perhaps unnecessarily?

1	It's normal for me to win (it may have been a fluke that I've won so often in the past).
2	Maybe the other players have been 'letting' me win up to now.

B. Converge

1	Last night was the only time I ever lost money.
2	I wish I knew if my losing was luck-related or skill-related.
3	I don't have enough spending money this month.

STEP 3: PROBLEM DEFINITION

A. Initial divergence

A	'How might I become a better poker player?'

B	'How might I increase my winnings or cut my losses?'
C	'How might I be seen as a winner?'
D	'How might I maintain my normal playing style?'
E	'How might I best spend my free time?'
F	'How might I get through this month with less personal money?'

B. Initial convergence

'How might I increase my winnings or cut my losses?'

C. Final divergence

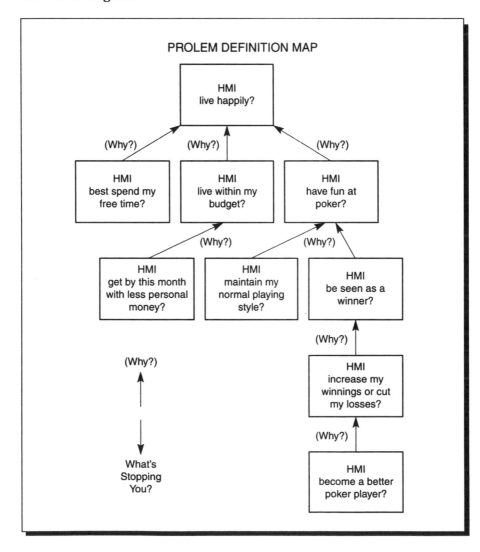

D. Final convergence

'How might I get through this month with less personal money?'

STEP 4: IDEA FINDING

A. Diverge

Selected problem definition:

'How might I get through this month with less personal money?'

Skip lunch	Eat at McDonald's every night
Don't smoke	Don't eat out at all
Use charge card	Buy big jar of peanut butter
Borrow	Put wife to work
Rob bank	Ask neighbor to help
Use bank loan	Get food stamps
Get second job	Cheat at cards
Have garage sale	Hold up variety store
Ask wife for money	Write bad cheques
Sell good junk	Travel business rest of month
Dip into savings	Get a personal loan
Car pool	Go to credit union
Sell car	Join the army
Cut out kids' allowance	Join the weekend reserves
Rob piggy bank	Test-drive cheaper car
Pool match	Drive cab at night
Sell can collection	Get donations for poker fund
Find something I can win at	Eliminate entertainment
Arm wrestle at a bar	Get metal detector for coins
Put kids to work	Test-drive company van
Rent out half the house	Charge admission to a party
Take in boarders	Install toll booth at I-55
Ask car pool to buy me sandwiches	Get raise

Pay bills late	Make $50 bills
Diet	Keep potluck dinner proceeds
Cut spending	Cut out beer
Have carpool substitute	Skip haircut
Reduce long-distance calls	Run NBA play-off pool and rake off profits

B. Converge

Skip lunch
Use charge card
Dip into savings
Skip haircut
Run NBA play-off pool and rake off profits
Pay bills late
Run garage sale

STEP 5: EVALUATE AND SELECT

A. Diverge

Possible criteria:

Dollars saved
Time taken to do
Amount of personal sacrifice required
Long-range effects
Effect on peers
Effect on wife
Degree of concealment from wife
Effect on debt position
Degree of added benefits
Effect on spending

| Effect on living standard |
| Legality |
| Morality |
| Effect on wife's self-esteem |
| Ease of implementation |
| Probability of success |
| Degree of personal interest in idea |
| Effect on health |
| Effect on job |

B. Converge

Criteria grid

SELECTED CRITERIA

SELECTED IDEAS	Effect on debt position	Degree of added benefits	Time taken to do	Degree of personal interest	TOTALS
Skip lunch	3	3	3	2	11
Use charge card	1	2	3	2	8
Dip into savings	3	1	3	1	8
Skip haircut	3	1	3	2	9
Run NBA play-off pool and rake off the top	3	3	2	3	11
Run garage sale	3	3	1	2	9
Pay bills late	2	2	3	3	10

STEP 6: PLANNING ACTION

Selected solution:

| Run NBA play-off pool and rake off profits |

A. Diverge

1 What new problems might this idea create?

> We may be seen as a gaming house.

2 Where might you encounter difficulties with this idea?

> This may be illegal.

3 Who might be negatively affected by this idea?

> People who don't win the play-off pool.

4 Who would benefit from this idea?

> Everyone would have fun.

5 How might you introduce this idea?

> At break.

6 When might be the best time to introduce this idea?

> Late in the week when everyone's looking forward to the weekend.

The 'movie theatre scene'.

> The whole gang is smiling and shaking my hand and saying what a great idea this play-off pool is.

What specific steps might I take to get the ball rolling?

Develop entry form
Collect money
Determine game schedule
Copy entry form
Evaluate winner

B. Converge

Idea selected:

> Run NBA play-off pool and rake off profits.

What Will Be Done	How Will It Be Done	By Whom	By When	Where
1 Determine game schedule	Check news papers	Me	After dinner	Home
2 Develop entry form	Pencil/ruler/ sheet of paper	Me	After dinner	Home
3 Copy entry form	Pencil/ruler/ sheet of paper	Me	After dinner	Home
4 Distribute entry form	Pass to known participants Ask them to pass to others	Me & particip-ants	Friday 4.30 p.m.	Work
5 Collect entry form and money	Phone – Ask stragglers to bring to me	Me	Friday 4.30 p.m.	Work
6 Evaluate winner	Read newspaper/ Watch TV news /Watch TV games	Me	After play-offs	Work
7 Payoff	Informally person to person	Me	After play-offs	Work

STEP 7: GAINING ACCEPTANCE

Whom do I need to convince?
No one but myself.

STEP 8: TAKING ACTION

Potential impediments that might prevent you from taking the first step?
None.

12

FOLLOW THE PROCESS
WITH OTHERS

A meeting without the minds

Looking up from his newspaper, Harry pointed out a headline to me. It was a story about an upcoming series of meetings of a major corporation's top management team. Harry shook his head and said, 'I sure hope their meetings are more productive than the ones we hold at our place.'

'What do you mean?' I said.

'You should see our senior management team in action,' he said. 'There are eight of us, all function heads, all very well-educated and capable. Lots of diverse experience. Most came on board having stood out as hot shots in other companies. But instead of getting the benefit of this broad range of experience, all we ever seem to do is jockey to look good.'

'Tell me about it' said Alice, rolling her eyes. 'We have the very same problem at our place.'

Harry continued. 'When we're working on a tough problem, we don't really think for ourselves. We just tell the president what we think he wants to hear. It's the easy way out. Nobody wants to rock the boat when the president already seems to have a solution in mind. And even if we disagree among ourselves, we usually manage to sound like we're agreeing. If someone challenges what someone else said, they back down right away.'

'And another thing,' he went on, 'None of us wants to show any signs of weakness. It's like those new engineers locked up in their labs. Everybody wants to appear strong, confident, knowledgeable. Nobody wants to confess to having any functional problems. So nobody ever asks for help from their teammates. And, of course, they never get any.'

'The whole purpose of teamwork to begin with,' Alice said.

'Exactly. Instead, we're like competitors, each trying to outdo the other in front of the boss. I'm sure we could be contributing so much more, but we never do. And I'm sure we're not the only people in the company with this problem.'

'In other words, meetings could be much more productive if only people knew how to behave in them,' I said. 'I guess another way of putting it is that they lack the process skills they need to work in groups. They know a lot about *what* they're talking about in the meeting, or the content. But they aren't very good at the process, or the *how* of talking about it.'

Harry said, 'That kind of sums it up. What versus how. That's the key, right?' ■

Summary of learnings

✈ *Beyond solving individual problems, you can use the process and process skills to improve teamwork and informal interactions with co-workers.*

✈ *Meetings are really a mechanism for solving problems with others.*

✈ *No matter what its content, a successful meeting requires participants to employ a common process and process skills. There are specific roles to play, and a defined meeting structure.*

✈ *A meeting's participants fill four main roles, including two process roles and two content roles.*

✈ *One process role is the process leader or facilitator. The facilitator does not take part in the meeting's content, but guides the meeting group through the Simplex process.*

✈ *The second process role is coach, played by all the meeting participants. In a debrief during or after the meeting, the meeting participants share feedback to review the group's process.*

✈ *The first content role of a meeting is the client. This is the owner(s) of whatever problem the group has been convened to help solve.*

✈ *The second content role is the participants. These people are selected either for their knowledge or to gain their commitment to a solution. A meeting held to solve a highly complex problem will likely have fewer participants than one held to solve a relatively simple problem.*

✈ *A successful meeting consists of three phases: preconsult, meeting and debrief.*

190 The Power of Innovation

✦ *In the first phase, the preconsult, the client selects a facilitator. The latter then guides the client through the first three steps of Simplex in order to better understand the client's needs. What results is a new definition of the problem to be addressed during the meeting itself. The preconsult also allows the facilitator to test for the client's true ownership of the problem, to ensure that a meeting is actually required, to select the meeting participants, and to plan the meeting's logistics.*

✦ *At the beginning of the meeting, the facilitator explains the process and process skills that the participants will need to use throughout the meeting.*

✦ *During the meeting, the facilitator leads the group through the Simplex process and models the use of the Simplex process skills for the participants. The participants offer knowledge, imagination and good judgment to the client. Besides taking part in the meeting, the client selects the best options as the process unfolds.*

✦ *During the final phase, the debrief, the group assesses how well it used the Simplex process skills during the meeting. This allows the group to continuously improve these skills from meeting to meeting.*

✦ *These process skills also apply to all teamwork situations and interactions with others. Learning these skills is the key to empowering others; they are the tools that allow you to coach and facilitate others in problem solving rather than doing all the work yourself.*

Once you've begun to apply the Simplex process skills to find and solve your own problems, you've taken a big step toward dramatically improving your performance. But you need to go further. You must now apply these process skills to problems that involve other people, in formal teamwork or in informal interactions with your co-workers. In either case, the best way to explain the use of these process skills is to look at how you should use them in problem solving meetings.

MEETINGS: TOOLS FOR SOLVING PROBLEMS

Meetings are really nothing more than tools for solving problems. Sharing information, figuring out how to implement new initiatives passed down from the top, handling gripes, creating new product and marketing ideas, finding ways to improve procedures, products and services, planning strategy, choosing from among options: each of these situations calls for problem solving that might take place in a meeting. If you need to share information with others, for example, your meeting challenge might be something like: 'How might I help others to understand this information?'; 'How might I persuade others to accept this information?'; 'How might I push others to act on this information?' A meeting is your mechanism for getting something done.

Many people dislike meetings. Even as teamwork becomes more important for organizations, we frown on meetings as a waste of time ('Not another meeting, all we do around here is hold meetings'). The problem is not so much the meeting itself as the way in which it is conducted. How can you expect to achieve quality results if you simply throw together half a dozen intelligent, complex people, all thinking a mile a minute, without any common process or set of process skills to guide them? Are these people trained in how to perform in a meeting? Do they recognize that others' thinking processes differ from their own? Do they have the social skills they need to interact effectively with others?

Expecting people to hold a successful meeting without these skills is like asking someone to solve a math problem without the ability to add or subtract. It's the same old dilemma of process versus content. Many people, even skilled problem solvers, fail to look on a meeting as a process and so jump directly into its content. But dealing with content alone won't guarantee you a quality result. No matter what the content, if you hope to hold a successful meeting, you need a meeting process and process skills. Successful meetings require three things: defined participant roles, a clearly defined structure, and specific behaviors and attitudes. Let's look at these elements in a simple example of a good meeting.

THE GROUNDWORK FOR A GOOD MEETING

Meeting participants play one of four roles. We can define these as two key process roles and two key content roles (Figure 12-1). The first key process role is the process leader, or facilitator. This individual's purpose is not to take part in the meeting's content, but to guide the group through the meeting using the Simplex process and process skills.

The first key content role is the client. This person is the 'owner' of the problem. Unless you've identified someone with a genuine need or concern that they can't handle well enough on their own, the meeting will be a waste of time. If you're the problem owner, the group cannot help you unless you have a real need and really want some help. The other group members need to know that you will take action after the meeting to help yourself.

Before talking about the other two meeting roles, let's look at the three phases of a good meeting (Figure 12-2).

There's more to the process than simply 'holding a meeting.' The meeting itself is actually the second phase. Before it comes the first phase, the preconsult, designed to complete a number of tasks.

Here, the client selects a facilitator who can divorce himself from the meeting content in order to lead the process (Figure 12-3). During their preconsult meeting, the facilitator leads the client through the first three steps of the Simplex process. He begins by assuming that how the client initially states his problem might not reflect what he actually wants. Exercising his process skill of deferral of judgment, the facilitator views the stated problem as nothing more than a fuzzy situation or starting point. He then leads the client through fact finding and problem definition, actively diverging and then converging during both steps. What results is a better understanding of the client's need, and a focused challenge that will become the starting point or new fuzzy situation for the meeting itself (Figure 12-4).

The facilitator uses the preconsult to test for true clientship. There are two parts to this 'test.' First, he must ensure that the client truly owns the problem. Is the individual there because he feels he should be, or only because his boss sent him? Second, he must determine whether there is actually more than one client. If so, the others should also take part in a preconsult in order to ensure that they have the same need and purpose. During the preconsult, the facilitator also makes sure that a meeting is actually needed. Sometimes the client discovers an insight during this phase that precludes the need to involve others.

During the preconsult, the client selects the meeting participants, the second content role. Participants are selected for the knowledge they bring to the situation, or because you need their commitment in order to make the solution work. (Sometimes it's a good idea to invite someone with little or no knowledge of the problem—someone who is detached and can bring a fresh perspective to

There are four key meeting roles: owner, participant, facilitator and coach.

1 Owner (Client) – This is the person who is 'hurting', the person who has to 'make it happen.' If there is no one hurting, or 'owning the problem,' you should go no further. There is no value in solving a problem no one is interested in. On the other hand, problem ownership could very well be multiple, (there could be several 'participants' who are also partially owners). The owner role is a CONTENT role. The owner is interested in the results and the details of the problem—the nuts and bolts or the 'WHAT' of the problem.

2 Participant – The participant is also a CONTENT role. The participants are selected for 'what' they can contribute in knowledge, originality, etc. They are there to help the owner find a solution to his/her problem.

3 Facilitator – The facilitator role is different. It is a PROCESS leadership role. The facilitator is concerned with 'how' the group is going to work together to attack the problem. That is the flow of the process steps, and the behaviors and attitudes needed to make the creative problem solving (CPS) process work. The facilitator's job is to help the participants help the owner and to help the owner help the participants develop a useful solution to the problem.

4 Coach – At any time, a member of the team could suggest a debriefing and give or get feedback about the team's process. Occasionally, a facilitator will request a coach to be present to give him/her and the team feedback on their process. The end of the meeting is a time for all participants to give and receive coaching.

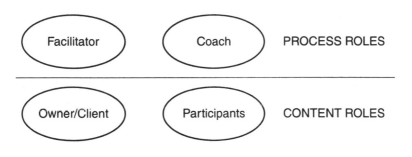

Fig. 12.1 Key meeting roles

bear.) There is no magic optimum number of participants for a meeting. Your preconsult will lead you to the right number.

Generally, the more critical the fact finding and problem definition steps, the fewer people the better. These are usually more complex problems, like plan-

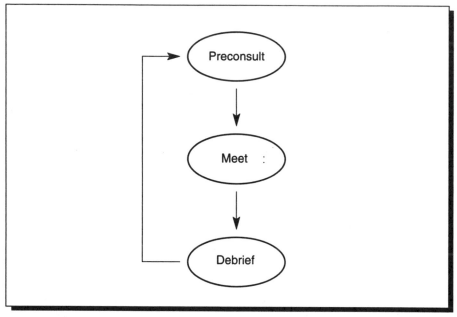

Fig. 12.2 Key meeting phases

- Confident and flexible in the use of the creative problem-solving process.
- Maintains an impartial stance to the content of the meeting.
- 'Polices' the separation of ideation and evaluation during the meeting.
- Encourages full participation by members in the meeting.
- Encourages the group to reach consensus during convergence.
- Assists the 'owner' in the planning of the meeting.
- Ensures the group debriefs its process at the end of the meeting.

Fig. 12.3 Key behaviors and attributes of an effective facilitator (process leader)

ning a strategy to resurrect a dying brand or to come up with new directions, new markets and new product plans. You're also better off with fewer participants when it's more important to converge on one best solution than to produce a variety of alternatives. You need diverse thinking, but if the group is too large, you won't have enough air time for everyone to speak their minds. For solving a highly complex problem, five to seven people might be the optimum number.

For less complex problems that are more clearly defined and that may require many potential solutions—'How might we convince adults that our

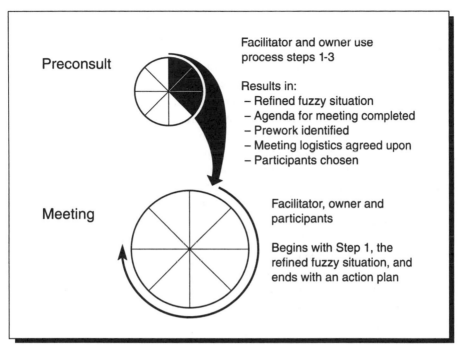

Facilitator and owner use
process steps 1-3

Results in:
- Refined fuzzy situation
- Agenda for meeting completed
- Prework identified
- Meeting logistics agreed upon
- Participants chosen

Preconsult

Meeting

Facilitator, owner and
participants

Begins with Step 1, the
refined fuzzy situation, and
ends with an action plan

Fig. 12.4 The preconsult

toothpaste is formulated especially for them?'—you're better off with more participants. This group can easily generate many equally valuable solutions, all usable and interchangeable. Perhaps 10 or more would be implemented at the same time. Here you don't need to zero in on a single all-or-nothing solution. For a relatively simple problem, you might invite as many as 20 or 30 people.

You use the preconsult to plan the meeting logistics. You must prepare an agenda, not just to lay out a shopping list of content items but to estimate how much time you'll need to complete each step of the Simplex process. It's difficult to do this with extreme accuracy, but making your best estimate is a worthwhile exercise. For complex problems, you should devote much more time to the fact finding and problem definition steps than you would for relatively straightforward ones. The latter may require only a quick check before you move into solutions. As the meeting progresses, you can always adjust your time allotments.

Now you have to decide where to hold the meeting and how to set up the meeting room. It's usually best to go off-site in order to get people away from the phones and the routine demands on their time. Putting people into a new environment also helps them think in new and different ways.

Use an open seating arrangement such as a semi-circle with the facilitator at the open end. The facilitator should have a flip chart for recording the information generated during the meeting as accurately and completely as possible. He should have a large wall handy for posting the sheets where his notes will be visible to everyone. This open arrangement reinforces the importance of openness to the meeting participants.

Avoid a large formal table—whether rectangular or U-shaped—that creates a structured atmosphere and that keeps people from using the vital process skills we've talked about so far. I'll never forget my first impression of the table used for contract negotiations at one giant automobile manufacturer. Managers and union representatives faced one another across a very heavy, narrow oblong table that seemed at least 90 feet long, like two football teams ready to do battle. The table was two-tiered, allowing everyone to keep their papers on the lower tier, hidden from the other side. Designed for a win or lose tug-of-war, it conveyed a lack of trust and teamwork—hardly the way to conduct creative problem solving for the benefit of both sides. (In a later chapter, we'll look at a successful example of union-management negotiations using the Simplex process and process skills.)

The client must now invite the participants to the meeting, letting them know the objective, location and time, and thanking them for their willingness to help. Arranging for coffee and refreshments to be available half an hour before starting time ensures a welcoming, relaxing atmosphere and a chance for people to discuss their thoughts in advance.

THE MEETING PROCESS AND PROCESS SKILLS

Now let's look at the second phase of the process, the meeting itself. The objective that you identified in your preconsult now becomes the fuzzy situation that the entire group will take through the Simplex process, from fact finding through to an action plan.

With an unskilled group, the facilitator must take some time to demonstrate the process skills that the group will need to use during the meeting. He might ask whether anyone in the group can offer a possible solution to the problem to get the meeting off the ground. When someone volunteers an idea, the facilitator immediately responds with a few killer phrases such as the ones we talked about earlier: 'That's a good idea but...'; 'I think we tried that five years ago but it didn't work'; 'It sounds all right in theory but I think we're looking for something more practical here.' This is an excellent way to demonstrate to the group the stifling effect of such killer phrases and how important it is to use the process skills of deferral of judgment, active divergence and active convergence.

There's another problem with the approach the facilitator just took: he leapt into the fourth step of the Simplex process, asking for solutions without having gone through the first three steps. Having pointed out this error to the group, the facilitator then explains why it's important to follow the process, starting with fact finding rather than jumping immediately to solutions. (Recall the story of the 'hot wax' formula from an earlier chapter.) This introduces the group to the Simplex process itself and to the fourth process skill of vertical deferral of judgment. Through this short exercise, a group can understand and appreciate the process and process skills that they will be using (Figure 12-5).

- Accelerated rate of change causes industry and people to constantly improve to remain competitive.
- People are often prematurely critical when confronted with new ideas, which can shut down the flow of productive thinking.
- People are traditionally taught to be very logical and, as a result, start thinking that every problem has only 'one right answer'.
- Individuals have different styles and methods of thinking and problem solving. These differences can make group problem solving inefficient unless synchronized somehow.
- Making change is enhanced if employees at various levels and in various functions are utilized to focus on specific problems.
- Management assumes that forming teams will instantly empower the workforce and get quick results.
- People can get so focused on being efficient (doing routine work) that they lose the skills required to be adaptable (change routines).
- Important problems that cross functions are often avoided: 'That's not our problem.'
- Interfunctional teams often argue about functional issues rather than focusing on the problem.
- Team leaders still think they are supposed to lead by their own preconceived plan and ideas.
- Leaders of meetings don't know how to act as facilitators, coaching the group to find its own way to innovate action.
- Groups sometimes tend to just 'hold' meetings, not solve problems. Information is hashed and rehashed without any resulting action.
- Groups often flounder because they jump into 'solving the problem' without first considering how they will go about reaching a solution.
- Meetings tend to be undisciplined discussions where facts, ideas, evaluations, action steps and problems are interjected randomly.
- Meetings tend to be unsynchronized. While some members are trying to generate information (facts, ideas, action steps, and problems), others are highly judgmental.
- Some people try to solve 'world hunger' in a one-hour meeting.
- Rarely will group members critique their meeting to examine how future meetings might be improved.

Fig. 12.5 The need for improved facilitation skills

Throughout the meeting, the facilitator leads the group through the process so the participants can help the client gain new insights and find a solution. More important, the facilitator must continuously model the process skills of deferral of judgment, active divergence and active convergence to encourage the client and participants to use these skills themselves. He frequently reminds the group which step of the Simplex process they are in and which process skill they should be using at any time. By drawing out these skills through probing questions, the facilitator ensures that participants interact and contribute as much as possible.

A participant's role is to help the client by offering knowledge, curiosity, imagination and good judgment. A good participant does not try to push his own views or accomplish his own hidden agenda. While participants' comments should influence the client, it's up to the owner of the problem to choose the best options during each step of the process. A good client will provide as much information as possible and accept participants' points of view. If everyone plays their role well and employs their process skills correctly, the client should leave the meeting with a clear action plan and the motivation to implement it.

While each person normally sticks to his assigned role, there are important exceptions. The facilitator might discover that he has important content to offer to the client. He can ask a participant or even the client to temporarily take on the process leadership role while he provides his ideas and knowledge as a participant; then he returns to his original role. To prevent confusion, the facilitator should state clearly that he is about to temporarily switch roles.

While individuals should usually maintain their distinct roles as participant or client, few people are either one or the other. A participant often has partial ownership of the problem from the outset. Or his ownership might grow during the problem solving process or as the problem itself becomes redefined. On the other hand, clients are often eager to share ownership with participants. Asking participants at the beginning of the meeting to rate their degree of ownership is a useful way to make this point. Everyone must understand where the ownership lies during all steps of the meeting. This makes it clear who will be making the converging decisions and who will be merely offering help.

DEBRIEFING: TOWARD BETTER MEETINGS

When the meeting ends with an action plan, it's time to carry out the third meeting phase, called debrief. Here the team assesses its use of the process skills during the meeting. With one member acting as facilitator, the group generates a list of answers to two questions: 'What did we say or do during the meeting that helped our process?'; 'What did we say or do that hindered our process?' The answers generate a discussion of how the group might improve these skills during the next meeting. As individuals better understand and practise these process skills, their meetings improve (Figure 12-6).

PRECONSULT
The preconsult is a premeeting to plan, which includes the process facilitator and content owner. During this premeeting, the objective (or refined fuzzy situation) of the team meeting, agenda, participants to be invited, and prework are defined. The facilitator uses steps 1-3 of the Simplex creative problem solving process to better define the fuzzy situation and determine if a group meeting is appropriate. Realistic expectations of the agenda are addressed.

MEET
This is the phase most people are familiar with. People tend to 'hold' many meetings. Effective meetings, however, are prefaced by planning in a preconsult and culminate in a debrief. They have a purpose, an agenda of how the purpose will be achieved, follow a process, and culminate in an action plan.

DEBRIEF
The debrief stage discusses how well the process, personnel and setting worked. It includes these general questions which may be customized to the group:

1 What did we do or say that helped our meeting process?
2 What did we say or do that hindered our meeting process?
3 What did we learn? (optional)

Fig. 12.6 How to conduct the three meeting phases

This final phase brings out the fourth meeting role—the second key process role—called coach. When a group debriefs, its members become coaches. They give each other feedback not about the meeting content but about their use of the process and process skills. Although it's logical to play this role after the meeting, you need not wait until then. The group can take a 'time out' at any point to debrief if someone feels it would be helpful to review the team's process. You might even assign someone to play coach for the entire meeting. Staying out of content just like the facilitator, this person gives periodic feedback to the team or to individual members to help the process along. By playing coach, the person learns to build his own process skills while helping the group. Whether the coach is a single individual or the entire team, the coaching role helps the facilitator manage the group's process and process skills.

Building your process facilitation skills will do more for you than simply improve your meetings. The same skills help you in any situation that calls for teamwork and interactions with others. For any leadership role you find your-self in—manager, co-worker, friend, parent, consultant—these skills are the secret to empowering others. You want others to take on ownership of impor-tant problems, freeing yourself to coach and facilitate the problem solving process rather than doing all the work yourself. The more you can transfer problem ownership to others, the greater their commitment to solving their own problems.

13

FOLLOW THE PROCESS
IN TEAMS

Monkey see, monkey do?

'You know the old expression monkey see, monkey do?' I said. 'A lot of the bad habits that top teams display in not working well together get passed down to lower level teams.'

'Let me guess,' said Alice with a smile. 'Another story, right?'

'Call it a telling example,' I said. 'I'm working with one company that's just gone through a reorganization. At each level in the organization, they've assembled interfunctional teams, each reporting in turn to another interfunctional team at the next level. But the top team complains constantly about the teams that report to it. Its members say that these lower-level teams don't really operate like real teams. They're more like groups of individuals all representing their own departments. They're a team in name only. They take unilateral actions and do a lot of arguing about decisions but they never reach consensus.'

'Sounds like the same old story everywhere,' said Harry. 'Wasn't that the big problem with trying to make matrix teams work?'

'Very much the same idea. And do you know what the real problem is? It's not so much the lower-level teams as the top team itself.'

'What do you mean?' Alice said.

'Despite its complaints, the top team behaves exactly like the lower-level teams. Its members hardly ever meet. When they do get together, they disagree a lot, they try to blame each other, they leave issues unresolved. They're always running out of time in the meeting and rushing off to catch their next plane.'

'No wonder the lower-level teams can't get their act together,' said Harry.

I nodded. 'The top team members are always telling their functional counterparts in the lower-level teams what to do to make sure they achieve their functional goals. They encourage them to take actions that are aligned with their functional goals—but then they pay lip service to teamwork. In the end it's obvious to everyone at every level that the real payoff lies not in teamwork but in achieving functional goals. Everybody wants to *talk* teamwork but there is very little incentive to *do* teamwork.'

Harry said, 'I guess it's that old dilemma: "Talking the talk is a lot easier than walking the talk."' ∎

Summary of learnings

✈ *Many factors make it difficult to assemble and maintain committed, effective teams. Using the Simplex process skills helps teams to function more effectively.*

✈ *Several additional skills help teams to use the four process skills effectively. These include three interpersonal skills—active listening, supporting team members, and speaking clearly and simply—and three team skills—achieving consensus, providing feedback, and building cohesiveness.*

By using the Simplex process and process skills to conduct meetings, you can help your organization's teams work much more effectively. There's nothing new about teamwork. What is new are the kinds of pressures that are forcing organizations to adopt the team approach. Increasing competition and more demanding customers, among other things, mean that organizations face much more complicated kinds of problems. If your organization hopes to fully understand these problems and come up with timely, quality solutions, then it has to draw on wider knowledge from a broader range of people—especially employees who deal directly with the organization's customers, products and processes.

THE PROBLEM WITH TEAMWORK

It's difficult to assemble and maintain committed, effective teams, for all kinds of reasons (Figure 13-1). Team members often just go through the motions, but then return to their 'regular jobs.' Group members cannot communicate clearly and simply, or can't adequately define terms. They assume that everyone knows what they mean, leading to frustration and wasted time. They don't recognize that individuals use different styles and methods of thinking and problem solving. If people are unable to synchronize these differences, then group problem solving will be inefficient. Groups that jump directly into 'solving a problem' without considering how exactly they will solve it eventually flounder. Focusing only on content and not process, their meetings often turn into undisciplined discussions; facts, ideas, evaluations, action steps and new problems are introduced at random. Instead of focusing on the problem at hand, interfunctional

- Members are unable to communicate clearly, simply.
- Assuming 'we all know what we mean.'
- Lack of awareness of differences in thinking and problem solving styles.
- Jumping directly into 'solving the problem.'
- Focusing only on content instead of process.
- Randomly mixing facts, solutions, evaluations, new problems, action steps.
- Arguing over territorial issues instead of focusing on the problem.
- Lack of facilitation skills, leaders promoting their own points of view.
- Failure to critique process.
- Fear of bold, innovative solutions.
- Members fail to support one another.

Fig. 13.1 Why teamwork is often uncreative

teams find themselves mired in territorial disputes. Meeting leaders lack skills in facilitating the group process. Rather than coach the group toward innovative action, they steer others toward their own points of view. Rarely do groups critique their meeting process to see how they might improve future gatherings. People often settle for holding unproductive meetings as an excuse for not developing bold, innovative solutions.

WHY CAN'T WE JUST GET ALONG?

Team members need to check egos and go-it-alone attitudes at door

We can all probably think of numerous ways in which teams fall short. Here are a few examples.

One manager emerging from an unsatisfactory team meeting said that people had arrived at the gathering armed with *their own plans of attack*. Instead of discussing what problem the team was trying to solve or considering alternatives, some individuals had spent their time trying to convince everyone else that their own plan was best. One member in particular had attempted to push his solution onto the group. As the only human resources representative among a roomful of engineering, production and marketing staff, this manager found herself uncomfortable because she didn't understand the background to this individual's solution. And because the solution had to be sold to senior management, she was reluctant to give in without obtaining more information. She began to ask questions to better understand the solution: How will this move affect our product's image? Have we done enough consumer testing? Have we done enough fact finding about all the implications of this move? Rather than view her uninformed questions as starting points to do some fresh thinking, some team members became frustrated with them. The individual pushing the solution misinterpreted her attempts to understand as an attack on his decision-making ability. Seeming to be in a great hurry to move ahead with a solution, the team members felt that the manager was blocking their progress.

In another company's meeting involving a senior management team, the team members—all diverse, capable, well-educated people—spent their time saying only what they believed the president wanted to hear. Instead of trying to draw upon their wide-ranging backgrounds and experience, *they simply jockeyed to look good*. The whole point of struggling together toward a richer answer for their problem was missed. Rather than share their problems—an admission that they actually struggled with problems—each member wanted to appear strong, confident and knowledgeable. What came out of the meeting was an inadequate solution lacking any real commitment. The reverse of this problem yields equally poor results. Sometimes a new team member wrongly assumes that solutions that worked in other situations will work for this new team. Instead of fact finding to learn more about the new organization or team, he simply pushes his views on others. He is unwilling to be flexible and adapt new solutions to fit the new culture.

A member of another senior managemen team described how employees always scrambled to line up behind potential *'power brokers.'* The senior team members rarely met or shared information. The president worked with them only as individuals, never as a group. Rather than build good solutions based on a solid understanding of customers and company needs, employees just 'did their jobs' as members of separate empires run by the senior managers. Nobody questioned strategies or worked together toward better solutions; they just waited for instructions to follow.

Some leaders worry too much about being seen as autocratic. They withhold their own opinions and provide little feedback during discussions. For some people, this attitude is a plus ('Isn't the president a nice man, he's always so pleasant'). Others aren't so sure ('He seems nice but sometimes I wonder what he's really thinking'). A leader who abdicates in this way builds resentment if employees feel he's contributing less than he could. Without the leader's participation and feedback, employees lose confidence and struggle to prove themselves in a vacuum.

The management team in one organization held a strategic planning session to come up with ways to achieve its stated goal of becoming more culturally diverse. Strategic planning is ordinarily a very creative activity; it's hardly a strictly analytical exercise. Participants need to look into the past and the future, then try to set goals and directions without a clear road map. They need a common creative process and good process skills in order to guide their thinking. But this management team had no such process or process skills. The members bounced back and forth in a random discussion of broad strategic issues and narrow tactical suggestions. Members used killer phrases liberally, even though the meeting had been billed as a 'blue sky' session.

To help focus the group, one manager suggested that its members consider the question, 'How would we know 10 years from now whether we had achieved our goal of cultural diversity? Would our management ranks include, say, 80 per cent non-whites?' Instead of building on this question in order to focus their discussion, the other managers immediately began to pick apart the example itself. Rather than diverge to consider different measures of success ('How might we measure our success?'; 'What might be our diversity goal?'), the group felt compelled to evaluate the manager's single example. Lacking the process skills of deferral of judgment and active divergence, the group couldn't build on the example. It got mired instead in content.

After this experience, other members clammed up for fear of having their own ideas picked apart. The meeting eventually broke up without reaching a concrete measure of success or a plan for achieving it. What trickled down to the organization's employees were many promising but vaguely stated goals from above—'start with the customer,' 'people empowerment,' 'quality first'—without clear operational plans to follow and specific targets to achieve. Skeptical about the senior managers' commitment to their own goals, employees continued to operate in the same old way.

The chair of another company's personnel committee lamented that the group's members showed little patience for dealing with complex issues. *They didn't want to take the time to clearly define their challenges.* Unwilling to linger in fact finding, they preferred to jump toward a result by choosing from among only a few preconceived options. They couldn't understand why they should diverge beyond a few obvious ideas. Any idea that was different or less than perfect they took as a final result that they could then pick apart. The two committee members who did understand the creative process and process skills found themselves odd men out. Discouraged from providing their unique points of view, and seeing the others defending their own positions, they decided that their ideas must be inferior and so contributed less than they could have. Unhappy with the group's results, the chair often simply made her own decisions later.

TOWARD MORE PRODUCTIVE TEAMS

You've probably seen similar examples of team behavior in all kinds of organizations. Not only are managers dissatisfied with their teams' results, but the team members themselves become disillusioned. The common lesson is that organizations hoping to make their teams more productive must meet several critical challenges, as follows (Figure 13-2):

- How might each member make a valuable contribution?
- How might each member support team decisions?
- How might members commit to implementing the team's own recommendations?
- How might the team focus on clearly defined challenges?
- How might the team develop and consider many alternative solutions?
- How might the team define how and when to implement its solutions?
- How might the team members listen to, share, and accept each other's ideas?
- How might the team members identify and resolve conflicting priorities and interests?
- How might team members agree on what's important?
- How might the team members assign themselves clear action steps?
- How might teams work well together?

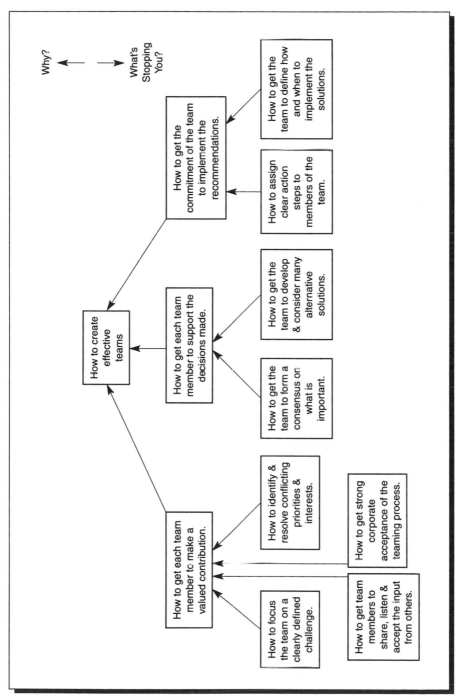

Fig. 13.2 How to create effective teams

INTERPERSONAL SKILLS FOR BETTER TEAMWORK

If team members hope to meet these challenges, they need to learn a few skills besides the Simplex process skills. In an earlier chapter, you practised your own skills in applying the entire Simplex process to your own work-related problem. When you're working in a team, you have to use the same skills, but you need to employ another set of interpersonal skills at the same time. These skills include active listening to others, supporting team members to help them say what they're thinking, and speaking clearly and simply to help others understand your thoughts (Figure 13-3).

Active listening means deliberately paying attention to what others are saying. The point is not to agree or disagree with their comment, but to try to completely understand what they're saying. Don't interrupt except to encourage clarification. Ask open-ended questions that permit speakers to enrich their thoughts. Value whatever is said, and avoid judging by your words or actions. Summarize their comments out loud to make sure you've understood.

Supporting others means automatically accepting that they're saying what they really think. Whether or not you agree isn't important. What's important is that you hear everyone's point of view. Don't debate or try to persuade team members to alter their comments to suit your thoughts. Otherwise, you will never enrich your own thinking or the thinking of the team. Effective problem solving comes from expressing differences of opinion or fact, not from suppressing them. Assume that others have useful information and ideas, but that they might not want to express them, perhaps because they lack self-esteem or they assume that everybody already knows their ideas. Speaking in friendly, warm terms encourages others to share their thoughts and feelings. They will contribute more readily to the team if they believe you will build on their ideas and respond openly and spontaneously to their thoughts. When you do offer

Interpersonal skills
1 Active listening
2 Supporting others
3 Speaking clearly and simply

Team skills
1 Achieving consensus
2 Providing feedback
3 Building cohesiveness

Fig. 13.3 Interpersonal and team skills needed for effective teamwork

your own thoughts, make sure others realize you are trying to enrich the pot, not deliberately challenging them.

Speaking clearly and simply means several things. Express your thoughts in complete, simple sentences rather than single words or phrases. Avoid jargon that comes naturally to you but that may be foreign to your teammates. Use terminology that's familiar to them. If they realize that you're trying to help them understand, they will appreciate your efforts and listen more readily. Avoid ambiguous terms that might be easily misinterpreted, and stay away from flowery language that intimidates others. For example, rather than saying, 'We need to increase productivity,' say something more specific like, 'Our customers are asking for a 10-per-cent reduction in defects,' or, 'We need to reduce costs by $1 per case to achieve our profit targets.' In this case, don't assume your teammates work with your definition of productivity. For different people, the word 'productivity' might mean how hard a person works, how many units per hour are being produced, the number of people it takes to produce a unit, reduced downtime, less idle chitchat at the water cooler, fewer breaks, working on important goals rather than 'busy work,' or any combination.

TEAM SKILLS FOR BETTER TEAMWORK

These interpersonal skills help team members to use their process skills in the group. They encourage the team members to defer judgment, actively diverge, and actively converge when they're working together. But just as the members must learn these interpersonal skills, so the entire team must learn an additional set of team skills: achieving consensus, providing feedback, and building cohesiveness (Figure 13-3).

Achieving consensus is the best way (but not necessarily the shortest way) for team members to converge together. Consensus doesn't mean getting the members' unanimous agreement on one of several options. It means putting together the team's best thinking to make a choice that every member will support—even if it wasn't the member's own first choice. Nor does consensus mean taking a simple vote, or living by 'majority rules.' While this approach saves time, it deters thinking things through carefully. Just because the majority was thinking the same way about a situation, it doesn't mean that any of them thought it through carefully or that they had all the important information (how many voters carefully analyze all the options or issues before casting their vote in a federal election?). When the team takes the time to hear and adapt everyone's best thinking, it is more likely to make the best choice, or even create a new one. When new information is provided by a minority, for example, it can spark fresh thinking by an open-minded majority.

Here are four guidelines for reaching consensus (Figure 13-4):

When groups of people solve problems together, the group members must diverge and converge together. Group convergence results are best when the group works toward and achieves consensus. Consensus may be difficult to reach. Consensus means that although not every selection or decision will meet with everyone's complete approval, each decision must be agreed upon by each group member ('I can live with it') before it becomes a part of the group decision. Try, as a group, to make each choice one with which all group members can at least partially agree. Here are some guidelines to use in reaching consensus:

1 View differences of opinion as helpful rather than as a hindrance.
2 Provide your best thoughts, no matter how different or unusual.
3 Don't change your mind just to avoid disagreements.
4 Avoid deciding without healthy discussion.

Fig. 13.4 Four guidelines for achieving consensus

- View differences of opinion as a help, not a hindrance. Don't argue for your choice just because it's yours. While keeping an open mind, focus on making a good decision, not on trying to prove your point. Deferring judgment on differences of opinion while the team converges helps members listen to one another and assemble their different viewpoints into the most creative end result, instead of simply pinpointing whose idea won or lost. The final decision belongs not to one person, but to the team as a whole.
- Offer your best thoughts, no matter how different or unusual they seem.
- If others have different viewpoints, don't change your mind just to avoid disagreement. Find out why the disagreement exists, then support the decision that best accounts for everybody's viewpoint. If you think a teammate is making inappropriate assumptions, find a neutral way to voice your questions or doubts. You can turn differences in viewpoints into a positive thing: 'It's really interesting to me that you and I see the same alternative so differently. Tell me more about how you see it. I'll bet I've missed something that could really add to my understanding.' The other person might respond positively and want to know more about your viewpoint in turn.
- Avoid deciding from among options without holding a healthy discussion. Trade information to ensure that everyone is using the same criteria to judge options. If people view options in different ways, you have to discover why the difference exists. Usually it's because people think different criteria are more or less important or because they lack the same level of understanding of the options. You won't get at these differences by simply flipping a coin or holding a vote without discussion.

It's especially difficult to build consensus in high-powered senior management teams whose members have gotten where they are through hard work and competition with others. They have learned to point out the flaws in others' choices as a way of showing their superiority. If a team member is focusing on getting a promotion rather than working toward true consensus and the best result, he may follow his own hidden agenda. The problem gets worse if the boss, fearing being labeled a tyrant, hesitates to drive the group toward consensus. Empowering individuals is one thing; abdicating authority is another. If the boss doesn't play a full role in building consensus, team members may simply jockey for political position instead of putting their hearts into teamwork.

Another important team skill is *providing feedback* to other team members and to the team itself. Just as ground control keeps a space shuttle on its correct launch path by making adjustments based on electronic feedback from the vehicle, so a creative team keeps its performance on track by providing continual feedback on its use of the creative process skills. Recall our discussion of the feedback process of debriefing during a meeting and its delivery through the process role of coach. When a team receives helpful coaching, its members will do more of whatever benefits their team performance and less of whatever detracts from it. Whether you're working in a formal meeting or not, this principle of continual feedback is central to effective teamwork.

As most teams focus strictly on content rather than process, most team members lack skill in giving each other helpful process feedback. They may even shy away from providing feedback. Why?

How to improve feedback

Many of us are used to getting only negative feedback (in school, at home, on the job), given only in a judgmental manner. Many performance appraisal systems, for example, work only by evaluating your past performance—especially by pinpointing your failures—rather than by looking at ways to improve your future behavior. We then react defensively to feedback, and find it difficult to subject others to the same negative experience. Few of us understand that the purpose of feedback is not to judge but to help us improve. Positive feedback is equally important: it's just as helpful to learn what you are doing well as to hear what you could improve (Figure 13-5).

Here are seven more principles for improving your skills in giving useful process feedback.

- Most important, your feedback must be based on trust and intended to help someone else. If your feedback is merely self-serving, keep it to yourself. As others learn that your feedback is intended to help them improve their performance, they will trust you more. And they'll be more likely to risk changing how they work. Not only does feedback based on trust directly improve results, but it further builds trust among teammates. It's a self-ful-filling process. Research shows that trust is an important factor in building high-calibre teams. In these teams, people actually ask for feedback instead of shying away from it.

- Feedback is most effective when it's requested. When you ask someone else for their feedback, you make it easier for them to respond truthfully, for better or worse. They are also more likely to follow your lead and solicit feedback for themselves.

- Feedback should be descriptive, not evaluative. Describe someone's behavior in a factual way, not in a way that evaluates them. It is much more useful to say, 'When Tom began discussing the financial repercussions of Fred's idea, you appeared to lose interest, and Tom seemed upset about it,' rather than to say, 'You don't listen well.' The latter attacks the person's self-esteem, and puts them on the defensive.

- Not only was the former approach more likely to motivate the listener to improve, but it was also much more specific. When feedback is specific and includes examples, the recipient is more likely to know exactly what to do. If you are the recipient, check the feedback for clarity. It's better to take the time to pinpoint exactly what was meant than to alter your behavior based on mis-understood information. The more specific the feedback, the more clear it is.

- Time your feedback so that the person is most likely to act on it. Feedback usually works best shortly after a particular incident occurs. If you wait too long, the individual may be unable to clearly connect your comments with his behavior. This isn't always the case. It might be more useful to wait until the person appears especially receptive to feedback or even asks for it. If they appear to be in a defensive mood, you might wait for a better time. Effective teams often provide a regular time for debriefing, which allows people to prepare themselves to give and receive feedback.

---

1 Positive feedback equally important.
2 Based on trust and intended to help.
3 Most effective when solicited.
4 Descriptive, not evaluative.
5 Specific (with examples).
6 Well timed.
7 In a manner that relaxes yourself and the recipient.
8 Avoid overloading.

Fig. 13.5 Eight principles of giving useful feedback

- Offer feedback in a manner that relaxes both parties. Remember that feedback is intended to help someone learn and change behavior. Recall that learning is much more effective when the learner is relaxed. Some people might use humor to create a relaxed mood. Others pay attention to their tone of voice, keeping it soft, friendly and measured. Pick relaxing or neutral surroundings. Instead of calling someone into your office, you might meet for lunch or coffee.
- Avoid overloading people with feedback. We can only remember so much at a time. Avoid feedback that in effect asks the recipient to make impossible behavior changes. You might encourage an introverted individual to be a little more energetic in leading a brainstorming session. But you can't expect them to become the life of the party.

It's one thing to know these principles of giving useful feedback. It's another to gain the skills you need to apply them. And not only must you apply the skills yourself, but you must lead others in doing so, either in teams or individually. If you model good feedback behavior, others will follow your lead.

To help you model this behavior with a group, use the two debriefing questions we discussed in the previous chapter on leading meetings: 'What are we saying or doing that is helping our process?'; 'What are we saying or doing that is hindering our process?' Encourage the group to consider these questions not just after meetings but during any form of teamwork. Reminding the team members to defer their judgment and actively diverge, ask them to come up with as many answers to the two questions as they can. Then encourage them to discuss and clarify what they feel are the more relevant points. Doing this helps the team improve its process skills. A third useful question is, 'What are we learning about our process and process skills?'

If you're giving feedback to one individual, you can modify these questions: 'Here is what you say and do that I really like in your interactions with others... (list as many positive behaviors as you can)'; 'Here are some things you might try to do differently to improve your interactions with others... (list a few of the most important opportunities for improving behavior).' Even better, ask the individual to tell you first what they feel they are doing well and how they feel they might improve. In other words, ask them to pose these two questions to themselves. Then add your own thoughts to reinforce theirs and to contribute anything they might have missed. When they're invited to participate like this, people are more likely to act on your feedback.

A third important team skill is to *develop high team cohesiveness*. Team members should feel strong bonds to other members and to the team itself. Team cohesiveness is necessary for good problem solving and creativity. Cohesive teams share their members' diverse experience more completely, and support differing viewpoints and risky, novel ideas. This helps to avoid 'group think,' which encourages members to follow the crowd into inadequate solutions instead of offering possibly controversial viewpoints. This false harmony is often a sign of a team lacking cohesiveness.

When used correctly, the process skills of deferral of judgment, active divergence and active convergence increase team cohesiveness. And just as heightened trust and better teamwork feed on one another, so greater cohesiveness improves the team's use of these skills. As team members learn the benefits of moving in sync between diverging and converging, they practise these skills even more. Quality results come not from the work of any one individual but from the efforts of the entire team. And no one cares or wants to know who should get credit for any particular idea. The process of achieving quality results becomes as exhilarating as the results themselves.

One way to develop this 'one-ness' is to provide feedback to the team as a whole instead of to individual members. If an individual behaves poorly, the entire team automatically behaves poorly. When good ideas surface or when good process skills are used, the leader must commend the entire team, not just the individual who came up with the idea or displayed good process skills. When a team meets to solve a problem caused by someone's mistake, the discussion focuses on the mistake made by the team, not by the individual. And when the team presents its results to senior managers, it does so as a unit.

In this and the previous chapter, we've talked in theory about how you can use the Simplex process and process skills to lead meetings and work in teams. Now let's look at three real-life examples.

WHOSE SIDE ARE YOU ON?

Bargaining team takes 'win-win' approach to contract negotiations

First, here's how Simplex was employed in union-management contract negotiations to generate imaginative solutions that would have been stifled by the more traditional adversarial bargaining process. A company's union members and managers wished to avoid the kind of negotiating deadlocks and subsequent strikes that had shut down the plant four times within 10 years. Looking for a more collaborative approach and more creative solutions, they agreed to try out the Simplex process and process skills.

The bargaining process is usually a 'win-lose' contest, as we've illustrated in the conflict resolution model in Figure 13-6. What one side wins, the other automatically loses. When negotiations get really heated and both sides fail to compromise anywhere along the bargaining line, some of the pie is actually thrown away. During work stoppages, for example, neither the company nor its workforce makes money. Both sides end up in the 'lose-lose' area. When both sides achieve nothing better than simply moving up and down the bargaining line, it's a sign that they are taking a limited view of the problem. As they jockey toward a compromise somewhere along the 'win-lose bargaining line,'

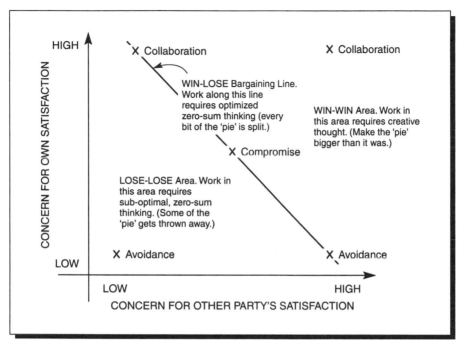

Fig. 13.6 Conflict resolution model

all that matters in the end is who got the larger share of the pie. Moving beyond the bargaining line into the 'win-win' area requires creativity. In this example, the participants learned to creatively define their problems, opening up room for new 'win-win' solutions (making the pie larger).

We began by giving the 14-member negotiating team 1 1/2 days' worth of training in the Simplex process and the process skills. As we've already discussed, these skills allow a team to build cohesiveness and trust, to extend its fact finding beyond the obvious, and to avoid preconceived solutions. In order to apply these skills to the negotiating process, the team decided to adopt a few simple, specific tactics. Whenever anyone used a killer phrase, for example, someone would ring a bell. The team also imposed nominal fines for interruptions and poor listening behaviors. They applied the Simplex process to their negotiations in a two-phase approach.

Starting with fuzzy situations

Viewing each of 25 contract items under negotiation as a fuzzy situation, the team started with fact finding in order to creatively define the 'problem' represented by each item. Using the Simplex process skills, the team was able to reach beyond superficial information. Instead of suppressing their biases, assumptions, hidden agendas, and differing values and points of view, team members laid them out on the table as valid information to be fed into each problem definition. Each side stated its entire opening position while the other side simply listened. The team then conducted divergent fact finding, using prompter questions like, 'What else do we know about this fuzzy situation?' and 'What don't we know but wish we knew about this fuzzy situation?' Team members interacted freely, entertaining all questions and answers and recording them on large sheets of newsprint posted around the room. Whenever the group lapsed into adversarial tactics, it called a halt in order to examine its process. Whenever the group was stymied, it engaged in freewheeling in order to generate new facts. Everyone was free to discuss anything that came to mind that might be remotely related to the particular issue.

Once the group felt it had pulled out all the facts, it converged to develop key themes by consensus. Using these selected key themes, the team again diverged to generate many optional problem definition statements. It then reached consensus on the most fruitful problem definitions to solve later in phase 2. The team completed phase 1 for all of the contract items in turn before going on to phase 2.

For example, one contract item had originally been stated as 'additional vacation time.' Creative fact finding uncovered the fact that many people hadn't been taking their full vacation time, for two reasons. They believed (mistakenly) that their job might be eliminated during their absence. And they felt they just couldn't afford to take vacations anyway. Following the Simplex process led the group to such interesting problem definitions as: 'How might we help people feel more secure about their jobs while on vacation?' and, 'How might we help people take more affordable vacations?'

For each problem definition selected for each contract item in turn, the team alternately diverged and converged to create solutions and action plans to revise the items. The team first arranged the items by order of priority. Then, item by item, the group generated solution ideas for each 'how might we?' statement from phase 1. They used several of the idea generation techniques that we discussed in earlier chapters to free the team members' imaginations and develop possible solutions.

Whenever possible, the team members immediately implemented workplace actions, wrote up new procedures, or made plans to gain acceptance from their respective areas. Each team member was assigned workplace actions along with specific timetables for completion. When members felt they might face a challenge in gaining acceptance for their actions, the team members created ideas to help them. Individuals who were assigned specific tasks to implement actions in the workplace were asked to report on their progress during subsequent team meetings. Thus, phase 2 corresponded to the second and third stages of Simplex (problem solving and solution implementation).

Within about two months, the group had applied both phases to all of these 25 contract items, resulting at least in agreement-in-principle for each. For many of these items, specific changes to contract language and workplace actions had already been implemented. Using Simplex had allowed the group to develop a more harmonious, co-operative atmosphere throughout the bargaining process.

There's an important lesson to take from this example. Creative problem definition allows two groups that believe they have few common objectives—or even feel they have opposing objectives—to find out what they actually have in common. In fact, this point is central to the definition of a team: without common goals and objectives, or problem definitions, there is no team.

DREAM TEAM?

'Foes' team up in creative approach to improve bottom line

This lesson also came out of a second example of creative problem solving and teamwork. Here, seven top corporate managers and seven top franchise owners had been assembled in a team to improve the entire organization's efficiency. For years, relations between the corporate managers and independent franchises had been strained by mistrust, conflicting goals and miscommunication. Many franchise owners thought the corporate managers wanted to weaken them financially so that the company could eventually buy them out at bargain prices. They felt that the company was being run by a bunch of Ivy League whiz kids who developed marketing programs without any real knowledge of the company's consumers. For their part, the corporate managers complained that the franchisees were reluctant to accept their new programs and plans, even after careful, sophisticated research. Time and again, the corporate managers found themselves apologizing for neglecting—albeit unintentionally—to tell all the franchisees about new activities until after the fact. Each side blamed the other for mistakes.

After undergoing separate training in the Simplex innovation process and process skills, the two groups met for two days along with an expert facilitator. The meeting succeeded, partly because the team members made a real effort to use the process skills, no matter how painful. But the real key to success was a strategic problem definition map that the group developed after fact finding (Figure 13-7). The members agreed that their most significant challenge was, 'How might we build two-way trust in order to come up with mutually agreed goals?' They felt that solving this problem and implementing the solutions would take them 80 per cent of the way toward achieving their overall goal, which they re-defined as, 'How might we help each other improve operating profitability?' Figures 13-8, 13-9 and 13-10 show the team's three best solutions, the key criteria that the team used to select these solutions, and the action plan created to implement the first solution: 'Do joint strategic planning and joint operating planning.'

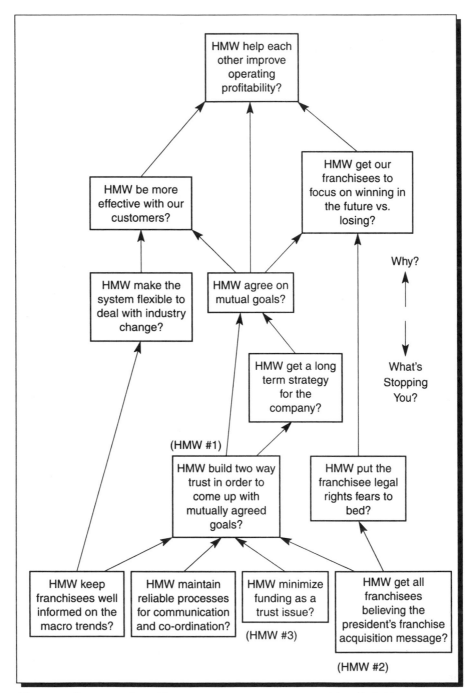

Fig. 13.7 Corporate-franchisee top management team problem definition map

Solution 1
Do joint strategic planning and joint operating planning.

Solution 2
Jointly develop a reliable process for two-way communication and co-ordination of the system.

Solution 3
Share profit and loss statements among the different franchisee and corporate units.

Fig. 13.8 Best three solutions for the challenge: 'How might we build two-way trust in order to come up with mutally agreed goals?'

The following eight criteria were selected as the most important to help evaluate the list of ideas.

1 To what extent is it a win/win situation for both groups?
2 Acceptability to broad franchisee body.
3 Executional feasibility.
4 Payoff: How much impact on improving trust?
5 Impact on success in marketplace.
6 Long-term impact.
7 Amount of motivation created.
8 Amount of shared commitment to the idea.

Fig. 13.9 Criteria selected as most important for evaluation of ideas for solving problem definition #1: 'How might we build two-way trust in order to come up with mutually agreed goals?'

TAKEN TO TASK

Task force maps out key challenges; breaks long-time impasse

In a third example, a long-term project team created an 'operational excellence program' that unified and motivated another organization's franchise-owned

What	How	Who	When	Where
1. Describe the contents of the current corporate strategic plan to this franchisee group	Hand carry	Dan Smith (corp. V.P.)	Next Monday June 3	National franchisee meeting
2. Pick the franchisee participants who will do the strategic planning	Meet after dinner on June 3	The franchisee participants who are here today plus Charles Adams	Monday June 3	National franchisee meeting
3. Pick the corporate participants	Discussion between George (the President) and staff at regular monthly meeting in June	The President	June 13	Chicago
4. Advise the date for the first joint meeting	Dan call John (franchisee designate)	Dan	By June 17	Office to office
5. Layout how the annual planning process works today (approximately) for sharing at the first team meeting	Dan to co-ordinate	Dan	TBD	TBD
6. Hold the first joint team meeting and make plans for joint involvement in developing the annual operating planning process	Co-ordinated by Dan & John	Dan & John	TBD	TBD

Fig. 13.10 Action plan for solution #1: 'Do joint strategic planning and joint operating planning'

and company-owned bottling plants. This diverse group, called the GMP (Good Manufacturing Practices) Task Force, used fact finding and a problem definition mapping process to select the three or four key challenges that would drive their subsequent activities.

The task force had been floundering for several reasons. There were long-standing differences over procedures for evaluating plants owned by franchisees and those owned by the company. The franchisees also resented having to be evaluated by company auditors. Similar to our earlier example, the franchisees suspected that the company planned to shut down their operations so that it could take them over. Both sides believed that the inspection system was ineffectual and lacked any real purpose. Thanks to these problems, the task force's initial meetings had gone nowhere.

The team had been struck to create a clear, meaningful audit process for both kinds of facilities, with a scoring system that would motivate all plants to score as highly as possible. Realizing that they lacked a process to achieve these goals, the team members brought in a Simplex facilitator to help them. After a preconsult, the team received fundamental training in the Simplex process and process skills. The team met several times over the next few months, repeatedly working its way through the process from fact finding to action. Fact finding uncovered a number of points, as follows:

- We lack a common clear understanding of what's important in a plant evaluation program.
- We lack agreement on basic values that we hope to achieve through common standards.
- We lack a common clear understanding of what's important in achieving excellence in plant operations.
- We agree that the outcome we'd like is a compelling, self-motivating tool that creates value for our people, our manufacturing processes and our customers.
- Excellence will likely be defined in terms of our basic values, whatever they may be.
- It's important to agree on what goals should be met, and how to measure how well they were met.

These facts led to the problem definition map shown in Figure 13-11. The team selected the most critical challenges to solve (circled on the map) and placed the most important of them in a sequence that became the team's project management plan. These critical challenges were as follows:

- 'How might we develop and agree on a common set of values about good manufacturing practices?'
- 'How might we determine the basic requirements that each plant *must* meet and the optional requirements that each plant *should* meet?' (Solving this

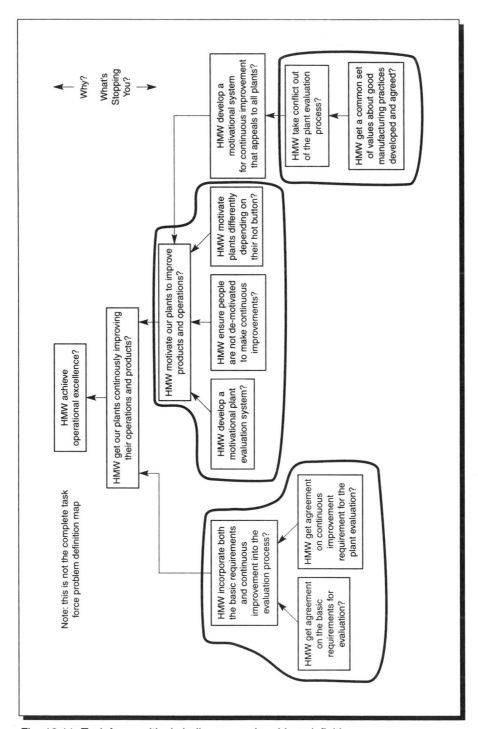

Fig. 13.11 Task force critical challenges and problem definition map

challenge would allow the group to incorporate both basic requirements and the option of continuous improvement into the new plant evaluation process.)

- 'How might we devise a system that removes the conflict from the plant evaluation process?'
- 'How might we motivate all of our plants to continuously improve their operations and products?'

Having placed these challenges in order, the group focused on implementing solutions to each. The result: the group developed a unique operational excellence program that overcame its long-standing problems.

In order to meet customer requirements, more companies are looking for corporate rather than just functional excellence. And for that, they need *new thinking skills*—especially among teams. Just as many companies created research and development departments about five decades ago to take control of product innovation, so companies today need to take control of process innovation. They can't leave process innovation to chance. What's needed is a new corporate function that builds teamwork across the entire organization and helps the organization to deliberately and continuously improve its processes and procedures. The function can be called different things, such as a 'corporate innovation office' or a program that aims to improve costs, methods or profits. Whatever its name, it calls for new thinking skills among teams.

14

ALIGNMENT: FOLLOW THE SIMPLEX PROCESS TO DEFINE YOUR KEY CHALLENGES

The missing link

'Something else about the top team at this company I was telling you about,' I said to Harry and Alice. 'Whenever they do hold a so-called meeting, there's a lot of saluting and a great show of support for the boss's idea or the plan that was just hatched. But that's as far as it goes. When its members go back to their respective departments, they don't take any action to follow up. It's just business as usual.'

Alice said, 'I've seen that kind of thing in all kinds of places: businesses, agencies, universities, governments. All the departments have their own goals and procedures to meet the goals. Whenever a new strategic plan comes down from the top with new goals and directions, no one down below can align them with their own departmental goals.'

'I know what you mean,' Harry nodded. 'Seems leaders can't make the link between the people developing the strategy and goals, and the people who have to execute the program to meet the goals. The people making the strategy have the power but they're not in any position to implement the programs. The people who do have to implement the programme don't have the power to make the strategy.'

Alice gestured as if to take Harry's comment one step further. 'So the people closest to the customers have nothing to do with making the strategy, while the folks making the strategy are the furthest from understanding the customers.'

'It's a real problem,' I said. 'Once they leave a strategic planning meeting, people can't get commitment to the changes back in their departments. Without commitment at the top, nobody else right down to the bottom of the organization can become committed to the change. Instead, different departments jockey back and forth, unwilling to give an inch. And the new strategic goals get further and further watered down.'

⇨

'So what can you do about it?' Harry asked.

'It's a tough problem,' I repeated. 'But I think you can overcome it. One way is for top managers to learn how to become better facilitators of problem solving groups. Then they can make sure that their own teams work well together instead of just going through the motions. This way, they can make sure that lower-level groups will creatively develops goals that are aligned with higher-level goals. It takes skill in leading groups of people through the creative process, and in getting people excited and positive about change.' ■

Summary of learnings

➤ *Instead of simply addressing whatever problems crop up or choosing only the most appealing ones, try 'working smarter, not harder.' Simplex helps you to define your critical challenges and focus on solving them.*

➤ *The 'why-what's stopping' mapping process is a strategic tool for defining the challenges important to you and to the organization. You should frequently update your own 'why-what's stopping' map as events unfold.*

➤ *Skills in the 'why-what's stopping' mapping process help you to align your selected challenges with the organization's strategic challenges. It also guides your daily activities toward solving internal and external customers' problems—the ultimate purpose of your job.*

➤ *This alignment helps you find and solve the problems that will help make the organization more competitive.*

W e ended the previous chapter by discussing how organizations need to appoint a special corporate function responsible for making change so that improvement and innovation aren't left to chance. Many organizations will be slow to do so. This gives you a golden opportunity to take the lead, to become that 'special function' by mainstreaming innovation, by proactively seeking out important problems, solving them, and implementing the solutions within your own department. Fail to seize the opportunity, and you lose the chance to distinguish yourself within your organization. So how to begin?

Once you begin to use the Simplex creative process, you will find no shortage of problems on which to apply it. Rather, your challenge will be to select the right problems to address. It's all too easy to tackle problems as they crop up or to pick only problems that you want to solve. And it's easy to have your priorities dictated by other people who don't fully understand your objectives and responsibilities. Instead, you need to take control. You need to define your own critical challenges and focus on solving them, even if it means putting other problems aside. In this chapter, we'll look at ways to help you define your critical challenges—the key to the well-known adage 'work smarter, not harder.' (Obviously, your own critical challenges must align with your organization's key corporate challenges. With any luck, your organization has already identified these corporate challenges, making this alignment clear. If not, you will also have to define those corporate challenges, something we'll look at in the next chapter.)

HOW TO DEFINE YOUR KEY CHALLENGES

A key tool for defining these individual and organization-wide challenges is the 'why-what's stopping' mapping process that we discussed earlier. As you ask the question 'why' of a particular problem definition, working your way up the map, you align your own challenge more closely with more strategic goals. Going in the other direction—asking the question 'what's stopping me' of the problem definition—you work your way down to identify more specific challenges. You must create your own strategic 'why-what's stopping' map, and return to it frequently to keep your efforts focused on your critical challenges. And you need to update your map as circumstances change.

How can you ensure that your own selected challenges are indeed relevant to the entire organization? You need to start with two assumptions. One is that organizations exist only to provide goods and services that solve *customers' problems*. There's an important difference between addressing customer needs and addressing customer problems. If you ask a customer what he needs, he'll only tell you what he thinks you can give him. Ask him instead about his problems, and his answer gives you the chance to create a new solution, and hence a new product or service. The second assumption is that your job exists only to help your organization solve its customers' problems. The 'why-what's stopping' mapping process ensures that these two assumptions direct everything you do, every minute of every day. It doesn't matter what your position is in the organization. By discovering and defining personal challenges that align with your organization's strategic challenges, you can concentrate on finding and solving the problems that will make your organization more competitive.

Further complicating things, no organization's critical challenges will remain the same. For an organization to remain competitive in the face of external changes—economic circumstances, technological advances, customer needs—its critical challenges also change. Let's look at an example of how to use the 'why-what's stopping' strategic mapping process to define your own critical challenges that relate directly to maintaining your company's competitive edge.

DEFINING YOUR KEY CHALLENGES: AN EXAMPLE

A potato chip manufacturing plant had been hit by a severe, prolonged recession. One manager had recognized that the challenge 'How might I help my company maintain a competitive edge during this recession?' ranked somewhere near the top of his personal 'why-what's stopping' map. Using his creative problem definition skills, he began to map out his other challenges by asking, 'What's stopping me from helping my company maintain a competitive edge during this recession?' His answer was that customers had less money to spend and thus were looking for greater value in their purchases. He came up with a more focused challenge: 'How might I help the company increase value to its customers during this recession?' By continuing this questioning process in both directions, he eventually produced his strategic map (Figure 14-1).

Then he looked for the one challenge that would allow him and his department to best help the company achieve its own strategic goal (maintaining its competitiveness during the recession). He eventually selected one of the more tactical challenges on his map: 'How might I reduce waste in my manufacturing operation?' This challenge wasn't at the top of the map. Several intermediate challenges eventually linked it to the more strategic ones. But he chose it because it appeared to represent the best balance of tactical and strategic interests. The challenge was focused enough that he could do something about it, and yet broad enough that his actions would help to achieve the overall goal.

He then treated this challenge as his new fuzzy situation. The manager first explained the project's goal and rationale to employees by showing them his 'why-what's stopping' strategic map. He showed them how this challenge was aligned with more strategic goals by asking the 'why?' question. Then he led them to discover more tactical challenges by asking the 'what's stopping?' question. The map clearly demonstrated to employees how finding waste sources would allow the company to reduce the waste and, ultimately, to maintain its

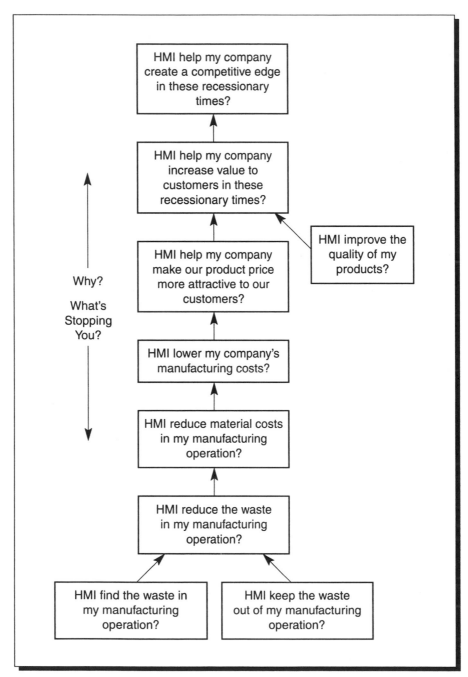

Fig. 14.1 How a manufacturing manager defined his critical challenges using the 'why-what's stopping' mapping process

competitiveness. In fact, most employees were able to take the map one step further. They realized that achieving the overall competitiveness goal would help to secure their own jobs (Figure 14-2). Sharing his thinking in this way helped the manager obtain their co-operation and participation.

Rather than take a straightforward trip around the wheel, the group cycled through fact finding several times in many ways to break down the fuzzy situation into its component parts. The first fact finding step was to conduct a so-called 'material balance,' a process to identify waste generated during manufacturing. Under this process, waste is defined as the difference between the quantity of raw materials entering the plant and the quantity of finished product leaving it.

The group used analytical procedures to identify and prioritize the sources of waste. Material was wasted in a number of ways, including being flushed down a drain, vaporized up a smokestack, or collected in containers to be sent to the dump. The group selected the three largest waste sources. Then it formed teams, each to take one waste source as its fuzzy situation. Each team began fact finding, using the six prompter questions that we discussed in an earlier chapter:

1 What do we know or think we know about this waste point?
2 What don't we know but wish we knew about this waste point?
3 What makes this waste point a problem for us? Why can't we resolve it? What are the obstacles?
4 What have we already thought of or tried?
5 If this situation were resolved, what would we have that we don't have now?
6 What assumptions or biases might we be bringing to the situation?

While asking these questions, the team members used the process skills of deferral of judgment and active divergence. As we mentioned in earlier chapters, these process skills are vital ones. They help team members respect others' viewpoints, avoid hidden assumptions and agendas, view challenges optimistically, express themselves openly, and share information freely. And they lead the group to new information and possible solutions. Too often, we accept a few readily available facts as sufficient. When we limit our fact finding to purely analytical thinking and techniques, we lose the opportunity to discover creative solutions beyond the obvious. In this case, using these skills helped each team to uncover many important but hidden facts beyond the information revealed by the material balance. Thus, each team broadened its understanding of its assigned waste source.

The manager knew that the material balance would tell him the amount of waste at each source and where it was going. But he recognized that the analysis wouldn't expose all of the hidden information about the causes of waste. One obvious fact, for example, was that all workers in one station trimming and paring potatoes before slicing appeared to be working diligently and quickly. But a hidden fact was that the station was actually overstaffed. People

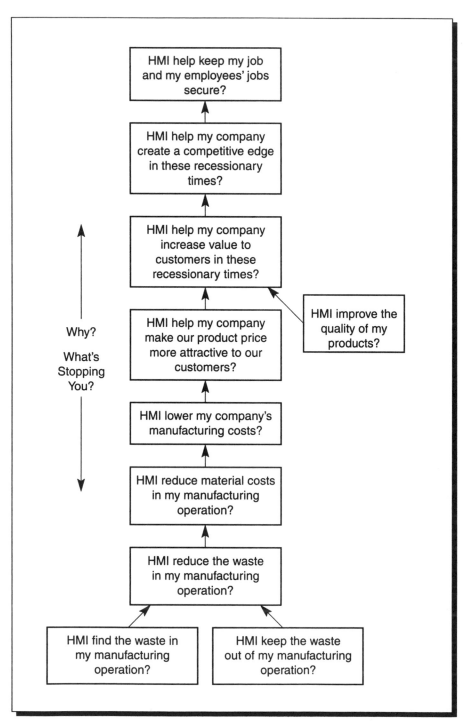

Fig. 14.2 *Using the 'why-what's stopping' process to help employees see how their work in reducing waste helps them to secure their jobs*

took on unnecessary tasks just to try to keep busy. Employees over-zealously trimmed and pared perfectly good potatoes, creating waste that kept other employees busy hauling it away. At a 'pick-out' station after the potatoes were sliced and baked, employees were discarding perfectly good potato chips just to appear busy.

The company had set up such an extremely efficient waste disposal system that it encouraged employees to get rid of waste and keep it out of sight. In fact, they prided themselves on keeping the plant clean. Chips seen lying on the floor were immediately swept up and discarded. But nobody saw 'invisible waste' like potatoes that were discharged to the sewer by the automatic potato overflow equipment. The system worked so well that the material balance had failed to detect where the waste was going. Few employees understood the costs associated with various waste materials. And the finished bags of potato chips were regularly overpacked by 1.5 grams over the marked bag weight of 22 grams—another fact not picked up by the material balance.

What made these facts invisible and, thus, so hard to identify? Had the manager not taken the lead and identified waste reduction as an important problem to solve in the first place, no one would have thought to begin this fact-finding process ('if it's not broken, why fix it?'). Employees feared that uncovering the fact that some people were merely doing 'busy work' might lead to layoffs. How could this manager expect people to freely use their knowledge and imagination to help the company if it meant they'd lose their jobs in the process? Instead of doing what so many others would do in his situation—lay off experienced, committed workers—the manager believed his job was to use these employees' talents in other ways. For example, he might ask them to create and implement waste prevention procedures in other parts of the plant.

Some facts were invisible because employees simply didn't know what to do with the information. The manager had to make a deliberate effort to uncover them. Further digging into why the potato chip bags were overpacked, for example, led the team to another fact. Proud of the company's commitment to high quality and customer satisfaction, no employee wanted the bags to appear less than full on store shelves. At some point, someone had made a conscious decision to overpack the bags so that they would look full. Everyone knew that the bags were overpacked. But no one had connected this fact with the seemingly unrelated challenge of reducing waste. Only when the manager took the lead to address the waste problem did people realize that the information was actually relevant.

Benefits of a creative process

In this example, the company's analytical and creative processes weren't necessarily at odds with one another. On the contrary, using the creative process showed the company how it could employ new analytical equipment to further increase efficiency. For example, uncovering the fact that employees were performing unnecessary trimming and paring led to a new challenge: 'How might we avoid unnecessary trimming and paring of potatoes before they reach the slicer?' The company might have solved this challenge by installing analytical equipment to measure potatoes' discoloration and irregularities before they reached the trimmers and parers so that they didn't have to examine each one.

Besides unearthing many important facts, the manager used the creative process to uncover important problem definitions. One of the plants' most important and long-standing challenges, for example, had been: 'How might we efficiently handle our waste?' This was hardly an appropriate challenge to address in order to meet the manager's strategic challenge of increasing value to customers during the recession. In fact, focusing employees' efforts on solving this specific problem had only made things worse. All the analytical devices that the company had installed to make the waste handling process more efficient had certainly helped employees eliminate more waste more quickly. But the devices had ultimately increased the amount of waste. Some employees became so intent on disposing of as much waste as possible that they actually relished creating more waste to get rid of. These analytical devices had been designed to optimize current (inefficient) processes, not to create new ones. In fact, they had hindered the creation of alternative processes, including the crucial one of reducing waste in the first place.

In this case, the company had been trying to improve the wrong process altogether. But even when a company installs analytical techniques in order to improve the correct process, it often confines its improvements to perfecting that particular process instead of coming up with a better one. It's like coming up with ways to perfect buggy whips in order to make the horse go as fast as possible. Inventing an internal combustion engine instead would be a brand new process for achieving the real goal: moving the carriage faster. This preoccupation with using analytical devices to make up shortfalls from the 'ideal' target often prevents companies from defining a more fruitful target and establishing a new process to get there.

Figure 14-3 shows how the team's focus narrowed from simply handling waste more efficiently to eliminating waste altogether. By meeting this more fundamental challenge, the company managed to keep its plant tidy—and reduced costs and increased profits. Following this process opened new pathways to increasing employee morale, self-esteem and job security.

Finding hidden challenges

As they gained skills in using the Simplex creative process, the manager and the team members got better at using existing analytical tools to reduce waste by identifying hidden challenges. The new facts that were unearthed when the focus shifted to reducing waste led to new challenges. Recall that a fundamen-

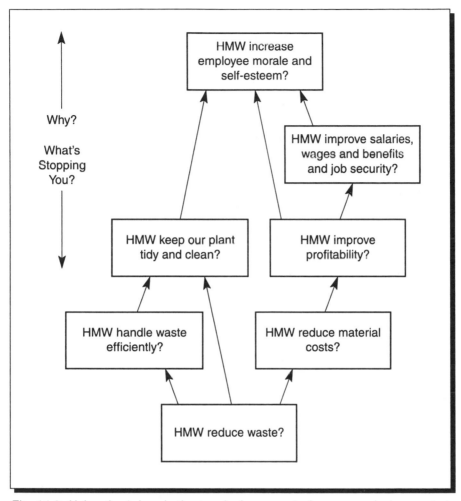

Fig. 14.3 Using the 'why-what's stopping' process to focus on reducing waste to ultimately increase employee morale, self-esteem and job security

tal principle of the Simplex process is to state challenges in the form of 'How might we?' questions, and to diverge before converging. This process allows people to express themselves without fear of evaluation, and to reflect the positive aspects of the situation, rather than the impediments to it. For example, one fact that the team uncovered—'If we pack target weight, our bags do not look full'—became multiple optional challenges, such as:

- How might we fill our bags without overpacking?
- How might we make the potato chip slices larger in area?
- How might we make our slices thinner?
- How might we make our bags smaller in volume yet appear larger?

The team could have picked any of these challenges. Selecting the first challenge, it developed a 'why-what's stopping' problem definition map (Figure 14-4). Successively broader challenges emerged during this process: 'How might we keep our bags looking full to our customers without overpacking?'; 'How might we keep our customers satisfied without over-packing?'; 'How might we keep our customers satisfied?' By asking, 'What's stopping us from filling our bags without overpacking?', the team determined that the potato slices were too heavy and too thick to fill the current bag volume without exceeding the bag's marked weight. This fact led to the breakthrough challenge, 'How might we achieve the right combination of potato slice weight and thickness to fill the bag without exceeding its marked weight?' Two other challenges that might have proven useful were: 'How might we make the slices thinner (and therefore lighter)?', and 'How might we increase each slice's surface area without increasing its weight?' Analytical tools were already available to achieve these goals. But they would have sat on the shelf if the team had not uncovered these new challenges. Focusing on these challenges turned up several additional challenges that permitted the company to consider employing other analytical tools. For example, a subsequent broader challenge, 'How might we keep the bags appearing to be full at our existing target weight?', even permitted the company to use gas to inflate the bags without altering their size or shape. Thus, creative problem definition broadened the team's options. Different challenges allowed it to use different sets of analytical tools.

Framing productive challenges

One of the teams chose to concentrate on another waste source. Starch, a by-product of the plant process, had always been flushed down the drain. Because the company had already tried and failed to eliminate this waste source, some people were reluctant to tackle it again. Here's how this team used creative process skills to turn negative attitudes and facts into productive challenges. Two key facts—one positive, one negative—were as follows:

- 'If we could sell our waste starch, we could avoid the burden of handling it.'
- 'We already tried to sell our waste starch locally five years ago, but no one wanted it.'

Deferring judgment and actively diverging, the team raised several positive challenges from these facts, including:

- How might we find new uses for starch?
- How might we find a buyer for our starch outside the local area?
- How might we make our starch for local industry to buy?
- How might we redeploy our starch handling crew in more productive ways?

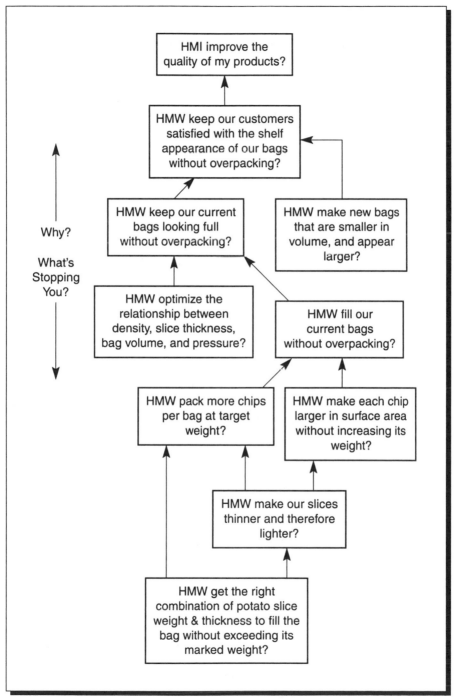

Fig. 14.4 Using the 'why–what's stopping' process to uncover challenges above and below the initial challenge

Once the teams had selected their most productive challenges, each moved step by step around the wheel to develop solutions and action plans. In order to gain acceptance for the new solutions, our manager involved his fellow managers and his boss in the process during action planning. With the team members and their managers acting as partners, it was more likely that all the action plans would be successfully implemented.

Over a period of time, the teams implemented many solutions to the three largest waste sources, which had been costing the company more than $12 million a year. By taking this initiative to save money, our manufacturing manager actually allowed his company to lower its prices. Thus it increased value to its customers and gained a valuable competitive edge during the recession. With many of the plant's processes improved, the groundwork had been laid for higher sales and profits during future prosperous times. By managing his work creatively to select the most important challenges to manage from his 'why-what's stopping' strategic map, this manager showed leadership in mainstreaming innovation. He dramatically improved his own performance, and produced short- and long-term benefits for the company.

WHAT CAN I DO?

Purchasing director goes beyond the call to involve others in innovation

Here's a second example of how a manager took the lead to mainstream organizational innovation, rather than wait for someone to create a special 'innovation or continuous improvement department.' In this case, a company's purchasing director was able to stimulate continuous improvement and innovation outside of his own department. He saw the purchasing function as the link between various company departments and the company's suppliers. In his unique position, he could encourage people from these areas to co-operate in finding and solving important problems that cut across functional lines.

For example, he realized that his suppliers knew enough about his company's business to help it become more competitive and profitable. What they lacked was an opportunity and forum to contribute their ideas. He trained his suppliers to arrive at meetings armed with specific ideas for improving his company's business. During these meetings, he posed challenges to them, such as, 'How might you help us reduce costs?', 'How might you help us implement new ideas more rapidly?', and 'How might you help us improve our packaging and product quality?' He involved them in finding and solving the company's important challenges by setting up teams including the company's technical experts and these suppliers, and training them in Simplex (Figure 14-5). He knew that, unless someone led the way to mainstream such innovative activi-

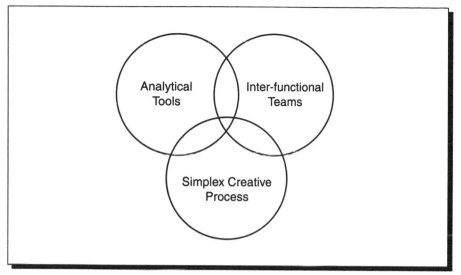

Fig. 14.5 *The necessary ingredients for involving people in finding and solving important problems*

ties, the company's outmoded ways of dealing with other departments and its suppliers would continue. (This example might just as easily have worked in the opposite case. A supplier might actively involve a customer in joint innovation by asking the customer to share its most important problems in joint problem solving teams.)

15

ALIGNMENT: FOLLOW THE PROCESS TO DEFINE YOUR ORGANIZATION'S KEY CHALLENGES

'Head office says we have to do it this way'

Alice had been thinking. Finally she said, 'That stuff you mentioned about the distance between customers and the decision-makers really rings a bell. Especially when you think about technology— seems to me businesses install a lot of expensive equipment without even thinking about the customer at all.'

'What do you mean exactly?' Harry said.

'Last week I took a few spare minutes to run into our new neighbourhood post office. I only wanted a few stamps. Figured I'd be in and out. It took forever. It didn't matter if you wanted one stamp or 100, everybody had to wait while the clerk fiddled with the computer, punching in one set of numbers after another. Some sort of inventory control system, obviously.'

'What did you do?'

Alice shrugged. 'What could I do? By the time I got to the front of the line, I was pretty frustrated. All I wanted was one package of stamps. I even had the exact change. But the clerk couldn't just give me them. She had to go through the routine, punching in enough numbers to fill a ledger book. I said,' 'This doesn't really do me much good. Couldn't you just give me the stamps and finish that later?" She said, "Sorry, but you can't have your stamps until I've put in all the inventory data."'

'So then what?'

'I asked to see the store manager. She said: "Sorry, but head office says we have to use this new computer system. I really can't do anything about it." Seems to me that businesses too often install technology that improves their own internal efficiency but that doesn't account for the effect on the customer. Shouldn't it be the other way around?'

'I couldn't agree more, Alice,' I said. 'These kinds of efficiency improvements save money in the short run. But we need to make sure they don't cost us customers in the long run. You need to make sure that whatever changes you make are aligned with corporate goals, with customer satisfaction at the top of the list.' ■

Summary of learnings

✦ *The 'why-what's stopping' analysis helps you align your organization's internal challenges with external customer-focused challenges.*

✦ *If you remember that your organization's primary challenge is to improve customer satisfaction, you can demonstrate effective organizational leadership beyond your department. Applying the 'why-what's stopping' process to this primary challenge helps individuals align their own challenges with those of the organization's customers.*

✦ *Customers' problems become the organization's critical challenges. Thus, your company's goals are defined by putting yourself in your customers' shoes and creating their problem definition maps. The Simplex process and process skills help you to identify your key customers and define their most critical challenges. Any challenges that your organization's employees tackle should aim to solve the key customer problems you've identified.*

So far, we've talked about how you can use the creative process to define your own critical challenges. And we've discussed how you can lead your department co-workers in solving these challenges to improve your company's performance. It's this kind of leadership behavior that will make your department stand out within the organization, and that will mark you as a candidate for company vice-president. But what kind of leadership behavior will it take to make you president? For this, you'll have to look outside your organization to define the critical challenges that the entire company must solve in order to satisfy its customers.

Many organizations, even successful ones, only look inward. They make changes to improve their internal costs and efficiencies without considering how their actions will affect external factors like customer problems. They fail to look outward. Here's an example of how to use the 'why-what's stopping' analysis to link an inward focus on increasing efficiency to a much more productive external challenge: how to increase customer satisfaction. Although this example comes from the banking industry, its lessons apply to almost every other kind of business.

LINK YOUR CHALLENGES WITH YOUR CUSTOMER'S CHALLENGES

'Stickhandling for customer satisfaction'

Bank trains employees to find creative ways to cut costs—and make customers happy too

Compared to many other businesses, banks are leaders in their willingness to invest in new technology. However, they often make these investments for the wrong reasons. Instead of looking first for ways to solve important customer problems, banks more often start by looking for ways to improve internal efficiency. Sometimes, of course, these two motives coincide. For example, the automated teller machine offers solutions to three problems: reducing labor cost, reducing customer waiting time, and making banking hours more convenient. However, this meeting of internal and external factors usually happens by chance rather than by design.

It's better to start by asking what customer problems must be solved, and then letting internal efficiency improvements fall out in the process. Recognizing this fact, some banks train their employees to identify important customer problems, and then to seek out and evaluate new technology that might solve them. Only after ensuring that the solutions increase customer satisfaction do they think about how the technology might increase internal efficiency.

In order to encourage this approach, an organization must develop its employees' skills in using the Simplex process, particularly in customer mapping.

Employees must learn to do customer mapping before investing in any new technology under consideration. Even better, the organization should make customer mapping a continual process. Then employees can identify ahead of time what new technologies they might need. In this way, the organization adopts technology because it solves customer problems, not just because it's available. The customer mapping process imposes the necessary discipline to ask, 'How might this new technology improve the customer's efficiencies?', rather than simply, 'How might this new technology improve our internal efficiencies?'

For example, introducing automated teller machines permitted banks to cut staff and reduce operating costs, thereby improving internal efficiencies. However, by allowing more convenient banking hours and reducing waiting time in lineups, the machines also solved a more important problem: improving customer satisfaction. Here's how a bank might have used customer mapping to ensure that its employees looked not just at ways to improve efficiency, but how to increase customer satisfaction.

Starting with the typical inward focus, the initial challenge might be: 'How might we reduce operating costs?' Asking the 'what's stopping' question produces the narrower challenge: 'How might we reduce the number of tellers on our payroll?' Repeating the question produces the yet narrower challenge: 'How might we automate the teller's job?' (Figure 15-1).

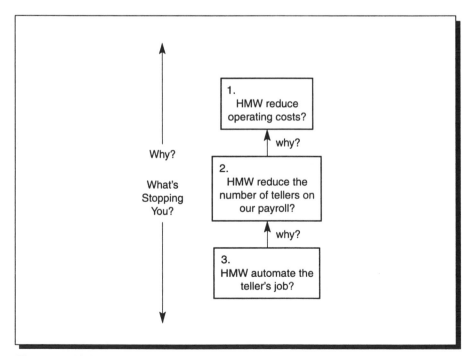

Fig. 15.1 Using the 'why-what's stopping' process to uncover more specific challenges that increase efficiency

You'll recall from an earlier chapter that asking the reverse question 'why' of each new narrower challenge leads you back up to the broader challenge. This acts as a check to ensure that you have placed the successive challenges in the right order in the hierarchy. For example, one possible answer to the question, 'Why would we want to automate the teller's job?', is that the bank wants to reduce the number of tellers on its payroll. Hence the broader challenge, 'How might we reduce the number of tellers on the payroll?', is positioned correctly in the hierarchy. (Similarly, one answer to the question, 'Why would we want to reduce the number of tellers on the payroll?', would lead to, 'How might we reduce operating costs?', one step upward in the hierarchy.)

Now asking the 'why else' question of the most narrow challenge ('Why else would we want to automate the teller's job?') leads you to a different broader challenge that also focuses externally on the bank's customers: 'How might we reduce customer waiting time?' (Figure 15-2). Asking 'why' again along this new external path yields new customer-focused challenges, such as: 'How might we make banking more accessible and convenient for our customers?' and 'How might we increase customer satisfaction?' (Figure 15-3). You can check your procedure by asking, 'What's stopping us from increasing customer satisfaction?' Answering this question leads you back down the hierarchy to the narrower challenge: 'How might we make banking more accessible and convenient for our customers?'

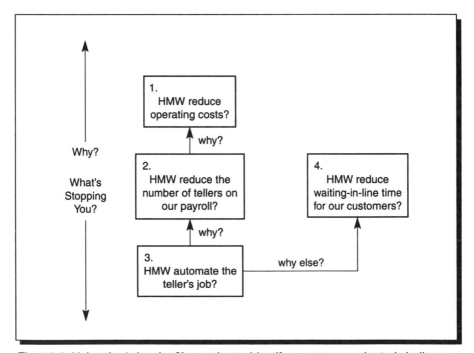

Fig. 15.2 Using the 'why else?' question to identify a customer-oriented challenge

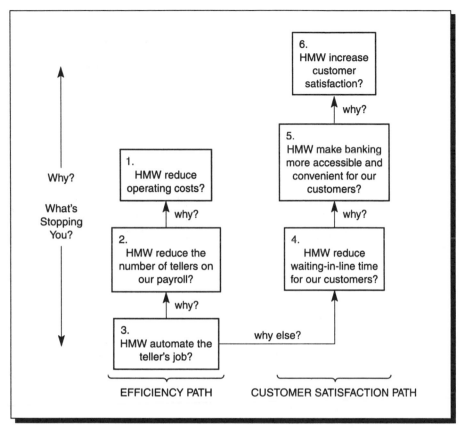

Fig. 15.3 Continuing to ask 'why?' to establish a customer satisfaction path

At this point, the relationship between the two pathways begins to emerge. If you ask, 'What else is stopping us from increasing customer satisfaction?', at the same time as you ask, 'Why would we want to reduce operating costs?', you uncover the problem definition that links the two: 'How might we reduce the costs of banking to our customers?' (Figure 15-4). By continuing this questioning process, you uncover the additional challenges along both internal efficiency and external customer satisfaction paths (Figure 15-5). These new challenges include the following: 'How might we increase short-term profits?'; 'How might we attract new customers?'; 'How might we keep customers coming back for more and new services?'; 'How might we increase long-term profits?'

The pathways will ultimately come together in a single challenge: 'How might we ensure that we are an effective organization?' (Figure 15-6). This single challenge links the long-term profit effects of increasing customer satisfaction to the short-term profit effects of reducing operating costs. (This echoes the point from earlier chapters that effective organizations require both short-

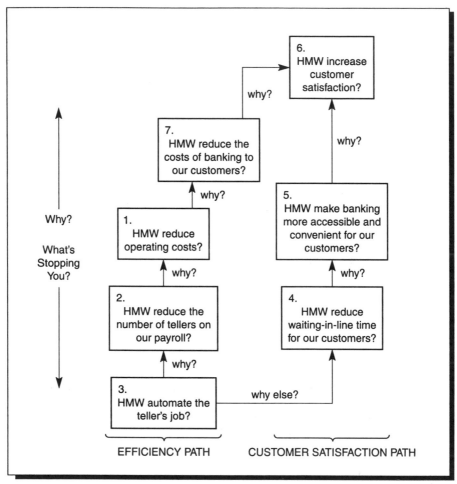

Fig. 15.4 Using the 'why?' and 'what's stopping?' questions to connect the efficiency path and the customer satisfaction path

term efficiency and long-term adaptability.) By training its managers to use the Simplex process, particularly the 'why-what's stopping' customer mapping, the bank made its employees routinely think beyond narrower internal efficiency to consider external customer satisfaction.

It's this kind of strategic thinking that will allow you to demonstrate effective organizational leadership far beyond your department's boundaries. The secret is to keep in mind your organization's primary challenge, 'How might we improve our customers' satisfaction?' Then you apply the 'why-what's stopping' process to unearth the answer, 'We haven't determined our customers' problems.' Asking this question in turn leads to a further challenge: 'How might we determine our customers' problems?' This kind of thinking sparks the use of

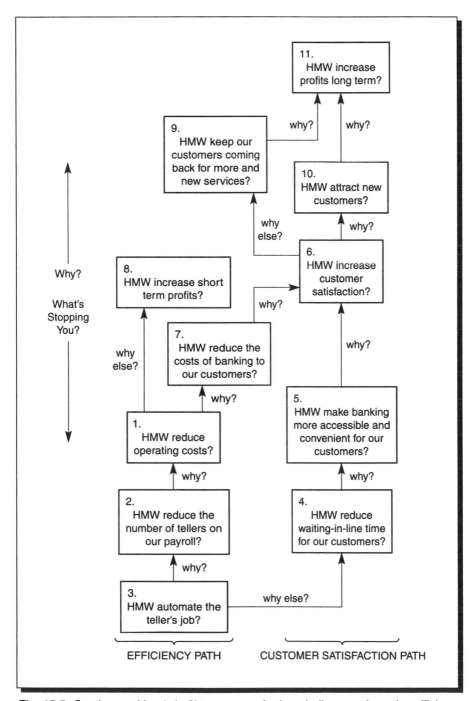

Fig. 15.5 Continue asking 'why?' to uncover further challenges along the efficiency path and the customer satisfaction path

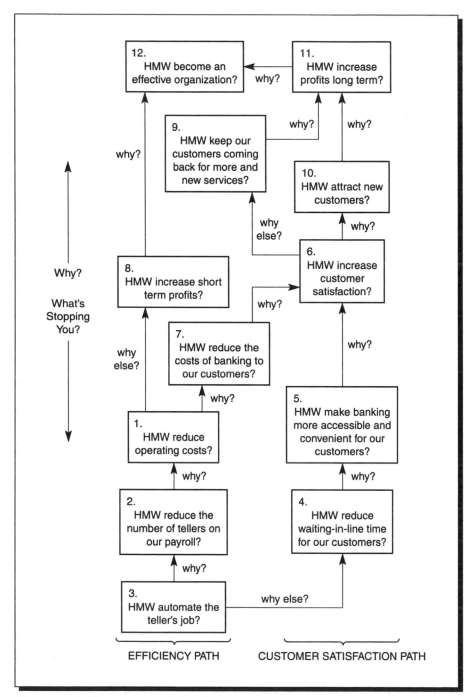

Fig. 15.6 Asking 'why?' until the efficiency path and the customer satisfaction path converge

the Simplex creative problem solving process. And it leads you to creative action in the form of new and improved products and services, new and improved internal procedures, and brand new customers.

STRATEGIC PLANNING: HOW TO IDENTIFY KEY EXTERNAL CHALLENGES

Here's another example of using the 'why-what's stopping' mapping process to identify critical external challenges. By conducting a strategic planning session, a mental health association had come up with a list of important issues to address, as follows:

- It lacked resources to carry out the necessary task of raising its public profile.
- Without a clear focus, its members were stretched too thinly.
- Its volunteers' commitment had slipped.
- Many of its programs and activities were not being assessed regularly enough.
- The association had too little input from users of its services.
- Communication was spotty across the organization.
- The association perceived an important need to expand housing for individual clients.
- The association knew that it would have to continue its provision of direct services.

With the help of a consultant versed in the Simplex process, a team of executives, volunteers, donors and clients identified the association's key challenges. The team began by diverging to list the association's customers. Then it converged to select the three most important customer groups: the public, resource providers and the association's staff. Again diverging and converging, the team identified each customer group's key problems, and framed them as challenges.

Using these challenges as a starting point, the team members employed the 'why-what's stopping' analysis to create customer maps for the three customer groups (Figures 15-7, 15-8, 15-9). They agreed on the most critical challenges in each map (starred in each figure). Using these challenges in turn as new starting points, the team again employed the 'why-what's stopping' analysis to create a single strategic map that represented all of the association's most important challenges (Figure 15-10).

By following this mapping process, the team was able to incorporate a lot of diverse information about the association and its customers into a single document. It also organized this information into a clear mission statement, and a hierarchy of goals, objectives, programs and tactics, all stated in challenge form ('How might we'). Within this hierarchy, the challenges nearer the top represented the association's goals and mission. The challenges nearer the bottom

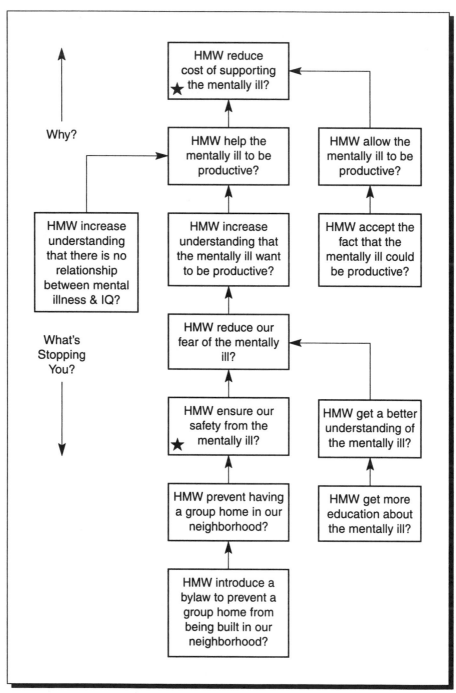

Fig. 15.7 Using the 'why–what's stopping' process to create a mental health association's customer map for its community

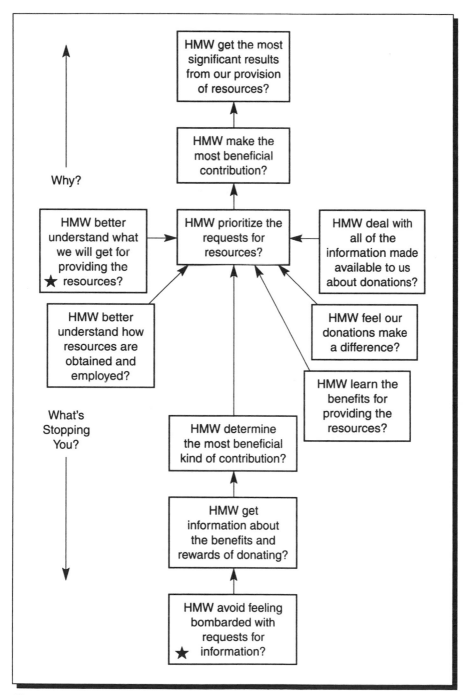

Fig. 15.8 Using the 'why–what's stopping' process to create a mental health association's customer map for resource providers

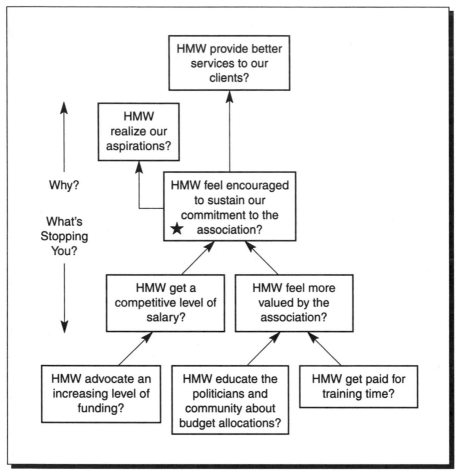

Fig. 15.9 Using the 'why–what's stopping' process to create a mental health association's customer map for itself

provided more specific directions for achieving these goals. In a way, this hierarchy is like a road map. Solving these challenges in the correct sequence would permit the association to successfully accomplish its mission.

CREATING THE STRATEGIC ACTION PLAN

From the road map, the team selected the association's most important challenges and placed them into sequence to create the strategic action plan shown in Figure 15-11. This strategic plan consisted of challenges, not solutions. Framing strategic challenges forced the team to not implement preconceived solutions.

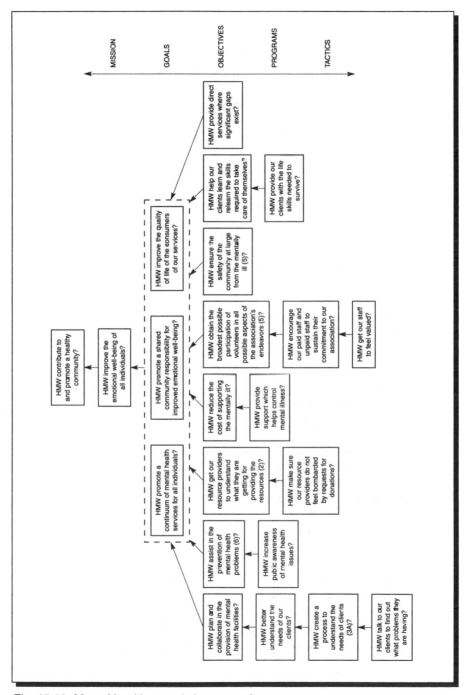

Fig. 15.10 Mental health association strategic map

1 HMW get our staff to feel more valued?
   – Program design by end of fourth quarter, 1992
   – Team leader is George with Tom, 1 manager and 1 staff member as team

2 a) HMW create a process which enables the resource providers to understand what they are getting for providing the resources?
      – Program design by fourth quarter, 1992
      – Team leader is Josephine
   b) HMW help our resource providers to better understand what they are getting for providing the resources?
      – Program completion end of fourth quarter, 1995
      – Team leader is Josephine

3 a) HMW get a process to understand the needs of the consumers?
      – Process design is to be completed by third quarter, 1992
      – Team leader is Paula with Program Members as team participants
   b) HMW better understand the needs of the client?
      – Program implemented by third quarter, 1993
      – Team leader is Paula

4 HMW increase public awareness of mental health issues?
   – Program design by end of second quarter, 1993
   – Team leader is the new hire
   – Team members include Josephine, a Volunteer Committee Representative, and a Community Relations Representative

5 HMW obtain the broadest possible participation of volunteers in all aspects of the association's endeavours?
   – Definition of the plan by first quarter, 1993
   – Team leader is Tom with George assisting

6 HMW assist in the prevention of mental illness?
   – Program design by fourth quarter, 1993
   – Team leader is the new hire working with consumers and Josephine

7 HMW plan for and collaborate in the provision of mental health services?
   – Program design by end of fourth quarter, 1994
   – Team leader is Beatrice working with consumers and Paula

8 HMW provide direct services where significant gaps exist?
   – Review and revise the process by fourth quarter, 1994
   – Team leader is George with involvement of the clients

Fig. 15.11 Strategic action plan for addressing the association's critical challenges

Armed with this action plan, the association then formed project teams to create processes, programs and plans to solve each critical challenge. Each team was assigned a leader selected from the strategic planning session. This ensured that team members adopted strong ownership of their challenge, and understood why the challenge was critical and how it fit into the overall strategic plan. Key members were selected for each team, and each team was assigned a deadline for creating the processes, programs and plans for each challenge. The group expected that solving the challenges would take anywhere from one to five years.

One year later, the association had already made significant progress on all of the challenges, for two reasons. Stating their tasks in challenge form had allowed the teams to come up with a lot of creative solutions. And the teams' activities had been focused on only the few critical challenges. Since then, the association has implemented several solutions, and its members now operate as a cohesive, creative unit. The 'why-what's stopping' analysis enabled a diverse group of executives, volunteers, donors and clients to adopt a wider view of the association and agree on how best to focus their energies. The process allowed the team to delegate responsibility to many smaller project teams that were truly empowered to solve the right problems and implement creative solutions.

Thus, you must allow your customers' problems to lead you to your company's critical strategic challenges. You have to extend your company's own 'why-what's stopping' mapping process to incorporate the most important challenges of your current and potential customers. You construct a strategic 'why-what's stopping' map for each of these customers' main problems. Then you select one or two challenges from each map as your company's own challenges. For each selected challenge, instead of asking, 'How might our customer ...?', you ask, 'How might we help the customer ...?' Your company's goals are defined by your customer's problem definition map. And any challenges that your employees tackle should aim to solve those customers' problems, directly or indirectly.

Understanding what you have to do to help customers solve their challenges will lead you to develop new internal processes and new and improved products and services. Instead of simply asking your customers what they want you to deliver to them, you learn about their challenges or problems ahead of time. Then it's up to you to come up with brand new products and services to meet them.

16

ALIGNMENT: FOLLOW THE PROCESS TO EMPOWER OTHERS

Working nine to five

'Customer satisfaction,' sighed Harry. 'You know why we're so poor at it? It's because everybody feels like it's someone else's job. No one looks at the problem of satisfying customers as a whole.'

'What do you mean?' I said.

'In some of our plants, people don't realize that the main purpose of everybody's job is to make sure customers get what they need when they need it. But that's a job that seems to belong to nobody. They all look after their own jobs well enough. Everybody goes through the motions, does what's expected of them. But come five o'clock, they're gone. The customer might still be waiting for an answer. But if he calls at five-thirty, he's out of luck till tomorrow. Nobody stays to pull it all together. Thing is, you can't pin it on anybody in particular if the whole project falls flat. After all, they've all done their job.'

'So most people don't see the big picture?'

'Right. Nobody feels ownership for making the entire project come together. They're doers of their own work, not facilitators of the company's work. Nobody seems to understand how the problems they're solving day to day align with the company's overall goals. But it's like you said earlier: it's customer satisfaction that we're after'.■

Summary of learnings

➜ *To empower others to solve your department's important challenges, there are five strategies for involving them: transfer ownership; be a facilitator rather than a doer; pick up your end; establish structures that encourage creativity; and show employees how these important challenges align with strategic company goals.*

➜ *The employee suggestion systems used in many Japanese companies are good examples of structures that encourage employee creativity and that emphasize how employees' challenges align with corporate goals.*

———————————

In the previous two chapters, we discussed how to exercise 'working smarter, not harder' leadership. The key is to define the critical challenges you are directly responsible for, and the critical challenges that your entire organization should address. In the first case, you looked inward to identify the key challenges that your department might solve to help meet important organizational goals. In the second case, you looked outside your department to identify your organization's key customer challenges (in effect, you put yourself in the shoes of your organization's customers). Whether you look inward or outward, you identify critical challenges that you then have to lead in solving. In doing so, you take the lead in mainstreaming innovation, and thus distinguish yourself.

HOW TO INVOLVE OTHERS IN SOLVING KEY CHALLENGES

However, you won't be able to solve all of these critical challenges alone. You'll need a lot of help. You'll have to involve other people in taking responsibility for many of these key challenges or their components. These people may include your subordinates and employees, your peers, perhaps even your superiors. Beyond simply enlisting your subordinates' support, you must actively involve them in meeting these critical challenges. Here are five strategies you can use to get others actively involved (Figure 16-1).

Transfer ownership: Let people in on challenges, not solutions

If you ask people to simply implement your solutions, how much commitment will they feel to making them succeed? People naturally work harder at their own projects than at someone else's. You must transfer to others your ownership of these challenges. The earlier you do so, the more ownership they will feel. When you're willing to share problems early, you give people the freedom to do their own fact finding and to define the problem in their own way—the

---

1 Transfer ownership: delegate challenges, not solutions.
2 Be a facilitator, not just a doer.
3 Pick up your end.
4 Set up structures that encourage others to buy in.
5 Show others how their challenges align with strategic company goals.

Fig. 16.1 Strategies for involving others in meeting your critical challenges

secret to transferring ownership. You must learn to hand off challenges to others, not make them wait for your own solutions. To borrow a few terms from an earlier chapter on meetings, rather than be the client, you must be the facilitator and the coach.

Involving people early during problem finding permits them to exercise their full creative potential. Recall the Japanese employee suggestion system that we discussed earlier. If a manager comes up with a new idea, he figures out what particular problem the idea might solve, then seeks out an employee willing to take on that problem. The employee's subsequent solution often turns out to be different from the manager's original idea although both solutions might be equally good. But the employee is now committed to making his solution succeed—more than he would have been to making the manager's solution succeed.

By transferring ownership of problems, these managers facilitate change rather than impose it. They know that the primary objective of these employee suggestion systems is not to create new products or methods, or to reduce costs or raise profits, but simply to motivate people. They know employees are motivated by the sense of accomplishment, recognition and growth that comes from exercising their creativity on the job.

Be a facilitator, not just a doer

Transferring ownership of critical challenges means you must learn to interact with others as a coach and facilitator. You have to give them the help they need as they think their way through each of their challenges. You must let them figure out their own solutions and their own implementation plans, and support them throughout the process.

Recall that a good meeting facilitator stays out of the meeting content. His role is to induce the client to focus his process skills throughout the Simplex process on solving his problem. Similarly, a creative leader induces others to focus the Simplex process and process skills on meeting their challenges. He becomes a consultant in the process of solving the challenge, rather than giving orders or doing the work himself. Creative leaders facilitate rather than direct; they consult rather than give orders. Having transferred ownership, they then help others to achieve their own goals. These creative leadership skills hardly fit with the traditional management style that most organizations employ, but they can be learned.

Pick up your end

Your goal is to involve others in using Simplex to solve the critical challenges you have identified. You must continually demonstrate your own commitment to using the creative process and process skills in meeting your own challenges.

In other words, you must act as a role model in using the process. How can you ask people to do something that you are unwilling to do?

Suppose you decide to send your subordinates for training but feel that you are too busy to attend the sessions yourself. If you don't understand what your subordinates have learned, they will have difficulty implementing their learnings, and will have to work around you. If you want others to gain skills in using the Simplex process, but they see you failing to pick up your end, how likely are they to use the process in order to meet those critical challenges?

You must also demonstrate that you're willing to do your own share to meet an important challenge. Make it clear that, without their help, you would have been willing to tackle the challenge yourself. Don't let others think that you are simply dumping the challenge onto them merely to get rid of it. When you abdicate responsibility, you send a clear signal that you don't believe the challenge is a worthwhile one. Why not hand over to employees the responsibility for managing the challenge, while remaining willing to help out as needed?

CONTINUOUS CREATIVITY IS KEY

Japanese suggestion system stresses means, not ends

You can encourage employees to apply the Simplex process and process skills to their critical challenges by setting up simple structures that make it easy for them to buy in. Think again of the Japanese employee suggestion system. The purpose is to get employees into the habit of continually coming up with new ideas, thinking creatively and continuously improving processes and products.

The system makes it easy for employees to find problems, and to work together to solve them and implement the solutions. Workers jot down their dissatisfactions with their jobs and company products (their 'golden eggs'), then post them on a wall poster under a column called 'problems.' Co-workers who read about a particular problem that interests them can then join forces to help solve it. Once they solve the problem, they post the solution in the second column on the chart. In a third column, the group chronicles its implementation. Only when all three columns are complete—when the individual or team has carried out problem finding and problem solving, and is ready to implement a workable solution—can workers submit the idea as a suggestion. At this point, it's automatically accepted by a supervisor. With about 96 per cent of suggestions immediately put into practice, employees get a clear message that the organization really values their ideas.

There's more to the structure of these systems than a wall chart. Another component is a system of cash rewards for each suggestion. Most cash awards are relatively small (the equivalent of about $5). It's the recognition people get that is the real reward. Supervisors' performance appraisals include their ability to motivate their employees to create suggestions. Some companies even establish informal monthly goals for numbers of suggestions per employee. Work groups are assigned a team leader who fills in where needed or gets help for the group in order to ensure that it can meet its daily production and still generate a flow of ideas. The group is not so preoccupied with maintaining daily production that members fail to generate ideas, or vice versa.

These Japanese suggestion systems are structures that encourage employees to use their creativity. Traditional North American systems, by contrast, are structures that actually discourage employee involvement.

In many North American systems, the purpose is plain: encourage a few employees to suggest a few big ideas that save the organization lots of money and earn the individuals major cash awards. Rather than stimulate the process of creative thinking and a flow of ideas, the object is to save as much money as possible. Employees simply dump ideas into a suggestion box without having to evaluate them or explain what problem they are trying to solve, and then wait for managers' judgments. The wait is usually long, and most ideas are rejected anyway. Managers dislike the task of judging the ideas, and actually fear the amount of change that the suggestions represent. As they have not been discussed or shared with other employees, individual suggestions are often difficult to understand. But employees have no incentive to work together. After all, other employees might want to share in the reward. Or they might claim the idea as their own.

In these organizations, mainstreaming innovation—the process of finding and solving problems and implementing solutions—is a foreign concept. Promotions and rewards are structured to favor individuals who show skills in avoiding problems, not in finding them. Many managers feel they have no time for innovation. They're too busy doing their 'regular jobs' of fire-fighting and meeting short-term profit and cost goals. And they expect their employees to do the same—to focus on solutions, not problems. In North America, 'constructive discontent' often receives no more than lip service.

Show people how their challenges align with strategic company goals

Recall our example of the manufacturing manager in the potato chip plant. He took pains to align his employees' tactical challenge of reducing waste—and reducing manufacturing costs—with the strategic company goal of increasing customer value during the recession. More than that, he made sure that employees could see and understand how these challenges aligned. Not only should your tactical challenges be aligned with your company's strategic plan, but this alignment must be readily seen and understood. People must clearly understand how every challenge they manage fits into the more strategic challenges of their department and organization. Even more important, they have to understand how their own challenges connect to their customers' key challenges. How?

SEEING THE BIGGER PICTURE

Japan's suggestion systems force employees to think big

In the Japanese employee suggestion system, managers guide employees in selecting problems to solve that are aligned with larger strategic goals. These larger goals are communicated downward continuously. Virtually every employee belongs to a 'quality circle team' (this is often the employee's natural work team). About every six months, upper management assigns each team a major 'theme' problem that directly aligns with a specific corporate need; a theme, for example, could be how to reduce the number of defects in a particular product. Quality circles also align problem solving with strategic goals through their connection to the employee suggestion system. During its regular meeting, the team might discuss many problems, not all necessarily related to the theme. These problems might be 'off theme' for the group. But they might be perfect candidates for the employee suggestion system. From this new pool of ideas, individuals often pick new problems to turn into completed suggestions.

In these organizations, the employee suggestion system and quality circles feed on one another. The quality circle team receives credit for every suggestion that one of its team members submits individually. Under North America's 'Lone Ranger' approach, however, the two systems have been difficult to integrate. In fact, because they've worked at cross purposes, quality circles have often failed. Individuals hoping to make money from the suggestion system are unwilling to share their ideas, and their rewards. So they're reluctant to follow the team-based approach to innovation needed to make quality circles work.

In Japan, employees must seek their manager's advice on the suitability of a problem before posting it. This ensures that the chosen problems align with important departmental or organizational needs. Managers themselves are trained to act as coaches in selecting the right problems and in solving them. For more complex problems, the manager makes sure that employees get the time and resources they need to solve them. The 'boss' becomes a facilitator rather than a doer. Along with the payment for each completed suggestion, employees get something even more important: praise and recognition from the manager.

Managers themselves are appraised regularly on their ability to improve employees' problem finding and solving skills. The usual measure is the quantity and quality of implemented employee suggestions. The employee suggestion system thus becomes an important part of the company's Management By Objectives (MBO) program. Think of the MBO program as a pyramid. Each management level in the pyramid agrees with the level above it on specific, important goals it will meet each year. At any level, a manager's performance appraisal is based on how well he met his stated goals. Above him in the pyramid, his boss is appraised in turn on how well he met his own predetermined goals. When these goals are aligned from the beginning, success at one level automatically makes success more likely at the level above. If managers use the suggestion system to guide their own employees' choice of problems, then any problems that the organization addresses—right down to the bottom of the pyramid—all line up with the top organizational goals.

By aligning its problem finding and problem solving efforts like this, one typical Japanese company with 9,000 employees implemented 660,000 suggestions in one year. These included about 6,000 suggestions for new products or product improvements alone. The remainder were suggestions for new or improved procedures, such as simplifying jobs or accelerating processes.

For these companies, aligning the creative efforts of individuals and teams with strategic goals makes the individuals and teams more productive. Individuals feel more motivated and have a greater sense of cohesiveness within their teams and throughout the entire organization. In fact, companies work to make sure that all employees recognize how their goals and creative efforts fit with both strategic company goals and other teams' goals. For example, as their projects reach certain milestones, teams routinely make presentations to the rest of the organization's employees during working hours. During an event held in the company cafeteria, for example, the plant manager might act as master of ceremonies, giving praise, recognition, and expert commentary. This reminds all employees of how their individual and team efforts align with overall organizational goals.

17

GET GOING: START THE SIMPLEX PROCESS YOURSELF

'It's all in his head'

Alice said, 'You know, Harry, that business about having to pull the whole thing together, making sure the customer got what he wanted, makes me think of how important it is to do what it takes to get the job done. People need to take action on their ideas. Otherwise, nothing new happens.'

Harry nodded his head. 'That's really the point. I'm always amazed at how few people realize what it really takes to make changes in an organization. It's a real struggle even to make small changes. Still, some people think all you have to do is just announce a change, wave a wand, and it'll magically happen.'

'We used to have a president who would announce a new slogan or new program about every six months,' Alice said, 'but it was always all in his head.'

'What do you mean, all in his head?' I said.

'It got to be a standing joke. The slogans usually had to do with empowering people, pushing down decision-making, that kind of stuff. But the president never acted in the way the slogans or programs meant you to act. He spoke the language alright, but he acted like a dictator. We all knew that after all the speeches and seminars, it would just be business as usual when we got back to work. Everyone else was supposed to do things differently, except him. In the end, nobody did anything differently.'

I nodded. 'So he had nice ideas, but he never took the pains to plan out how they'd be implemented or to actually do what he wanted everyone else to do. You've got to do more than just come up with a problem to solve or a solution. If you're going to follow the creative process, if you want to make any kind of valuable change, then you've got to implement the change.' ■

Summary of learnings

✦ *Once you've identified your important challenges, you need to move them forward through the Simplex wheel. Each time you address a challenge, make sure you end what you're doing with an action plan that specifies your next steps. If you rank your action plans in order of importance, you get the greatest impact on your performance.*

✦ *Action planning for each challenge gives you a written record of your actions, and allows you to quickly bring others up to speed on the status of any challenge.*

✦ *Updating your action plans allows you to work on several challenges at once and permits each one to unfold at its own pace. You can move back and forth from one challenge to another, no matter which step of the Simplex wheel it is in, and even cycle back and forth between steps within the wheel.*

✦ *Action planning for managing challenges as a whole is on a larger scale than the individual action plans you make to implement solutions for each challenge.*

✦ *Action planning for managing your challenges requires identifying obstacles you're likely to meet in moving them around the Simplex wheel. Place these obstacles in order and then create ways to overcome them.*

Recall that the purpose of this book is to help you meet a key challenge: to dramatically improve your personal performance and distinguish yourself within your organization. Until· this point, we've developed a solution to this challenge. You've learned about a creative process, Simplex, that helps you find and solve important corporate problems and implement the solutions. In other words, you've learned about a process for mainstreaming innovation in your work. You've also learned a set of process skills that will help you make this creative process work. And you've learned how to use the process and process skills in defining the critical challenges that you and others need to address.

Now we've reached the point where you have to implement this solution. Implementing change doesn't come easily for any person or any organization. You must spur yourself—and others—to take whatever actions are necessary to put into practice what you've learned. If you fail to turn these words into action, then you might as well leave this book on the shelf. In these last four chapters, we'll discuss how to implement what you've learned, including how to push yourself and others to act, how to improve your innovation skills, and how to get started.

A PLAN FOR IMPLEMENTING YOUR SOLUTIONS

We said earlier that the trigger to the implementation phase of the Simplex process is the action plan. Not only does the action plan specify exactly what steps you're going to take, but more important, it motivates you and others to actually get moving. Similarly, what you need now is an action plan that will help you to implement the creative process and process skills yourself. This means you'll have to carry out three action planning steps, as follows:

1 For every challenge you address, always create an action plan, and update it each time you address the challenge.
2 Organize all your action plans for all your challenges, and rank them in order of their potential impact on your performance.
3 For each action you take, assess its impact on your performance.

Let's look at each of these three steps in turn.

Why do you have to keep a current action plan for each challenge? For many people, action planning is something you do only occasionally, when you're working on major projects. But there's more to it than that. A well-maintained action plan is your ticket to managing many challenges at the same time, no matter how large or small. If you don't discipline yourself to create and update a simple action plan while you're managing a challenge, then any new information you uncover or any new problem or idea you find will likely disappear under the flood of day-to-day activities. A simple, concise, up-to-date action plan acts as a record of your previous steps. It allows you or your team to quickly get up to speed on the status of any initiative at any time.

Maintaining a current action plan for each challenge allows you to work on several initiatives at one time. You can lay aside any one action plan to address another as necessary, and then return to the original plan later. Each challenge then unfolds at its own creative pace. You don't need to worry that you're missing a key milestone on one project just because you're engrossed in reaching milestones on another project.

Maintaining multiple action plans is like keeping several challenges cycling through separate Simplex wheels at the same time. At any one time, each initiative will likely be in a different step of its own wheel. But because you're following separate action plans for each challenge, you can move back and forth from one challenge to another, no matter which step of its wheel it happens to be in. And rather than follow a one-way route around the wheel for each challenge, you can cycle back and forth between steps within the wheel. While you're evaluating and selecting or planning action, for example, new facts that you hadn't considered earlier might crop up. So you'll need to return to the problem definition step to restate the challenge in a more fruitful way. With separate action plans, you can move back and forth like this on a particular challenge without 'dropping the ball' on other challenges.

By the way, we talked in an earlier chapter about how to creatively plan action on a particular problem as the sixth step in the Simplex process. But here we're talking about planning action on a larger scale. We're looking at how to manage an entire project—one that might contain numerous problems—through the Simplex wheel. This action plan for a larger project might integrate several smaller action plans on particular problems that crop up as you move through the wheel. For example, the larger action plan might specify what steps your team must take to move from the fact finding stage to the problem definition stage. Between team meetings, the plan might detail the preparations you need to make to help establish the right criteria for completing the evaluation and selection step. The plan might specify how to bring a senior manager into a meeting to help the team decide from among alternative solutions or optional problem definitions.

HOW TO CREATE—AND SUSTAIN—
YOUR ACTION PLANS

So how to create the action plans for managing all of your challenges? Just as few of us recognize the need for creativity in implementing a single idea, few of us recognize the need for creativity in managing several challenges through to completion.

For any challenge, you'll face many obstacles during your trip around the wheel. It's important to identify these obstacles, using the process skills of deferring judgment, actively diverging, and actively converging. Involving a group in this exercise is a good idea: you gain other perspectives, you can quickly assess the amount of effort you'll need to launch your new initiative, and you can mobilize the group.

Having identified the key obstacles, you can now place them in a logical order to overcome them. Begin with any key obstacle that you've identified. First look backward by asking yourself, 'What other obstacle would I have to overcome before I can address this obstacle?' Then look forward by asking yourself, 'Once I overcome the first obstacle, what other obstacles will I run into?' As you repeat this questioning process in both directions, you will find that your key obstacles become shuffled into a logical sequence.

With these obstacles now in logical order, ask yourself, 'How might I overcome each obstacle?' Defer judgment and actively diverge to create alternative approaches for overcoming each obstacle. Then actively converge to select one approach. Just as you placed the obstacles in order, place in order the approaches you'll follow to overcome them. Turn each selected approach into a very specific, simple, concrete action step. Organize these steps into an action plan, and start implementing it. Following this procedure allows you to remove the obstacles and gradually move a challenge around the wheel. Of course, in order to move the challenge, you still have to do the necessary creative work within each step and between the steps, ultimately ending up with an action plan that is implemented.

Each time you return to a critical challenge to move it further around the wheel, don't drop that challenge until you've developed an action plan. Even if you do nothing more in addressing the challenge than to dig up a few new facts, discipline yourself to stick with the challenge until you can answer the question: 'What's the next specific step(s) that I must take?' Document these steps to ensure that you always have an up-to-date action plan when you come back to that challenge. By keeping the action plans for all your challenges current, you can organize and integrate them into an overall action plan that is always current and that guides your efforts.

So which action plan should you tackle first on any given day? The best way to decide is to assess their potential impact on your performance, rank the plans in order of importance, and then start with the plan on the top of your list. But don't burrow so deeply into one or a couple of plans that you neglect others. Ensure that you're making the right selections by getting continuous feedback on how your actions are affecting your performance. Are things happening as they should? Are results being recognized?

If you hope to dramatically improve your performance and distinguish yourself in your organization, you have to do what few others are likely to do: mainstream innovation. As you take action to implement valuable changes, it's important that you monitor your success, and that you enjoy doing so.

18

GET GOING: INVOLVE OTHERS IN THE PROCESS

'They say they want innovation, but . . .'

'That reminds me,' said Harry. 'So many organizations trumpet innovation, talk about how badly they desire it. The truth is, most of them don't do anything to reward innovation.'

'Sounds like another story,' I said.

'Last month I talked with a guy at our Rotary Club. A real up-and-comer, only 35 and he's already a division manager. But he's really fed up with his job. Seems his company has been preaching a lot of principles that are supposed to represent what it values. Motherhood stuff mostly. People are our most important asset. We're going to be a defect-free culture. That kind of thing. The one that really bothers him is: We will reward innovation.'

'What's that all about?' said Alice.

'He says it's like one part of the company is busy dreaming up these slogans and values, but nobody else is doing what the slogans say you're supposed to do or setting up any reward systems to make sure they happen. He says he's suggested all kinds of creative ideas. But every one has hit a stone wall. Sometimes his ideas are even ridiculed by his superiors. And he's hardly alone—it happens all over the company.'

'So what's he doing about it?'

'Well, about a month ago he had a long talk with his boss and the president. He said: "If innovation is such an important principle around here, how do we measure it? What are the mechanisms for measuring and rewarding it?" His superiors got really defensive. He never did get an answer. He heard later through the grapevine that they see him as a bit of a maverick and tough to deal with. So he's looking for a new job.'

'That company is going to lose a lot of good people,' I said. 'Trouble is, the next place he goes might not be any better. Just like you said earlier, Harry, a lot of organizations say they want innovation. But few know how to get it.' ■

Summary of learnings

✈ *As you involve other people in implementing the innovation process, you will encounter further challenges. Not everybody has the same creative problem solving process style. Different departments and teams also have varying styles—so do organizations. And, like individuals, organizations have long-standing roadblocks to innovation.*

✈ *These style differences stem from varying relative preferences for the four quadrants of the Simplex process: generating, conceptualizing, optimizing and implementing.*

✈ *All individuals and organizations gain knowledge and understanding in different ways. Some learn by doing, others by sitting back and analyzing. And all individuals and organizations use what they learn in different ways. Some prefer ideation, others prefer evaluation.*

✈ *Variations in how individuals, teams and organizations gain and use knowledge and understanding blend to yield different creative problem solving process profiles. Understanding these differences helps you shift style in order to complement the process preferences of others. It also helps you help others to learn, and helps you decide whom to ask for help in ideating or evaluating.*

✈ *Understanding differences in these process profiles allows you to help others, including customers, make best use of the Simplex process.*

✈ *Innovative organizations and teams require people whose collective process styles cover off all parts of the innovation process. Your dominant style is less important than your flexibility in shifting among styles when necessary.*

✈ *In trying to involve others in innovation, you will encounter individual roadblocks, such as attitudinal, behavioral and thinking barriers to creativity. You will also encounter organizational roadblocks: limited time available for innovation; limited or invisible incentives to innovate; over-management;*

inadequate upward communication of ideas; inadequate downward communication of goals and strategies; physical environment not conducive to innovation; inadequate outside contact; outdated organizational design; lack of technical critique by peers; turf issues; and lack of support for training in and application of creative processes.

✦ *Organizations must structure themselves to encourage people to lead vertically (within functions) and horizontally (across functions) at the same time.*

✦ *Other ways to overcome these organizational roadblocks include: pointing out successful applications of Simplex; rewarding people's efforts to apply Simplex; modeling use of Simplex; providing resources for training and application; coaching; involving others early in making changes; listening well; setting clear innovation goals aligned with strategic goals; incorporating innovation into performance appraisal structures; organizing diversified teams; introducing Simplex to the organization beginning with top managers; guaranteeing job security for innovators; and investing in skills training to keep valuable employees.*

As you manage your critical challenges through the Simplex innovation process, you will find that you need other people's help. These people may be your co-workers, but may just as often belong to different departments. They may be your subordinates or even your superiors. As you try to involve other people throughout the organization in implementing the innovation process, you will face three challenges, as follows:

- How to recognize and manage differences in innovation process styles among co-workers?
- How to recognize and manage my organization's innovation process style, and the differences in process styles among my organization's departments and teams?
- How best to help others overcome long-standing organizational and individual roadblocks to the innovation process?

THE CREATIVE PROCESS: RISE ABOVE YOUR DIFFERENCES

In an earlier chapter, we noted that everyone has a different creative problem solving style. Your particular style reflects your relative preferences for each of the four quadrants of the Simplex innovation process: generating/initiating, conceptualizing, optimizing, and implementing. Your behavior and thinking processes cannot be pigeonholed in any single quadrant. Rather, they're a combination or blend of quadrants: you prefer one quadrant in particular, but you also have secondary preferences for one or two adjacent quadrants (Figures 18-1, 18-2). Stated another way, the creative problem solving profile shows which particular steps of the Simplex creative process you gravitate toward.

Entire organizations also have their own innovation process profiles. An organization's profile reflects such things as the kinds of people it hires, its culture and its values. For example, if an organization focuses almost entirely on short-term results, it may be overloaded with implementers but have no conceptualizers or generators. The organization will show strengths in processes that deliver its current products and services efficiently. But it will show weaknesses in processes of long-term planning and product development that would help it stay ahead of change. Rushing to solve problems, this organization will continually find itself reworking failed solutions without pausing to conduct adequate fact finding and problem definition. By contrast, an organization with too many generators or conceptualizers and no implementers will continually find good problems to solve and great ideas for products and processes to develop. But it will never carry them to their conclusion. You can likely think of many examples of companies showing this imbalance in innovation process profiles.

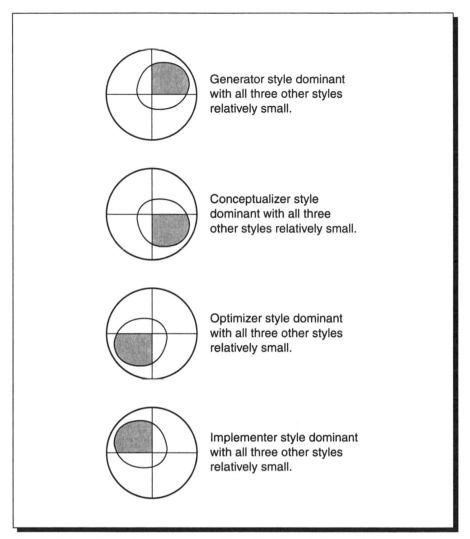

Generator style dominant with all three other styles relatively small.

Conceptualizer style dominant with all three other styles relatively small.

Optimizer style dominant with all three other styles relatively small.

Implementer style dominant with all three other styles relatively small.

Fig. 18.1 Creative problem solving profiles with different dominant styles

What causes these differences in orientation? They usually stem from differences in how knowledge and understanding—'learning'—are gained and used. No two individuals, teams or organizations learn in the same way. Nor do they *use* what they learn in the same way. As shown in Figure 18-3, some individuals and organizations prefer to learn through direct, concrete experiencing (doing). They gain understanding by physical processing. Others prefer to learn through more detached abstract thinking (analyzing). They gain understanding by mental processing. All individuals and organizations gain knowledge and understanding in both ways but to differing degrees. Similarly, while some indi-

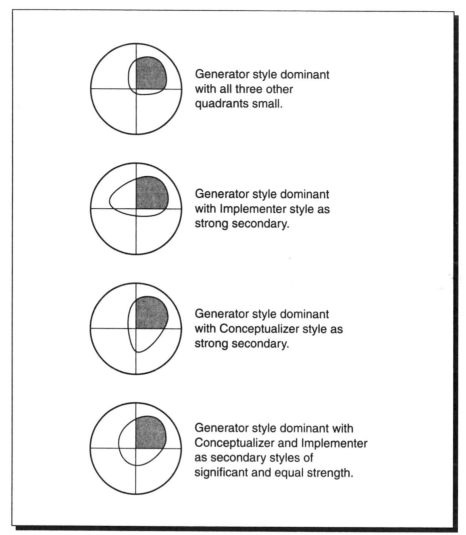

Generator style dominant with all three other quadrants small.

Generator style dominant with Implementer style as strong secondary.

Generator style dominant with Conceptualizer style as strong secondary.

Generator style dominant with Conceptualizer and Implementer as secondary styles of significant and equal strength.

Fig. 18.2 Creative problem solving profiles with dominant generator style

viduals and organizations prefer to use their knowledge for ideation, others prefer to use their knowledge for evaluation. Again, all individuals and organizations use their knowledge in both ways but to differing degrees.

How an individual or organization combines these different ways of gaining and using learning determines their innovation process profile. When you understand these differences, you can shift your own orientation in order to complement the innovation process preferences of others. Equally important, you can take various approaches to working with people. You can decide on the optimum strategy for helping someone else to learn something. And you

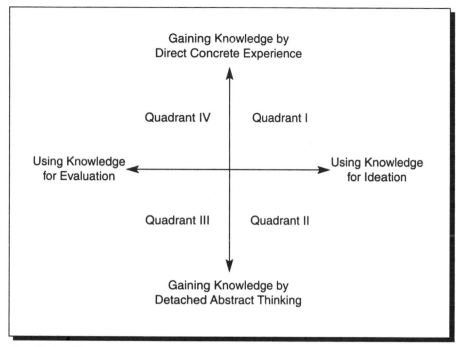

Fig. 18.3 Differences in gaining and using knowledge that cause differences in innovation process profiles

can decide whom to turn to for help in ideation or evaluation. Understanding these differences also helps you interact with other people to help them make best use of the Simplex creative process. For example, you can help strong optimizers discover new problems and facts, or present new problems and facts to them. You can help strong implementers better define challenges, or present well-defined challenges to them. You can help strong generators/initiators evaluate and select from among solutions and make plans, or present to them evaluated solutions and ready-made plans. You can help strong conceptualizers to convince others of the value of their ideas and push them to act on them, or push their ideas through to acceptance and implementation for them.

HELPING CUSTOMERS THROUGH THE INNOVATION PROCESS

Taking this idea one step further, if you understand your customer's innovation process profile, you can help that customer move through the innovation process. You can also shift your own orientation to help the customer with his innovation process.

Suppose you're trying to help your customer make a valuable change by adopting or implementing your new idea. As we discussed in an earlier chapter, your first step is to explain to the customer just what problem he faces that your idea will address. This is the first step of the Simplex innovation process, problem finding. Next, you must discuss facts and develop a mutually understood definition of the customer's problem that your idea will address. These are the next two steps of Simplex, fact finding and problem definition. Now you're ready to present your idea as a solution to an important customer problem.

You can tailor your approach to different customers by employing your skill in assessing their different innovation process profiles. Suppose one customer prefers generating and conceptualizing. He gravitates toward the first three steps of the innovation process (problem finding, fact finding and problem definition). In planning your approach, you would likely decide to spend less time on these areas with him than with a second customer who prefers optimizing and implementing. With the latter, you would likely devote more preparation time to identify and define his appropriate problems that your idea addresses, and only seek his agreement and approval. In fact, as he has little patience for uncovering facts or defining problems, he would likely appreciate your having done this chore for him. With the former customer, you could count on involving him in uncovering facts or defining problems along with you to help him see how your idea might solve his problems. As he normally has less patience for action planning and implementation, however, you would spend more time preparing an action plan for him to fine-tune and implement.

'TOGETHER, WE CAN CARRY OUT THE PROCESS'

The point here is that an innovative organization requires a healthy balance of members whose orientations complement one another. This balance gives the organization a continuous supply of new problems, new ideas, new solutions, and new processes, products and services.

Maintaining this healthy balance is most important on the organization's interfunctional teams. While there are many exceptions, people who work in similar occupations or departments usually gravitate toward one dominant quadrant. Because their secondary preferences differ, their individual profiles may differ. But they have more in common with each other than with people in other occupations or departments who rely on different ways of absorbing and using knowledge.

For example, people in research and development departments, and training or organizational development departments often favor the generator/

initiator style. Employees in market research or engineering design often favor conceptualizing. People in accounting, finance and administration gravitate toward optimizing. And people in manufacturing production, logistics/distribution/warehousing, sales, secretarial or administrative support, social/health services/case worker, customer relations and manufacturing maintenance favor implementation. No matter which process style an individual prefers, however, a team's members have to learn to use their differences to advantage. When you're assembling a team, especially one involved in continuous improvement and innovation, you must put together people who enjoy working in different steps around the Simplex wheel: finding new problems and opportunities; clarifying and refining those problems and creating ideas; developing practical solutions and plans; and making new solutions work.

Whether you're working in teams or not, helping individuals learn to shift among orientations also ensures that the entire organization has a complete blend of process styles. In fact, your dominant orientation is less important than your ability to shift among orientations. Your preference for certain quadrants within the Simplex innovation process are not static 'traits' but rather dynamic 'states.' You can learn to work in any of the four quadrants in order to complement others in a given situation.

Suppose you prefer implementation. If you find yourself working on a project with another implementer, try to balance things by temporarily adopting a conceptualizer style. Instead of concentrating on implementation, you might try to ensure that your team properly defines its goals and creates plenty of fresh ideas. As a consultant and professor, for example, I find myself frequently shifting orientation to balance diverse groups of colleagues. My industry clients have often gotten where they are by exercising implementation skills. In that case, I can best serve them by providing new ideas, directions and theories that they in turn can implement. My fellow academics, on the other hand, are brimming with new ideas and theories. What they often need from me is the push to transform these ideas and theories into finished products in the form of articles, books, courses or seminars. If you can shift roles like this, you gain an invaluable skill in using the Simplex process and in managing your critical challenges through the innovation process.

At worst, individuals with opposing process profiles might have trouble working together, or teams or organizations might show weaknesses in certain parts of the process. But even if you manage to work around these opposing process preferences, you still face two more kinds of roadblocks. One kind consists of individual or personal roadblocks. These are barriers that each of us erects during the conditioning process we all undergo as we mature. (These are the attitudinal, behavioral and thinking barriers to creativity that we discussed in an earlier chapter.)

ORGANIZATIONAL ROADBLOCKS TO CREATIVITY

Our discussion so far has addressed what you can do to overcome these personal barriers. But you encounter another kind of roadblock throughout your working life. These organizational roadblocks to creative thinking take several forms, as follows (Figure 18-4):

Limited time available to spend on being innovative

Many people feel they barely have enough time to do their 'regular' jobs, never mind taking the time to be innovative. They perceive innovation as something apart from their work, something 'extra' that further complicates their jobs, something less important than meeting routine deadlines and goals. As growing global competition forces organizations to become fashionably 'lean and mean,' individuals who find themselves spread thin feel they have even less time to create ideas for new procedures, and new goods and services. The organization ends up with very few new ideas and very few people who are receptive to making them work.

Limited or invisible incentives to innovate

Many people just don't see any real personal benefit from becoming innovative. Reward systems like performance appraisals and promotions are often based solely on measures of short-term efficiency and profitability. For most jobs, efficiency components can be measured easily and almost instantaneously:

---

1 Limited time available to spend on being innovative.
2 Limited or invisible incentives to be innovative.
3 Over-management.
4 Inadequate upward communication of ideas.
5 Inadequate downward communication of goals and strategies.
6 Physical environment not conducive to innovation.
7 Inadequate outside contact.
8 Outdated organizational design.
9 Lack of technical critique by peers.
10 Turf issues.
11 Lack of support for training on, and application of, creativity/innovation processes.

Fig. 18.4 Organizational roadblocks to creative thinking

'How many units did I make this week?'; 'How good were the units I made?'; 'How much did it cost to make the units?' It is much more difficult to measure performance on criteria of adaptability and innovation: 'How many new, worthwhile future opportunities to improve our long-term business prospects did I discover this week?'; 'How many new methods and technology ideas did I investigate?'; 'How many good ideas did I think of this week to improve my job or our procedures or products?'

Because these adaptability and innovation components are difficult to measure in the short term, and because their results only become apparent in the long term, few organizations try to measure them, much less reward individuals for them. Several years might pass between the time you sense an opportunity and the time someone else acts on it. By then, it's hard to remember who thought up the opportunity, and almost everyone claims credit for its implementation. Small wonder that people have little incentive to go beyond their current responsibilities.

NEVER MIND THE MEETING

Managers trying to think long-term find themselves penalized

In one manufacturing company, for example, supervisors who attempted to encourage innovation actually found themselves penalized by the company's traditional cost accounting system. Senior managers had encouraged supervisors to hold voluntary weekly meetings with their employees to improve communications and to develop new ideas for improving products and procedures. But the managers had neglected to change the company's reward system to reflect this goal.

Some supervisors attempted to carry out the process. They held their regular meetings, shutting down the production line for one hour a week to do so. But other supervisors decided not to bother; instead, they kept their lines running full tilt. This difference immediately showed up in the weekly cost performance summary. The latter group achieved lower costs per unit of production and were regarded more favorably by their superiors. Senior managers had expected that the team meetings would yield instantaneous improvements. They hadn't realized that many of these improvements wouldn't appear for several months or even years. The result: after a short time, none of the supervisors held any team meetings. They had learned that, while their superiors encouraged innovation, no incentive existed to try. Rather, they were punished for trying to innovate.

Over-management

Even in departments designed for innovation—product development, research—people often complain that their supervisors are too quick to critique, censor, or kill their ideas. They say they are forced to work under too many guidelines and that they lack freedom to explore fresh lines of thinking. Instead, their supervisors want to know almost immediately what bottom-line benefit or product idea will result from innovation. They feel guilty about visiting the company library just to spend time reading about current events, their competitors' activities, or existing and potential customer trends. (Research shows that managers in successful organizations make extensive use of their libraries. They place greater emphasis on gathering information, looking for opportunities, and just plain learning—the problem finding phase of the Simplex innovation process.) Instead, employees bury themselves in their laboratories, confining their activities mostly to 'keeping busy' and pursuing short-term goals and objectives. They believe they have little time for problem finding, only for problem solving.

When an organization questions its employees' use of fact finding, it discourages them from looking ahead. The organization might get a few small ideas that improve current processes and products. But it fails to net the kinds of big ideas for entirely new processes or products that will transform the business. This short-term focus also discourages people from sharing new ideas out of fear that they may be inappropriate. Not wanting to be accused of 'shooting from the hip,' they suppress these ideas. So the organization loses out.

Inadequate upward communication of ideas

Many people near the bottom of the organizational pyramid or hierarchy feel they need more direct communication with upper management. They see middle managers censoring and restating their ideas, so that top managers hear something different than what was actually said. They see middle managers shy away from taking risks and from proposing anything less than a sure winner. In their eyes, middle managers are driven by fear of making a mistake rather than by any desire to take the lead and champion new ideas.

Inadequate downward communication of goals and strategies

People often fail to focus their innovation efforts because company priorities and directions are unclear. Top managers might clearly enunciate their goals and strategies. But often they are so poorly communicated downward or so heavily screened through the hierarchy that the full message doesn't penetrate to lower levels. People even pursue goals that have been completely misinterpreted.

NEW PRODUCT OUT TO LUNCH

Failure to check assumption proves costly

For example, the president of a mid-sized household detergent manufacturer once made a passing comment at lunch to the company's research director: 'Wouldn't it be nice if we had one more liquid detergent to sell?' What he really meant was that the company's overall sales were growing more slowly than he had hoped. While developing a new liquid detergent might have been one way to build sales, it wasn't at all what he had really wanted. But he'd inadvertently set the ball rolling.

The research director mentioned the conversation to one of his department heads over coffee that afternoon. By the next morning, a small project team found itself busy creating a new liquid detergent. The team members were unsure of the goals and objectives of the project. But they reasoned that, since the president himself had brought it up, it must be an important task. Some members tried to find an unfulfilled consumer need that might be met by a new detergent. Others simply jumped in with random product ideas. Frustration mounted, but about six months later, a product finally emerged.

Imagine the team members' consternation when both the president and the research director expressed surprise that the team was ready to present a new product. In fact, neither individual could recall the initial lunchtime conversation. During a subsequent debrief, the team discussed how it had managed to go astray. Its members said they had often wondered whether they were on the right track but feared appearing impertinent if they asked too many questions. They had been too quick to assume that the apparent goal of the project had been well thought out.

Many organizations make it difficult for people to align their work with company directions or goals. We've talked earlier about skills and processes to prevent this misalignment, such as the 'why-what's stopping' analysis. Innovative organizations have clear objectives, goals, rules, policies and guidelines that help employees choose useful goals to achieve and useful problems to solve. It's more difficult to set and communicate such clear goals and visions during periods of uncertainty and rapid change. But this is precisely when it's most important to do so.

Physical environment not conducive to innovation

In too many organizations, individuals still work in complete isolation from one another, holed away in small cubicles down long hallways. This office arrangement represents the classic bureaucracy. Work is preprogrammed and broken down into small pieces. If each person executes his or her small piece of the puzzle, the organization can deliver its products most economically. This arrangement promotes efficiency, but hardly encourages innovation.

People share their problems, information and ideas when the organization provides many open areas in which they can gather formally and informally at any time. In open office arrangements, for example, many people are separated not by walls but by small noise-buffering dividers. Other organizations arrange their offices around the perimeter of a large central atrium that extends from top to bottom of the building. In this 'open building' arrangement, individuals can see almost every other office in the building—even on other floors—as soon as they walk outside their own offices. This layout gives people the feeling of working amid a hub of activity and of belonging to a large team whose members are all headed in the same direction, no matter how diverse their expertise or individual projects. Innovation depends on having groups of people working together, putting together varying knowledge and innovation process styles, working beyond the confines of their offices or laboratories, dealing with diverse colleagues, and moving outside the office to deal directly with customers, outside experts, competitors, and professional societies.

Inadequate outside contact

Some organizations are so engrossed with keeping their internal activities secret that they virtually forbid outside activities like attending conferences or publishing findings. As a result, employees are intellectually undernourished. They fail to benefit from new ideas, knowledge and approaches. This results in fewer new ideas for products and services. It also means the organization incurs unnecessary costs to reinvent information that it might have gotten elsewhere.

Outdated organizational design

A surprising number of organizations are still structured along the outdated scientific management approach. Here, the organization arranges work around functional specialization—manufacturing, sales, engineering, marketing, R&D, finance, accounting. Each function pursues its own goals, and often works in a separate building or even a separate location. Managers succeed by pursuing functional goals, not overall organizational goals. Surrounded by specialists in the same field, they regard other functions as less important, or even as competitors. This arrangement hardly fosters the teamwork required to create new products and services. Many important organizational problems fall between the cracks. Some are not even addressed; others are bounced back and forth ('that's not our problem, it's engineering's problem'). Customers themselves are passed from one department to another when they phone in for information.

Each function's work is often broken down into smaller and smaller tasks, with people doing the same task day after day. The theory is that this builds expertise: by doing a simple task over and over again, a person becomes very good at it. But in practice, this design causes people to view their organization as a group of separate functional chimneys. They pursue narrow goals that benefit their own function but that prevent the entire organization from succeeding.

New interfunctional projects take forever to complete, as individuals complete parts of the project in sequence rather than in parallel. Individual functions wait to begin their tasks until others have completed their own satisfactorily. Suppose a product development department still has to conduct nine months' worth of testing before choosing from among three product options. The marketing department could begin developing three separate marketing strategies at the same time in order to be ready to fly with the one that product development finally chooses. But, reluctant to develop two strategies that are only going to be thrown away, marketing prefers to wait for the final decision nine months later. Suppose it takes six months from that point to develop the marketing strategy. The marketing department has managed to meet its own cost-containment goals. But the entire organization has lost about six months' worth of sales while customers were kept waiting. And if anything goes wrong to delay the project, different functions spend more time pointing the finger than working together to speed things up.

Innovation calls for a parallel team approach. However, most organizations have trouble organizing and maintaining teams. A 1993 issue of 'Fortune' magazine relates, for example, that, by organizing its functions into a single team working under one roof, the Ford Motor Company cut two years from its normal development time when it came out with the Taurus model. But the company was unable to transfer its successful team approach to other areas. After the individual who had spearheaded the Taurus project had been transferred to Europe, the organization simply reverted to its customary approach. Seven years later, Ford still faced the challenge of mainstreaming this team approach to innovation across all its new products. In order to become competitive—or more innovative —organizations must learn to encourage their functions to operate in teams. Instead of pursuing goals only within functional chimneys, individuals must pursue overall organizational goals.

When someone successfully leads others in meeting important functional goals, he exercises strong vertical leadership. Vertical leadership emphasizes technical excellence in a particular field, such as accounting or marketing. When an individual leads others to meet interfunctional, organizational goals, he exercises strong horizontal leadership. Horizontal leadership emphasizes teamwork and long-term thinking. Some functions might have to sacrifice short-term goals for the benefit of the entire organization. Horizontal leaders use informal networking to get things done, rather than hierarchical approval. They encourage people outside their own narrow domain to see the 'big picture.' Organizations need to structure themselves in order to develop strong vertical and horizontal leadership at the same time. Innovation cannot flourish under vertical leadership alone.

Some organizations have established matrix teams that try to achieve teamwork even as they maintain functional priorities. But these efforts have failed for several reasons. Functional priorities often take precedence over interfunctional objectives. The organization's reward system often favors individual efforts to meet functional goals, not teamwork to meet organizational goals. As they lead their teams across functional barriers, the few skilled horizontal leaders ruffle the feathers of others who are less flexible and more used to thinking vertically. Because promotions often follow functional lines, horizontal leaders often end up low on the promotion list. Until organizations place horizontal leadership and organizational goals on the same level as vertical leadership and functional goals, matrix teams will not work.

Figure 18-5, for example, shows individuals with various combinations of leadership skills. The individual represented by A exercises only high vertical leadership. His function meets its internal goals very successfully, but pays no attention to overall corporate and team goals. B exercises only high horizontal leadership. He encourages individuals and teams to meet overall corporate and

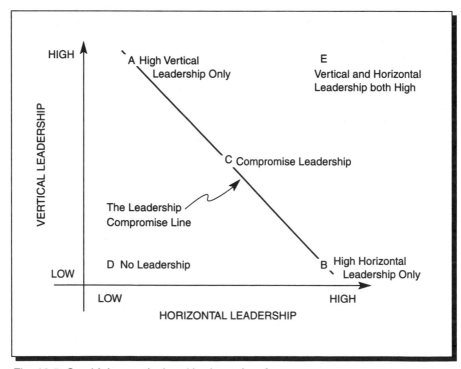

Fig. 18.5 Combining vertical and horizontal performance

team goals, but pays little attention to functional goals. C doesn't believe he can meet both functional and organizational goals at the same time, but that he has to sacrifice one in order to attain the other. So he bargains and makes compromises, and achieves moderate success in both. Exercising neither vertical nor horizontal leadership, D simply tries to survive from day to day without getting fired. E has learned how to excel in both vertical and horizontal leadership at the same time. He leads people to attain functional, team and organizational goals without sacrificing one for another.

Lack of technical critique by peers

People confined to narrow vertical functions (with a reward system that encourages them to pursue narrow vertical goals) get little opportunity to receive helpful critique and input from their peers in other vertical functions, or to offer feedback to those people. They complete projects more slowly and with less fresh thinking, and fail to understand how their work aligns with others' and with overall corporate goals. People also find themselves reinventing the wheel, unaware that colleagues have already completed certain projects or tasks.

Turf issues

Innovative projects often suffer from interdepartmental squabbling. Rather than co-operate as a team, the departments soon find opportunities to quarrel over who should receive credit for a certain project or who needs more resources. Achieving vertical functional goals becomes more important than reaching overall, organizational objectives.

Lack of support for training in and application of creativity/innovation processes

In earlier chapters, we discussed how engineering and business graduates, for example, might go too far when they learn to exercise highly structured, solution-oriented, analytical thinking. When they become managers of organizations, these individuals need to be careful that they don't rely solely on programmed problem solving methods and highly structured procedures. They need to become more comfortable with innovation. They need to recognize the value of learning new processes that help people to cope with uncertainty, ambiguity, poorly structured problems and other situations requiring non-programmed thinking skills. Because these processes are strange to them, they regard them skeptically. As an employee trying to involve your colleagues in the innovation process, you must prepare yourself to encounter this skepticism. Don't be surprised if your managers are slow to support the idea of investing in learning and applying creativity and innovation processes.

HOW TO INVOLVE OTHERS IN IMPLEMENTING INNOVATION

How to get around this formidable array of roadblocks? It might not be easy. But then, if it were a simple matter, then anyone could do it and you'd lose your opportunity to distinguish yourself. The secret to overcoming these roadblocks is to apply creativity to meet your challenge: 'How to involve others in implementing the innovation process?' Let's look at some ways to involve your co-workers in innovation (Figure 18-6).

- Use every opportunity to point out to your fellow workers successful applications of the Simplex creative process and process skills. If you produce a regular report of your activities every week or every two weeks, mention not only the results you achieved, but also the process by which you achieved them. *Talk about the successes* you've experienced in using the process and the process skills every chance you get—at lunch, during breaks, in meetings.

1 Tell others your success stories in applying the creative process.
2 Reward others' efforts to apply the process and process skills.
3 Model and demonstrate the process and process skills.
4 Provide resources for training and application of the process and process skills.
5 Coach and teach the process and process skills to others; provide feedback.
6 Involve others as early as possible in the change-making process.
7 Listen well in order to understand facts and build others' trust.
8 Set clear, specific innovation goals that are aligned with strategic objectives.
9 Include use of the process and process skills and teamwork as criteria in your performance appraisal structures.
10 Encourage others to become skilled innovation process facilitators.
11 Organize diversified teams to tackle problems that would normally fall between the cracks.
12 Introduce top managers to the Simplex innovation process and process skills.
13 Make sure people base their capital investment decisions on more than one criteria such as short-term costs.
14 Never let people think that they might lose their jobs because of the profitable new ideas they help to create.
15 During economic downturns, invest in people in anticipation of recovery.

Fig. 18.6 How to involve others in implementing the innovation process

- *Reward sincere efforts* to apply the process and process skills, either formally or informally. Rewards can be extrinsic, such as salary increases or promotions. They can also be intrinsic, such as opportunities for advancement and growth, challenging assignments, and public recognition and praise. For peers or even superiors, you can reward innovation efforts in other ways. Offer enthusiastic thanks and praise, especially in front of others. Spread the word about their contribution by copying their superiors on your thank you letters or progress reports. Share the credit for success publicly.

- *Model and demonstrate* your own working knowledge of the innovation process and process skills. You cannot empower others without first empowering yourself. You may be far from perfect at first. But when others see you take the risk to use the process and to try to make valuable changes, it won't matter whether or not you succeed each time. If you fail but pick yourself up and try again, others will be even more willing to try themselves—and even learn from your mistakes to do it better than you. Reward and support others who take similar risks.

- *Provide resources* for training and application of the new process and process skills. Let other people read this book. Discuss it with them. Encourage them to get additional training and offer your help in applying the process and process skills in their work. (In the next chapter, we'll talk about how we can all improve our process skills.)

- *Coach and teach* the process and process skills to others, and give them helpful feedback. Offer to sit in on meetings and act as coach while someone else acts as facilitator.

- *Involve others* in change-making—using the Simplex innovation process—*as early as possible* in the process. Don't wait until you've solved the problem yourself to present it to others (step seven). Instead, involve them in step one or two (fuzzy situation or fact finding) or even step three (problem definition). This is a much easier way to gain acceptance for an innovation.

- *Listen well.* If you work hard to understand facts as your subordinates and others perceive them, you will build trust. Others will be willing to experiment—even with unusual ideas—without fear of making mistakes.

- *Set specific innovation goals that are clearly aligned with corporate strategic objectives.* Make these goals clear to everyone you are trying to involve in innovation. Keep reminding them of these goals and their alignments with top company directions or goals. Establish common innovation objectives across departments to rally teamwork toward meeting important company strategic goals. Whenever possible, involve others in setting innovation goals.

- *Revise performance appraisal structures* to include the process skills that we've described in this book. Reward people for how (the process) they go about achieving results, including their teamwork performance. You might have to invent new approaches such as peer evaluation of individuals' team performance. Make sure that innovation performance is as important as other aspects of people's performance. Encourage your boss to base your own performance appraisal on the same principles.

- *Encourage others to become skilled facilitators.* They should be able to assist others in using the innovation process and process skills.
- *Organize diversified teams to tackle important problems* that would normally fall between the cracks. Talk others into helping you establish and maintain these teams. Try to get top managers assigned to such teams as full-fledged members or even facilitators. This will ensure the teams have the clout to make others take their innovations seriously across functional lines. Provide facilities and equipment to make it easy for these teams to use the Simplex creative process and process skills—including such basic things as a meeting room with easels and chart pads, magic markers, masking tape and other supplies.
- *Introduce the Simplex creative innovation process and process skills to your top managers.* Try to induce them to start developing their own skills. At the very least, make them aware of your innovation efforts so that you can draw on their support when you need it.
- Show people who are responsible for making capital investment decisions how important it is to use *several decision-making criteria* to balance long- and short-term effects.
- Educate as many people as you can on the importance of guaranteeing *job security for innovative change-makers.* Your organization must learn to reinvest people's talents into other valuable projects rather than let them become displaced by the profitable new ideas they help to create.
- During economic downturns find ways to *invest in people through skills training* in anticipation of better times. Having better trained people not only results in higher quality products, greater productivity and more innovation, but it can even mean lower costs in the long term. Severance packages often end up costing more down the road, especially when you consider the costs of hiring and training new people once boom times return.

19

GET GOING: BUILD YOUR SKILLS IN THE PROCESS

'But I did my training objective!'

'It's not only in innovation that organizations fail to practise what they preach,' said Harry. 'Look at what happens with training when companies launch a new initiative. Most managers are reluctant to make any changes to support the initiative in the first place. But they want to be seen as doing something constructive. So they take the easy way out by sending a few people to training in the new initiative.'

'Why is that the easy way out?' said Alice.

'Sparing a few bodies for a few days of training isn't going to make a big impact on their monthly profit and loss statement,' Harry explained. 'They just have to send enough people to fill up a training class. In the end, they don't have to do anything differently anyway. The training isn't used for what it's intended for: creating change. It's just an opportunity to pay lip service to the new initiative while they get on with the real business of the day-to-day stuff.'

'I've seen plenty of cases where companies waste a great deal of money on training because people don't behave any differently when they return to work,' I said. 'And as you said, Harry, the managers who sent the employees to the training in the first place don't really want them to act differently once they return. After all, they'd have to manage the new behaviors, wouldn't they?'

'I heard about a manager in one plant,' I continued. 'One day he announced to his team that he wanted to start an employee participation program. He explained that he wanted employees to take the ball and run with it—you know, starting from the bottom upward—that it was his job just to start the process and then step out. The result was almost a disaster. Because he didn't lead the way—setting goals, modelling the new behaviors—everybody just floundered for a few weeks, then went back to business as usual. You

⇨

should never start training unless you've targeted it toward a well-understood business need and unless you've put into place an infrastructure that allows the new skills to grow.' ∎

Summary of learnings

✦ *Training in Simplex allows individuals to learn to use more of their inborn creativity. Research in this training has demonstrated this in several ways.*

✦ *Simplex training improves people's performance in all three stages of finding problems, solving problems and implementing solutions.*

✦ *This training works only if it convinces people of the value of Simplex process skills and encourages them to apply them.*

✦ *Because individuals get swept up into the content of a real-world, relevant problem, they find it more difficult to apply the process and process skills than to hypothetical problems.*

✦ *Because individuals prefer different phases of the process, how well Simplex training works depends on which phase they are working in. For example, deferring judgment might be more difficult for an individual during problem finding than during problem solving or solution implementation.*

✦ *Simplex training works even for people who might naturally regard creative thinking with skepticism.*

✦ *Because trainees from a single work location can support each other's use of the process and process skills back on the job, the greatest improvements from Simplex training occur among intact work groups rather than relative strangers.*

✦ *For people from top to bottom of the organization, Simplex training makes trainees more willing to accept deferral of judgment and active divergence. While training improves these process skills for all process styles, the greatest improvement occurs among optimizers. Training might work best to improve an individual's least developed side, thus balancing ideation and evaluation.*

✦ *Individuals benefit from extending effort during ideation. They are more likely to find their best ideas among the latter two-thirds of all ideas generated.*

✈ *Training improves skills in evaluating ideas.*

✈ *Training in Simplex resembles climbing a skills progression ladder. At each of three successive levels, trainees learn to use the process first for individual benefit, then for team benefit, and finally for organizational benefit.*

––––––––––––––––

By this point, you should have gained a sense of how developed your own creative process skills are. 'Creative' is the key word here. We said earlier that each of us enters the world with creative capacity. As we mature, our ability to tap into this capacity is gradually conditioned out of many of us. Fortunately, it's not lost altogether.

My own research shows that you can learn to use more of your inborn creativity. Let's take a look at some of the results of this research, conducted in several organizations during almost two decades. All are examples of how the Simplex process and process skills can be trained and learned.

TRAINING IMPROVES EMPLOYEE CREATIVITY

'Nurturing the creative spark'

Training improves creativity, process skills

My first major experiment took place in the mid-seventies at Procter & Gamble Inc. in Cincinnati, Ohio (work that led to my award-winning doctoral dissertation). I wanted to see what effect Simplex training would have on employees working in applied research, including engineers, engineering managers and technicians. I had already been successfully conducting this training for several years, but had never formally documented its results and mechanisms. Would this training improve these employees' creativity? And how and why would it do so?

The participants underwent 2 1/2 days' worth of intensive training in using the process and process skills that we've discussed in this book. They interacted with one another, worked in teams, and practised the process and process skills on work-related situations. For example, after working alone to define a problem, they compared their points of view to discover that others had defined the same problem in different, and sometimes more fruitful, ways. They generated individual work-related problems, and developed solutions and implementation plans that would allow them to transfer their skills back to their jobs. Then they did the same as members of teams. They answered questionnaires that measured their process skills and attitudes. I observed them both before the training and after, including two weeks after their return to work.

From the outset, I had expected that this training would make them better at using the Simplex wheel—finding problems, solving problems, and implementing solutions. I had also expected the training to make them more willing to use the process skills of deferral of judgment, active divergence and active convergence (the ideation-evaluation process), and make them better at using them. More importantly, I had also expected that only those participants whose training made them more willing to use the skills would actually improve their use of the process—and I was right.

The results? The training improved the employees' performance both immediately and, later, on the job. They were less likely to jump to conclusions about the nature of a problem; more open-minded to new ideas and approaches; more open to new and unusual product ideas; less likely to engage in negative evaluation during idea generation; better able to develop a range of problem definitions before choosing a best one; and more likely to risk trying an unusual approach (Figure 19-1). They produced higher-quality ideas and more of them.

Not only was I able to document these results, but I also identified how the training worked and clarified some earlier research results. Before my experiment, most research on organizational creativity had been confined to showing that people could be taught to apply brainstorming rules to hypothetical problems (for example: 'List as many uses as you can for a wire coat hanger') and only in the problem solving stage. Very little of this research had involved real-world problems relevant to organizations. And when real-world problems were used, there were some contradictory findings. In two separate experiments, for example, one group of managers trained in creativity techniques produced more original ideas than a control group. But in the other, a second group that received similar training produced ideas no more original than those of the control group. But no one had tried to figure out why this discrepancy existed. More important, none of the research had attempted to identify or measure exactly how creativity training worked to produce results. Without knowing *how* it worked, no one could analyze *why* training did or didn't work.

Trainees were:
- less likely to jump to conclusions about the nature of a problem.
- more open-minded to new, unusual ideas and approaches.
- less likely to make negative judgments during idea generation.
- better able to develop a range of problem definitions before choosing one.
- more likely to risk trying an unusual solution.
- more likely to produce higher-quality ideas—and more of them.
- more likely to transfer effects of training to job if trained as intact work groups.
- more accepting of deferral of judgment and active divergence, whether the trainees were manager or nonmanagers.
- more likely to extend effort to find more and better ideas.
- better skilled in evaluating ideas.

Fig. 19.1 Results of training in creative process skills

What I discovered was that training success depended on improving people's acceptance and use of the three critical process skills of deferral of judgment, active divergence and active convergence (the two-step ideation/evaluation creative process). During the training, you had to convince them of the value of these process skills and make sure they applied them.

Giving people only brainstorming instructions, for example, provided enough process skills to allow them to solve simple, hypothetical problems like finding uses for a wire coat hanger. Brainstorming instructions are really minimal training. But because the artificial content of hypothetical problems didn't really matter to them, people found it very easy to defer judgment and actively diverge. But they still lacked the necessary level of process skills to solve real-world problems. With the latter, people often become so preoccupied with the problem's content that they find it much more difficult to defer judgment and actively diverge.

People working on real-world problems need more intense training—much more than simple brainstorming instructions. Participants in the successful real-world experiment above, for example, had received about nine times as much training as participants in the unsuccessful experiment. Besides the amount of training, other factors explain these groups' differing success rates. In the unsuccessful experiment, the groups were randomly assembled to include people who didn't know each other. The successful groups, however, consisted of people who not only knew each other but liked each other. We're unlikely to defer judgment and actively diverge within a group of strangers, especially when no or few members have skills in deferring judgment or diverging. In a group like this, killer phrases abound. Unless training truly teaches individuals to accept and apply their skills in the ideation/evaluation process, they can't be expected to produce more creative results. The amount of training you need to reach this point differs from one person to another.

This experiment showed something else. For any individual, how well they applied the training also depended on which of the three phases of the Simplex process they were in. For example, it might be harder to train a person to defer judgment (or actively diverge or converge) during problem finding than during problem solving or solution implementation. For someone else, however, the reverse might be true.

TRAINING IMPROVES USE OF PROCESS SKILLS

'The team that trains together . . .'

Intact work groups transfer training back to job

In a second experiment, I tested the effects of the same training on a large group of manufacturing production engineers, and got similar results. Half of the group came from various manufacturing locations; the other half came from a single location. I measured their acceptance of the deferral of judgment and active divergence process skills before the training, five weeks later on the job, and then 10 weeks later on the job. Both groups improved their acceptance of both process skills—improvements that were still evident even after 10 weeks had passed.

Simplex training works for different kinds of people—even manufacturing production engineers who prize practicality and who regard 'creative' thinking skeptically. These participants were quick to see the practical value of the process skills. Even more interesting, greater improvements showed up in participants who had come from the same location than in those who had come from various locations. Why? Participants who had received the training along with their co-workers supported each other in using these new process skills back on the job. But people who had not undergone the training with co-workers found much less peer support for using these 'strange' new process skills back on the job. Training intact work groups makes the training work better— its effects are more likely to stick on the job (Figure 19-1).

TRAINING IMPROVES PROCESS SKILLS, NO MATTER WHO YOU ARE

'From office to shop floor'

Training benefits white- and blue-collar workers alike

Going further, I undertook a third experiment to see whether this training produced differing effects among managers (first-line supervisors to vice-presidents) and non-managers (hourly workers, clerical employees, technical specialists, professionals such as information systems analysts). I also wanted to see whether training worked differently in individuals with varying creative problem solving process styles (i.e., generator, conceptualizer, optimizer, implementer). For managers and non-managers alike, training made them more willing to accept the process skills of deferral of judgment and active divergence (Figure 19-1). Training also improved these skills no matter what the individual's particular process style. But I saw the greatest improvement among one group in particular: the optimizers.

I found this result surprising at first, for two reasons. Optimizers by definition often prefer convergence over divergence. And they prefer to learn through abstract thinking rather than through the kind of concrete experience used in the training. After some further thought, however, the results made sense to me. With its emphasis on deferral of judgment and active divergence, and learning by concrete experience, the training was probably most jarring for optimizers not accustomed to using these skills or learning in this way. But perhaps for any individual, the training works best to improve their least developed side, either ideation or evaluation. (Incidentally, I have found similar results among Japanese, Latin American and European cultures. But I have yet to determine the effect of training on individuals with different process styles in other cultures.)

TRAINING IMPROVES USE OF ACTIVE DIVERGENCE—AND HOW

'Any more bright ideas?'

'Best' idea often saved for last: Study

In a fourth experiment, I tested one particular aspect of the process skill of active divergence: extending effort. As we discussed earlier, extending effort means deliberately pushing to generate additional information and options during ideation. My earlier experience had shown that people were often reluctant to actively diverge beyond a relatively small number of options. They believed most of their good ideas would surface early in the process, so saw no value in continuing ideation past a certain point. Earlier research, including my own, had already shown that extending effort improved the chances of coming up with a really good idea, and yielded more high-quality and fewer poor ideas. I wanted to see whether the 'best' idea could just as easily show up in the later stages of active divergence as in the early stage.

I did two studies, in which I trained intact work groups involving hundreds of managers and professionals from a range of organizations—nurses, hospital administrators, businesspeople, technicians and scientists. The first study focused on individual problem solving, the second on group problem solving. In both studies, I wanted to see how often the 'best' solution to a problem emerged during the first third, middle third or final third of all ideas generated. In both studies, the participants benefited from extending effort. They were more likely to find their best idea not among the first one-third, but among the latter two-thirds of the list. While your last idea might not always be your best, it does pay to persevere beyond your initial burst of ideas (Figure 19-1).

TRAINING IMPROVES USE OF ACTIVE CONVERGENCE

'I'll be the judge of that'

Training yields more ideas, and better ways to judge them

More recently, my research has looked at how training in the Simplex process improves the process skill of active convergence. Both before and after 2 1/2 days' worth of training, I assessed the evaluative skills of a large group of middle managers employed by an international consumer goods marketing and sales company. The individuals came from a wide range of functions—finance, manufacturing, operations, employee relations, distribution, marketing and sales. Before and after the training, they generated possible solutions to important work-related problems, and then evaluated those solutions. Not only did the training result in more and better ideas for solutions, but it also improved their skills in evaluating those ideas (Figure 19-1). (For more discussion of Simplex training, see appendix.)

Developing your skills in Simplex is like climbing a ladder of skill development, or a 'skills progression ladder' (Figure 19-2). Skills in Level I—individual effectiveness—include everything from mere exposure to the process to using

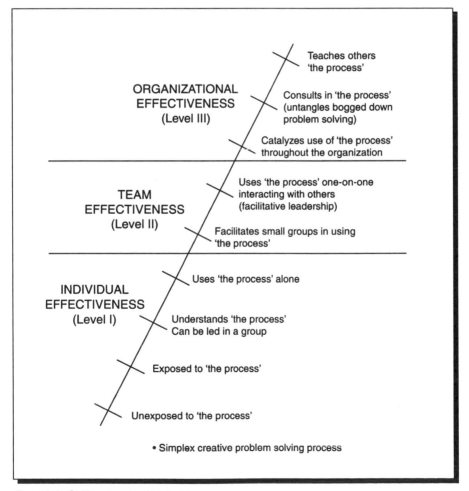

Fig. 19.2 Skills progression ladder

the process and process skills well enough to be led by a facilitator or to solve an individual problem alone. Skills in Level II—team effectiveness—include being able to facilitate others through the process, either formally in a small group or informally with individuals. Skills in Level III—organizational effectiveness—include promoting the everyday use of Simplex throughout the organization, acting as a 'Simplex consultant' to help others diagnose what's wrong with their problem solving, and knowing the process well enough to teach it to others. The more you practise, the higher you progress on the ladder. As you climb the skills progression ladder, you begin to see that developing the process and process skills needed for mainstreaming innovation is a life-long journey. Even after some 20 years of developing my own skills, I continue to be amazed by all the things I have yet to learn, and by how easy it is to slip back down the ladder without continual practice. It's like the old saying, 'The larger the island of knowledge, the longer the shoreline of wonder.'

20

WHAT'S AN EASY NEXT STEP?

'What's the next step?'

'Well,' said Harry as we began our descent, 'an awful lot of the things we've talked about seem to have a common thread.'

'What's that, Harry?' I said.

'It's the creative process,' he said, nodding to emphasize his point. 'A lot of the things we do to improve organizations involve skills in the creative process. And a lot of the things we do wrong have to do with not understanding the creative process and with our lack of skill in making the process work. This process you've told us about ties a lot of things together. The whole notion of putting as much emphasis on the process, or on *how* we do things, as on the content, or *what* we're doing, makes a lot of sense.'

Alice said, 'I don't think I'll ever look at a situation again without reminding myself to defer judgment, think divergently and think convergently.'

'And don't forget the fourth skill,' I added. 'Remind yourself to look for good problems to solve, then solve them, then take action. And even before you solve them, make sure you define them well. Do your fact finding before you define your problem.'

'Vertical deferral of judgment,' she said. 'See, I was listening.'

'So,' said Harry, 'what's my next step?' ∎

Summary of learnings

✈ *You can implement Simplex into your organization in one of two ways. You might integrate Simplex into an existing improvement initiative, or you might launch an improvement initiative based entirely on the process.*

✈ *In either case, integrate Simplex with a clear business need or goal, and a solid infrastructure that encourages people to use the new philosophies and tools regularly. Structures include performance appraisal systems, teamwork and reward systems.*

✈ *Introduce any improvement initiative as a process to be implemented, not merely as "content" to be presented.*

✈ *It's important to convince others that mainstreaming innovation is not such a "big change." Show people how they can integrate Simplex with existing tools and techniques. The specific tools and techniques you employ are less critical to innovation than following a process. Demonstrate how Simplex process skills can revitalize other management methods that are flagging.*

We said in earlier chapters that, if they hope to be effective, organizations must mainstream efficiency, adaptability and flexibility all at the same time. We talked about how difficult it is for most organizations to mainstream adaptability in particular. A proven way to mainstream adaptability is to implement the Simplex innovation process and process skills throughout an organization. We've already looked at what it will take for you to implement Simplex on your own, and to involve others. Now let's look at what it will take to get your entire organization started.

INTEGRATE SIMPLEX, OR IMPLEMENT IT FROM SCRATCH?

An organization can implement Simplex in either of two ways. The easiest way is to integrate it into an existing corporate improvement initiative, say, a total quality management program. Rather than reinvent the wheel, you introduce the process to enhance an existing (and perhaps flagging) program, thus averting the 'Oh no, not another program' reaction. You simply integrate Simplex into an existing infrastructure and business need. On the other hand, if your organization has no improvement initiative at the moment, then you can start afresh, establishing an innovation process based entirely on Simplex. In this case, you must identify a clear business need and establish an infrastructure that will encourage routine use of Simplex. No matter which way you implement Simplex, the creative process and process skills will die unless they clearly address an important business need and are integrated into a solid infrastructure (Figure 20-1). Many worthwhile initiatives have floundered because the organization lacked at least one of these three components.

The organization might have introduced a program without linking it to a specific goal that employees could understand and buy into. You have to spell out a clear business need that the 'program' is intended to address: lower costs, higher sales, fewer defects or customer complaints, shorter turnaround time or time to market, higher quality products or services. Many very successful companies have introduced a total quality management (TQM) program for no better reason than that they don't want to miss out on something or that everyone else is doing it. Launching the initiative without a clear goal is like setting employees adrift in a rowboat out of sight of land. The new initiative addresses no specific business need and employees have no way to measure success.

Other initiatives have floundered because the organization lacked an effective infrastructure to encourage people to use the new philosophies and tools regularly. In order to make these initiatives work, you have to make structural changes that give employees the time, place and motivation to implement the new ideas. You must alter performance appraisal systems to reward people

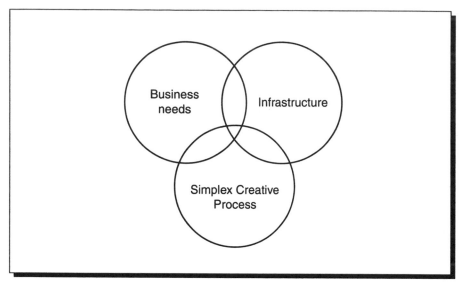

Fig. 20.1 The three necessary components of a successful organizational effort to mainstream innovation

who apply these new ideas. Teamwork is another 'structure' established specifically to address important problems that relate directly to the business need and to other vital company goals and objectives. People need to know they are going to be rewarded for implementing a new initiative, and must be given the necessary time and resources to do so. If they're going to make valuable changes, they must believe that the new initiative is part of their job, not just something 'extra.'

Even when organizations establish clear business needs and infrastructures for implementing new initiatives, they still hit roadblocks. For example, many organizations attempt to implement TQM programs without realizing just how much they are expecting of their employees. In effect, the organization is asking people to fundamentally change the way in which they work. Managers underestimate what it takes to alter people's change-making skills, attitudes and behaviors—the very process skills that we've talked about in this book.

The organization must encourage people to view problems as 'golden eggs' and to embrace the creative problem solving process in order to make continuous improvements. In order to help employees and teams use the Simplex process to deliberately find and solve problems and implement solutions, the organization must train them in the process skills of deferral of judgment, active divergence and active convergence. No improvement initiative or philosophy will work unless people acquire skills in working together, enjoy looking at things in new ways, and look positively on change. In other words, the organization has to introduce its improvement initiative as a process to be implemented, not merely as 'content' to be presented.

THE SECRET TO TOTAL QUALITY MANAGEMENT

'TQM takes time'

Total quality no overnight success

It was this very point that made TQM so successful in Japan. After the Second World War, the Japanese realized that the quality of their manufactured products lagged worldwide standards badly. They deliberately changed their management and production methods. Employees were encouraged to apply creative thinking to improve their work. Over the next few decades, Japanese products and services gradually became world leaders in quality.

During my sabbatical year in Japan, I asked many managers what effort it had taken to establish successful programs such as quality circles and employee suggestion systems. A typical reply was: 'It took us nine years to establish quality circles and even longer to set up our employee suggestion systems. People resisted at first, but we persisted, continuing to polish the programs and train employees. Finally, these new systems became permanent.' In other words, these initiatives were not expected to work overnight. But having decided to change, these managers deliberately invested the effort into acquiring the necessary change-making process skills to do so.

In many organizations, TQM fails because they're missing these process skills. TQM is usually presented as nothing more than a philosophy and a kit of tools, including statistical process control and flow-charting. Many other new managerial methods have become no more than passing fads for the same reasons. Management By Objectives, T-groups, and intrapreneuring can fail because the companies adopt the philosophy but pay lip service to translating theory into action. Most important, they underestimate what it takes to alter people's change-making skills, attitudes and behaviors.

The point of this entire book has been how to improve these skills. To mainstream innovation, an organization must integrate the Simplex process and process skills into its daily routine. And it must establish a clear-cut business need and infrastructure to encourage employees to use the process and process skills on the job. So how to do it? Let's look first at how to integrate the process and process skills into an existing corporate improvement program by discussing examples from four companies. As you read these case studies, look for ways in which their situations resemble yours. Obviously, none of them is exactly like yours. But perhaps you will be able to adapt one of their approaches as an easy next step to getting your own organization started.

USING SIMPLEX AS A 'TOTAL QUALITY PROCESS'

'What can I do?'

Employees learn to help company adapt to change

McCormick & Company Inc., a worldwide manufacturer of spices, flavorings, and seasonings based in Maryland, implemented Simplex back in 1987 as the base of its Total Quality Process. For this company, Total Quality Process represents two things: an ethic and a discipline. An ethic defines the core values that guide McCormick in its business. A discipline is the use of specific principles and methods to improve the business.

One ethic, for example, is employee involvement. A main principle of this ethic is that the 'experts' are really the people doing the work. Thus, the people doing the job are in the best position to improve it. How to translate such an ethic into day-to-day discipline? The company chose the Simplex creative problem solving process, for several reasons. The company wanted a process that could focus on groups, that valued everyone's ideas, that offered a structured process that everyone could learn and use, that encouraged horizontal rather than vertical thinking, and that required divergence in every step of the problem solving process. The Simplex process helped to translate into daily practice two other company ethics: open two-way communication builds co-operation and teamwork; and TEAM ('Together Everyone Achieves More'). The process skills of deferral of judgment, divergence and convergence helped people to openly share information, for example, and to build on others' ideas without unnecessary debate and argument.

For McCormick, mainstreaming the creative problem solving process addressed several specific business needs. The company had to adapt to changing markets and meet changing customer demands. More and more of its customers were industrial rather than retail. And on both sides, customers were demanding faster response and more product options. The company was also seeking new international business, meaning that it had to make changes in its supply chain. What had been a relatively stable business for many decades was about to become a relatively tumultuous one during the late 1980s and '90s. The company knew that it had to stay out in front of this change curve, and recognized a need to improve its employees' problem solving skills and creativity.

More specifically, one of McCormick's customers had recently invited the company to take part in creative problem solving on a mutual problem. In this new customer-supplier partnership (relatively unheard-of at the time), it was almost assumed that the supplier would have to work on creative problem solving along with the customer in order to keep its business. The partnership worked so well and the process was so instrumental that McCormick had decided to implement Simplex itself.

At the same time, the company had recognized that success rested on three necessary and interrelated principles that made up its Total Quality Process: customer focus, process management and employee empowerment. It identified the first two as technical components and the third as the 'people' component. Focusing on the customer meant talking to customers in order to uncover all kinds of 'fuzzy situations.' In fact, when you start understanding customers' expectations, and then measure the effectiveness of your own processes designed to meet them, you can't help but encounter problems to be solved. Then you have to be able to 'manage' these problems, to effectively select and address the most important ones. Without process management, you're quickly overwhelmed or you fall back on standard programmed solutions that don't do the job.

Making improvements based on customer needs

The company now makes improvements based on internal and external customers' needs using a number of existing infrastructures.

One infrastructure is a system of Multiple Management boards. The company maintains 16 boards worldwide, each containing three or four teams. A team investigates opportunities for improvement (taking six months to examine a particular area or opportunity) and recommends necessary process changes to senior management. Simplex training has improved the performance of these teams and boards. They now follow a common, formalized process and a set of process skills to find and solve problems efficiently. The company also set up process teams specifically to find problems to solve, based either on unmet customer needs, or on needs to reduce costs or to respond to changing markets.

Another infrastructure within the Total Quality Process is a so-called Quality Encounter. Customers and suppliers meet for fact finding and problem finding in order to communicate their expectations about products and services. It establishes what resources internal customers need in order to do their jobs and how well those needs are being met by internal suppliers. Most important, it points to opportunities for improvement and helps to unearth many problems that must be solved. Employees have no choice but to talk to customers and find different ways to define and solve important problems using Simplex.

McCormick's Total Quality Process provides other infrastructures for using Simplex. Interacting with customers and investigating processes points the way to important opportunities for creative problem solving. Without a process that enabled them to address these fuzzy situations, employees would simply have been overwhelmed or even paralyzed. The company had to do more than give employees vague instructions to 'go out there and improve quality' or 'run processes better' or 'talk to your customers.' Simplex offered the creative problem solving process skills that they needed to solve problems.

McCormick also revamped its managers' performance appraisal system so that it would reflect the total quality ethic and discipline, including problem solving skills. Part of the new system assesses managers for their problem solving and decision-making abilities. For example, managers are assessed for their ability to take innovative, creative approaches to problem solving or to make timely, quality decisions in an ambiguous or chaotic environment.

In order to implement Simplex throughout the company, McCormick first trained a core group of employees. These employees became 'champions' who carried the process until enough people had bought into it. If the process was to have any credibility among employees, it had to be presented as a way to meet specific goals. So these champions endeavored to apply the process to important business problems.

McCormick's senior managers decided to drive the process from the top down. They identified the corporation's critical success factors, then determined the strategic problems that stood in the way of achieving those critical success factors. These problems were then broken down into more detailed or closely defined problems to be tackled by lower-level teams. Driving the process from the top supported and empowered employees: they were given the authority to tackle not just smaller localized issues but truly important problems. This process—allowing the people at the top to decide what's important and then translating these priorities throughout the organization to front-line workers—is the key to employee empowerment. What's needed is alignment: if the process is driven from the top, then it's aligned throughout the organization. McCormick developed its own internal Simplex trainers and facilitators, most of them regular managers rather than professional trainers. The company has also trained its employees and teams in Level I and II skills. This has institutionalized the use of the process. Because they have internalized the process skills, employees use them continuously and naturally, not just in formal situations like problem solving meetings. Phrases such as 'How might we?' and 'Let's diverge' are a part of everyday conversation.

USING SIMPLEX TO INVOLVE ALL EMPLOYEES

'Top-down training'

How one company pushed a training program through the ranks

In 1981, I received a call from an automobile manufacturer. For several business quarters, this company had suffered heavy losses. Bound and determined to change the way it operated, the company had launched many initiatives. One of the most important was its decision to turn to its people—involving everyone in using their minds to improve quality and customer satisfaction and to increase innovation. The company had heard of my work at Procter & Gamble in involving managers in actually 'managing the business' rather than just 'doing my job.'

The company and its union had recently agreed in a letter of understanding to implement a joint program on Employee Involvement (EI) for its unionized employees. They jointly provided resources, including both unionized and salaried employees, that would diagnose important training needs and create strategies and programs to meet those needs. Its first step was to form problem solving groups in the plants guided by local and national joint steering committees. To build skills in problem solving, these groups had been taught standard analytical tools borrowed from statistical process control and total quality management programs (such as 'cause-and-effect diagramming' and 'cause-unknown diagnosis').

The company now wanted to expand Employee Involvement to include salaried employees, and to develop problem solving processes that were better suited for their jobs. It hoped that these employees and their managers would take more initiative in identifying opportunities for improvement and tackling them creatively. During a preconsult, we agreed that the Simplex process seemed highly appropriate for this purpose. This was confirmed during a preliminary training workshop designed to give several key employees some experience with the process and process skills. We agreed on a strategy to train a number of employees in applying the Simplex process and in training others in the company.

During this training, we had a chance to apply the process to a problem at a newly modernized plant that made a major component of the company's new front wheel drive automobiles. The plant was setting new records for quality and low cost, but one department was struggling. Only about one-third of its output met the company's high quality standards, and employees had to work heavy overtime schedules in order to keep up with orders. The plant managers had tried several quick-fix solutions to resolve the production and quality problems, but none had worked. We established a cross-functional team of 15 plant managers and supervisors in order to apply the Simplex creative problem solving process to the problem.

Along with one of the company's internal consultants whom I was training as a Simplex facilitator and trainer, I conducted the application session with this team. We set aside about half a day for training in the Simplex process and process skills, and two and a half days to apply the process to the team's fuzzy situation. During the training, we asked the team members to complete the Simplex creative problem solving profile. Recall from earlier chapters that this instrument reveals individual differences in preferences for various phases of the creative problem solving process. The team discovered a very revealing insight.

Of the 15 team members, eight showed creative problem solving styles heavily oriented toward quadrant 4, implementation. The other seven showed styles heavily oriented toward quadrant 3, optimization. No members had creative problem solving styles oriented toward quadrants 1 or 2, generation and conceptualization. In other words, the team was composed of people who preferred to jump quickly to action rather than spend time first in fact finding and problem defining.

When we discussed these results, the team members were able to identify many instances in which they had mistakenly made assumptions about this particular problem, leading to one failed solution after another. Rather than take the time to define the problem accurately, they had simply jumped from the fuzzy situation to one solution after another. They had spent all of their time alternating between quadrants 3 and 4, and none in quadrants 1 or 2 (Figure 20-2).

These action-oriented individuals agreed to spend two days in quadrant 1 and 2 activity, gathering facts and defining problems (Figure 20-3)—even though the whole exercise was against their nature. Three specific problem definitions emerged from this exercise. On the third day, the group was able to create simple but specific solutions to each defined problem that it could quickly implement. Within several months, most of the plant's production was high quality and was still improving.

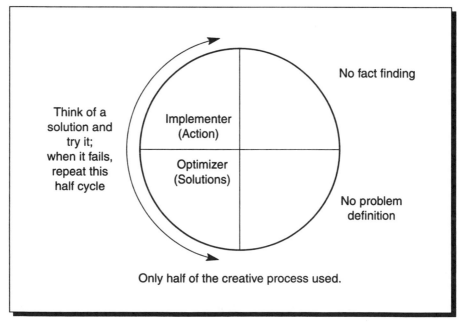

Think of a solution and try it; when it fails, repeat this half cycle

Implementer (Action)

Optimizer (Solutions)

No fact finding

No problem definition

Only half of the creative process used.

Fig. 20.2 The results of heavy orientation towards quadrant 3 and 4 thinking styles

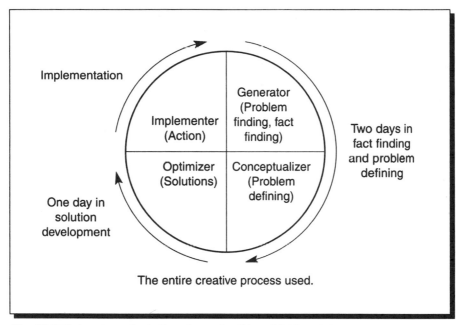

Fig. 20.3 Balancing orientations towards all four thinking styles

By hooking Simplex into the company's existing Employee Involvement infrastructure, the internal consultants easily grew and disseminated these process
skills. They found that managers and salaried employees were eager to learn
and apply the process.

USING SIMPLEX TO INVOLVE ALL EMPLOYEES

'What are we about?'

Company defines niche, appoints teams to roll out cost improvements

During the early 1970s, senior managers at the Procter & Gamble Co. in
Cincinnati, Ohio, had decided to extend a long-standing cost improvement program across the entire corporation. The program had originally been confined
to its manufacturing plants. But Procter & Gamble saw it as a way to counter
external pressures—double-digit inflation, an OPEC oil embargo, anti-trust
government activity that hindered acquisitions, growing environmental concerns—and maintain healthy profit margins and sales volumes. Instead of
relying only on making more money, the company decided to form cross-functional teams to identify creative ways to save money, and spend money more
effectively, on its products and operations.

Until then, employees hadn't usually operated in teams. Instead, people had been groomed to excel as individuals on marketing, accounting or other specialized functions on specific products. In order to get the ball rolling, the company president showed his own commitment to the cost improvement program and teamwork by writing letters to all managers clearly explaining the need and rationale for the new approach. He asked the general manager of each operating division to set goals and involve employees in implementing cost improvement programs in their divisions. After cross-functional teams were formed across the corporation, many of them received training and support in Simplex.

These teams then used problem finding to discover opportunities and set goals for cost improvement. Within four years, the teams achieved the president's overall company goal of increasing annual savings to 6 per cent of sales—an impressive amount, given that after-tax profit margins were normally about 7 per cent of sales.

Because the business need had been so clearly spelled out at the top, and because a new infrastructure (the teams) had been created, the entire corporation was primed to use Simplex in all kinds of projects: shortening product development time, reformulating brands, adopting new technology for improving manufacturing and sales operations, making advertising dollars go further, streamlining accounting and legal procedures, and simplifying communications among departments. Without a clear business need or infrastructure, it would have been much more difficult to introduce a seemingly 'out of the mainstream' process to many managers and departments.

USING SIMPLEX TO EMPOWER EMPLOYEES

'What do you think?'

Employees forced to look inward for answers to problems

Another example of welding Simplex into an existing structure comes from its use by Kimball International Inc. This Indiana-based manufacturer of consumer durable goods had flourished since its inception in the late '40s under the vision of a strong, entrepreneurial leader. Whenever employees needed guidance, they knew they could turn to him or his senior managers for the right answer to their problems. As the business had been running extremely well under an established set of procedures, there was little need for new or different ideas. People knew what to do and how to do it. By 1985, however, market conditions and competition had changed. The company needed to change its procedures and leadership style. Kimball had several new underlying business needs. The most important was that the business itself was changing. Its customers were becoming much more sophisticated, its markets were fragmenting into niches, and information technology had brought its own set of changes. In order to adapt to these changes, the company had to give its employees more authority to solve problems on their own and to form business units to manage particular products. No longer could workers simply turn to their leaders for the 'right' answer to any problem. They had to learn to concentrate on their work process, not just the 'content' of the particular product or market area. So how to empower employees?

The company's president began by opening dialogue with all employees on market conditions, competition, changing expectations of customers, quality expectations, cycle times to market, and what that meant to the organization. Because decisions needed to be made and problems solved at the level of the customer, the company removed middle management layers in order to flatten the organization.

One challenge was to convince workers that change was even needed. From the employees' perspective, the company was still financially sound. So why change? The senior executives believed it was important to start early and introduce changes gradually, rather than wait until a crisis forced the company to change overnight. On the plus side, its solid finances meant that Kimball could afford to make its changes without the kind of painful revolution and chaos that many organizations have experienced when forced to make changes at the last minute.

Employees needed to be given tools and thinking skills to enable them to make changes and solve problems. Before they could solve problems, for example, employees would need to know how to collect and analyze performance data. But rather than hand over a jumbled kit of tools and techniques for making changes, the company needed to pull them into a meaningful framework. Otherwise, employees would view them as little more a jumble of tools without knowing how or why they were to be used.

How to help 7,500 diverse employees used to doing things in a certain way to understand the company's new goals? Kimball began by writing a document that laid out a well-defined mission, vision, guiding principles, and goals or critical success factors (CSFs). Unit leaders took part in this exercise and in sharing the results with their units. Involving 200 to 250 of the top leaders, this process took about 18 months and included three or four rewrites. Every sentence was scrutinized to ensure that everybody understood what the words really meant.

Besides writing a document that would align the new thinking skills and tools with a common goal, the company wanted to create a symbol that would easily and effectively communicate its mission, vision, guiding principles, and goals. What resulted was '3D': the company had to explain its *direction*; *develop* its people, tools and resources; and *deploy* them effectively.

Using Simplex to integrate improvement processes

How could the company link its 3D goals and visions to the various tools that different departments had already adopted? Various departments, for example, had unilaterally adopted such practices as computer-integrated manufacturing, statistical process control, structured panel interviewing or Simplex creative problem solving. In order to find a way to explain to employees how all of these tools fit together, company managers met to apply the Simplex process itself to the communication problem. Their solution was a diagram that showed the relationships among all of the company's tools, guiding principles and goals. In the process, Simplex itself became far more than just a tool for solving problems. It became the process by which Kimball could use all of its other tools to mainstream innovation.

With its business need and infrastructure defined, Kimball has successfully mainstreamed the innovation process and process skills. Many process changes have resulted, including alterations to such 'sacred cows' as reward systems, organizational structure, benefits strategies, and hiring practices.

For some senior managers, making these changes meant a real struggle. Many of their employees simply couldn't believe that these sacred cows had become fair game for change. In some cases, employees were reluctant to suggest changes for other reasons. One senior manager, for example, had tried in vain to encourage his subordinates to suggest changes. He eventually realized that it was his own ingrained behavior patterns that were preventing employees from making suggestions. Simply put, they didn't believe he really wanted to make changes. So he asked his staff for suggestions on how to alter his own behavior.

One subordinate who had received Simplex training finally suggested that this manager attend an upcoming Level I workshop at one of the company's plants. During the training, the manager realized that Simplex could help him to change his leadership style. He continued through Level II training. Although his paternal leadership style made the training itself a challenge for him, he learned how Simplex skills could help him to develop his employees' thinking skills, self-esteem and self-confidence.

When he tried out the process skill of deferral of judgment back on the job, for example, his subordinates soon felt much more empowered. They realized that new ideas wouldn't be immediately quashed. Until then, none of his employees had felt able to use the tools that were part of 3D. His new-found skills in using Simplex allowed him to empower his employees. They finally felt free to 'open the toolbox.'

New teams get the ball rolling

In fact, this manager eventually played a key part in implementing Simplex throughout the company. After his own 'conversion,' he began to consider how he might introduce these process skills to his co-workers. Because he headed several diverse functions, he was able to start the ball rolling without having to ask for permission. He set up cross-functional teams to use Simplex in solving important problems. The teams' enthusiasm for the process proved contagious. So much so that the president agreed to take Simplex training himself along with Kimball's other senior managers.

These managers all received training in Levels I and II. A core group attended Level III workshops to improve their internal consulting, coaching and training skills, and to better understand how to mainstream Simplex. Level III training also helped managers to understand how Simplex could allow employees to use the 3D methodologies (performance measurement, cost of quality, information engineering, structured panel interviewing, manufacturing performance excellence, computer-integrated manufacturing, and statistical process control). This core group then devised a top-down, cascading training strategy for the rest of the employees.

Each of the company's autonomous business units decided how to implement Simplex among its own employees. During an extensive preconsult, a unit manager and one of the core managers used the 'why-what's stopping' analysis to show how Simplex might help the business unit reach its goals, and to identify additional training needs. Thus, each business unit developed its own strategies for implementing Simplex and the 3D methodologies.

Simplex permits reengineering

Simplex has done more for Kimball employees than simply open the toolbox. Using the process and process skills also helps them to select the right tools for a particular situation. The 'why-what's stopping' mapping process, for example, ensures that people have correctly defined their real problem before trying to use the wrong tool to solve it. Asking the question 'why' might lead an individual to discover that he needs a tool to reengineer a process or to create a new strategy. Asking the question 'what's stopping' leads him to tools that make current processes more efficient or that execute a current strategy more effectively.

Simplex also helps the company to incorporate diverse points of view during discussions among internal customers, suppliers and experts. Cross-functional teams have been able to directly address problems that had previously been ignored. Company auditors who once did nothing more than expose business units' mistakes now coach these units in order to improve their processes and help them become self-sufficient. The process allows people to work together better than before.

The process has become so widely accepted at Kimball that a full-time training director has been assigned to manage its implementation and integration with the rest of the 3D tools. In fact, Simplex has become a part of the company's performance feedback system. The performance improvement process for employees uses and highlights the necessary leadership style, thinking skills and behaviors of Simplex creative problem solving. Simplex creative problem solving has become a key ingredient of organizational development strategy. Many of the Simplex trainers, by virtue of skills acquired, individual initiative, and visibility, have advanced to positions of higher responsibility. This enables growing interest and continuous improvement as it is recognized throughout the organization.

We used the above four examples to illustrate how organizations integrated Simplex into an existing improvement initiative. Now let's look at how two organizations launched the process as a new initiative—in effect, as their new improvement 'program.' Neither of these examples will exactly mimic your situation. As with the above four, your job is to adapt their experience to create your own approach.

USING SIMPLEX TO FLATTEN COSTS

'A process for profits'

Company uses creative process to reap cost savings

By 1982, senior managers at Frito-Lay based in Dallas, Texas, had decided that they needed to further improve the company's productivity. Frito-Lay had always been profitable. During the inflationary '70s, the company's strategy had been to produce the highest quality snack foods and maintain its profit growth by simply increasing its prices to cover annual cost increases. By the early '80s, however, facing lower-cost, lower-quality competition, the company recognized that it had to do more than simply increase prices each year in order to retain customers. If it didn't make some imaginative changes, it could expect to see slower revenue growth even as costs continued to rise, resulting in a profit squeeze (Figure 20-4). The managers had already discussed standard solutions to their productivity problems with several consultants. But none had seemed suitable. Frito-Lay approached me to use the Simplex creative process to better define what the company needed.

During a preconsult, we used the Simplex process to develop a three-part strategy. First, we translated the company's desire to improve productivity into a simple, clear business need: to learn to offset inflationary cost increases in order to flatten costs. Second, managers aimed to encourage employees to find creative ways of meeting this business need by giving them Simplex training. Third, the company decided to create interfunctional teams of upper and middle managers; these teams would use the creative process to identify ways to save money, and spend money more effectively (Figure 20-5). These interfunctional teams would then hand off challenges to lower-level teams that had also received Simplex training. To make the business need more concrete, the company president set a specific goal: to save a total of $500 million over the next five years.

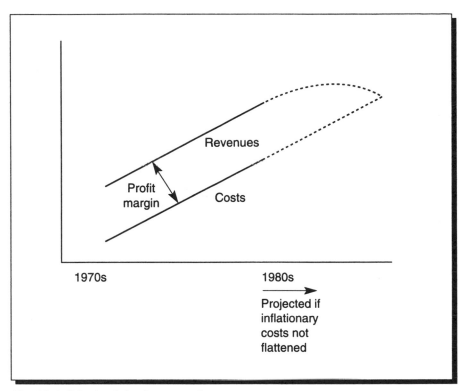

Fig. 20.4 Frito-Lay's business need

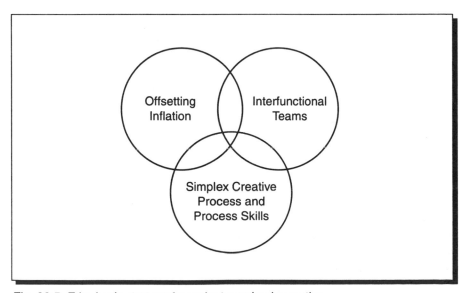

Fig. 20.5 Frito-Lay's strategy for mainstreaming innovation

To implement this strategy, senior managers visited the company's plants to explain the business need and to introduce the new initiative (called the 'Off$et Process'). More than 50 internal line managers eventually received training so that they could teach Simplex to other employees and lead the organization in continually finding and solving problems and implementing solutions. Because they understood the overall strategy, Frito-Lay employees were very willing to undergo this training and to apply it within the new teams.

The teams completed many kinds of projects, including the following: increasing equipment capacity; reducing rework; rolling out a new product in record time; shortening new technology installation time; and accelerating the introduction of product and packaging improvement ideas. The company realized its goal of $500 million in savings a full year ahead of schedule. At this point, Frito-Lay revised its business need from merely flattening costs to actually reducing them.

The company might have found it a much less difficult task to integrate this innovation process with an existing initiative. Without an initiative already in place, Frito-Lay faced a lot of up-front work in convincing employees to understand and commit to mainstreaming innovation. But positive results and continued encouragement from senior managers eventually won their acceptance of the process.

USING SIMPLEX TO REGAIN BUSINESS

'Making up lost ground, and then some'

How one company used creativity to make up for lost business

Here's another example of how strong leadership pulled Simplex into an organization as a stand-alone initiative, this time at Woodstream Corp., a Pennsylvania manufacturer of pest control products and outdoor sporting equipment. While the company had experienced little change in its products and processes before early 1989, the recently installed president suddenly found himself facing numerous changes, including the fact that the bottom had fallen out of one of its major businesses. Until this point, only a few senior people had ever been involved in solving problems. The president recognized that he had to involve employees in figuring out how to meet these challenges and to make the necessary improvements.

After a fairly lengthy search for a way to involve employees, he settled upon the Simplex process. He recognized the importance of balancing process and content, and the importance of using process skills in teamwork. Having found what he'd been looking for, his next challenge was to convince his staff to give the creative process a try.

He started by providing a Level I training workshop to a team of senior managers. The training convinced the managers in turn that they needed to train the other employees. This team mapped out the company's strategic needs using the 'why-what's stopping' analysis. For each of these strategic needs, the company established cross-functional teams (including people from various departments) to break down traditional functional barriers and solve company-wide problems. Later, focused work center teams (natural teams that work together at different work centers) were assigned to address narrower problems that required less interfunctional team play.

The next steps were Level II training for many key people and Level III training for senior managers. The company also held creative problem solving 'days' to celebrate its successes and to refresh employees' process skills. During a meeting held by one cross-functional team, a simple but powerful idea surfaced. This was a vehicle for problem finding called 'fuzzy boards.' On these boards, which are now located at each work center, workers write down problems or 'fuzzy situations' that they discover but cannot solve alone. Other employees then offer assistance; sometimes a team forms spontaneously to solve the problem. Solutions to the problem and action steps for implementing solutions are also written on the boards. Managers act as coaches. They inform employees of company goals and strategies in order to help them choose relevant problems to solve (recall the suggestion system used by many Japanese companies to encourage employees to post similar problems).

As further structural support, Woodstream's performance appraisal system incorporates employees' creative problem solving process skills and behaviors. Under the system, employees are rewarded for practising 12 important skills

and behaviors, as follows: flexibility; efficiency improvement; adaptability; buy-in to group convergence; leadership (change agent); consistent use of Simplex creative problem solving technology; advocating and believing in the participatory process (Simplex creative problem solving); attitude; sense of urgency; company-wide thinking; interpersonal skills; and communication (what, when, to whom). The company looks for the same attributes during interviews with job applicants.

Through these structural support systems, Simplex has become far more than a problem solving tool for Woodstream. The creative problem solving process is the cultural foundation for encouraging teamwork, instilling respect for fellow employees, and fostering the belief that every idea has merit.

Suppose that, like Frito-Lay and Woodstream, your organization has no specific improvement program already in place. How do you introduce creative problem solving as your organization's sole improvement initiative?

YOUR NEXT STEP

Consider taking the following steps. Use your creativity to identify an important business need or challenge that will grab the attention of your senior managers. Refer back to chapter 15 for ideas on how to define the critical challenges that your organization should be focusing on.

In order to demonstrate how useful the creative problem solving process can be, organize an application session including some of these managers to address one key challenge. Follow the steps outlined in chapter 12 to prepare for and conduct this problem solving meeting (remember to identify a true client for a preconsult). During the meeting, lead the group through the Simplex process. Don't forget to model the process skills (deferral of judgment, active divergence and active convergence) at every opportunity. The main purpose of the application session is to let the group members see for themselves the value of the process and process skills. It also gives them a look at how the entire organization could use this same process and process skills continuously to mainstream innovation.

Be prepared to explain the secrets of implementing the process and process skills by discussing the three necessary components of implementation in this chapter: business need, infrastructure, and the Simplex process and process skills. Then suggest that the group allow you to take the lead in creating an implementation plan. You might show the group a prepared example of an important business need and infrastructure that could work in your organization. You might even tell them about the examples we've discussed in this chapter. The point is that, because your organization is unlike any other, it must develop its own business need and infrastructure in order to make Simplex work.

Whether you use the innovation process to launch a brand-new initiative or integrate the process into an existing initiative, you'll have an easier job of mainstreaming innovation if you can convince others that it's not such a 'big change.'

One way to do this is to let people use the process and process skills on an important challenge as we just suggested. Another way is to show them how they can use existing tools and techniques within the Simplex process. For example, statistical process control techniques such as histograms and control charts for tracking quality are actually excellent fact finding techniques for a manufacturer. That's step two of the Simplex process. Other standard techniques like fishboning, flowcharting and force field analysis become even more effective fact finding and problem defining tools if they're used along with the process skills of deferral of judgment, active divergence and active convergence. The pareto analysis is a natural converging tool that helps in every step of the Simplex process.

IT'S UP TO YOU

In any case, it's up to you to explain to others the difference between a 'tool' or 'technique' and a 'process.' A process is a series of steps; these tools and techniques are simply methods of executing the steps. Many specific tools or techniques might work for you within any step of a process. The one you select matters less than ensuring that you perform the particular step of the process well. Stated another way, the first three steps of the Simplex innovation process—problem finding, fact finding and problem defining—are critical to innovation. The specific tools or techniques you use to accomplish them are less critical. In any situation, one might be as good as another.

If you're not satisfied with how well your organization has implemented other management methods, show people how the Simplex process skills can breathe new life into them. For example, if you're using Management By Objectives (MBO), you need to agree with your boss on specific goals that you should reach in the next year. Why not defer judgment and diverge together to create an imaginative list of potential goals, and then pare down the list after discussing relevant criteria? Then do a 'why-what's stopping' analysis to discover and map out even better goals (challenges). Still deferring judgment and diverging together, you can create ideas to solve the specific challenges you finally select as your goals.

For example, the goal of increasing sales in the Western region by 5 per cent becomes the challenge, 'How might I increase my sales in the Western region by at least 5 per cent?' Finally, exercise your converging skills together to select the best solutions, then develop an action plan that you can implement to reach the goals. Your boss then assumes the role of coach to check in regularly on your progress and help you. Use the process and process skills together to incorporate new facts that surface during the year, and to adjust your goals and action plans. Many of us try to implement good management processes like MBO without the necessary process skills to make them come alive. Almost any plan that you create to mainstream innovation throughout your organization will require your senior managers to adopt—and to encourage others to adopt—these process skills. In other words, senior managers must themselves appreciate and demonstrate the distinction between managing process and managing content. The everyday rush of short-term, urgent tasks might cause them to focus only on what they're trying to achieve rather than how they are going to achieve it. Others in the organization will simply follow their lead. Instead of proactively seeking out new problems to solve, employees will continue to react, and to apply outdated processes and solutions to whatever problems confront them.

Mainstreaming innovation, on the other hand, requires the organization to continuously and deliberately change *how* things are done. As we discussed in earlier chapters, top companies already know this 'big secret.' Xerox, for example, states this idea in its definition of total quality management as 'a long-term process aimed at fundamentally changing the way people work and manage so they can continuously improve the way they meet the requirements of their customers.' Top Japanese companies, for example, mainstream innovation by using the process of *kaizen* or continuous improvement: as soon as a product is made, it's time to begin improving it; never be satisfied with your job; find ways to make your job better. However, real change requires action. Managers must lead the process by example, not just words.

As we discussed in the opening chapter, being able to use an innovation process that starts with finding good problems to solve has never been more important. The pace of change continues to increase. Even as we confront new situations more often than ever, there seems to be less time to address them all. At one time, people could expect to face the 'same old problems' routinely. They could rely on a handful of tried-and-true solutions. It was easy to find someone to turn to when an unusual problem occurred, someone who had done it before. Not any longer. Small wonder that so many organizations freeze at this point.

Organizations that take the pains to master the innovation process become adaptable. They learn to manage change. While many organizations strive to be efficient and flexible, truly effective organizations go further: they are also adaptable. Thus, they stand out above the competition. Similarly, in order to stand out in your organization, you must be seen as an effective person. You must demonstrate efficiency, flexibility and, most important, adaptability at the same time. While many people can demonstrate efficiency or flexibility, very few have figured out how to be adaptable, or innovative. Here's your opportunity. If you hope to distinguish yourself and dramatically improve your performance, start mastering adaptability. Become innovative. In this book, we've tried to provide the ticket you need—the Simplex process and process skills. Now it's up to you to put them to good use. It's up to you to get started.

APPENDIX

You can obtain more information about the Simplex creative problem solving process, and training in problem solving, in several ways.

- Explore a three-level series of experiential training workshops for yourself and fellow employees. This systems approach to training develops participants' problem solving skills and encourages them to apply those skills back on the job to achieve meaningful organisational goals and strategies.
- You might establish a facilitator certification process. This process enables individuals to practise and receive training in problem solving skills so that they can model the desired skills, and provide coaching and feedback to others.
- The 'One Hour Problem Solver' is a software package recently developed to prompt the user through each of the eight steps of the Simplex process, allowing you to 'practise, practise, practise' without leaving your desktop computer system.

For more information . . .

If you'd like more information about Simplex training workshops or application sessions, and/or the 'One Hour Problem Solver' software package, contact:

The Center for Research in Applied Creativity World Headquarters

Canada:	Dr. Min Basadur 184 Lover's Lane Ancaster, Ontario Canada L9G 1G8 Phone: (905) 648–4903 Fax: (905) 648–7510	UK:	Dr Garry Gelade Phoenix 2000 Ltd c/o 1 Circus Lodge Circus Road London NW8 9JL Phone: 071-404-2944/ 071-289-6305
USA:	Dr. Min Basadur 8791 Hollyhock Drive Cincinnati, Ohio USA 45231-5013 Phone: (513) 522-2616 Fax: (513) 522-6317	South Africa:	Mr Rod Hooper-Box Jubilee Hall P.O Wits University Johannesburg 2050 Republic of South Africa Phone: (27–82) 448–9519 Fax: (27–11) 642–6011

South America: Mr Mauricio Sanhueza
                    Las Flores
                    11932 Las Condes
                    Santiago, Chile

      or P.O. Box 20028
                    Las Condes,
                    Santiago, Chile
                    Phone: (562) 243–1246
                    Fax: (562) 625–1000

The Center also has representatives in Asia and Australia.

Index

abstract thinking 37, 271
acceptance gaining 38, 53, 59
  creative solutions 107, 11, 117–120
  implementation struggles 310
  process skills 154, 187, 217
action 18, 39–40, 55, 59, 311
  creative solutions 52, 109, 111–16,
    120–124
  critical challenges 41–43
  leadership 236
  problem definition 89–90
  process skills 135, 263–66
    applied individually 152, 177,
      185–187
    groups and teamwork 193,
      196–9, 203, 216, 220–3
    without a creative process 29
active convergence 39, 50–1, 232–3
  creative solutions 101
  implementation struggles 266, 290,
    292, 294, 310–1
  leadership 236
  process skills 131, 133–41, 160–87
    groups and teamwork 193–7,
      209–10, 214
active divergence 35–7, 39, 50–1, 126
  creative solutions 116
  critical challenges 229–30
  implementation struggles 266, 291,
    292, 310
  leadership 236
  process skills 131, 133–57, 160–87,
    266
    groups and teamwork 192,
      196–7, 213–6
active listening 202, 208, 209

adaptability 2, 5–8, 16–8, 32, 63–64
  implementation struggles 299, 310
  involving others 276
  teamwork 204
agendas 193–5
  hidden 211, 215, 229–30
ambiguity 14–5, 35–7, 39–40, 173, 209
  implementation struggles 284
analysis 20, 22, 56, 90, 226–37
  brain functions 137
  implementation struggles 268,
    272–3
  leadership and teamwork 205,
    234–6, 304, 308
  paired comparison (PCA) 96, 102,
    104–8
  see also why–what's stopping
    analysis
applied action 29
appraisal systems, performance
    31–32, 114, 128–130, 212, 258
  implementation struggles 269, 276,
    286, 298–300, 304–5
assumptions 14–15, 28, 69, 93, 306
  critical challenges 229–30
  groups and teamwork 198, 209, 215
  ideas boxcd in 140–1
  problem finding 68–69, 72–4
attitudes 2–4, 9–16, 40, 129–30, 205
  implementation struggles 268, 275,
    290, 300–2, 313–4
  leadership 236
  problem-solving 61, 64–6, 68, 70
  successful meetings 191–200
awareness 133–58
  lack of 20, 28–9

bargaining 214–9
barriers 24–5, 66, 72, 268, 275
  fuzzy situations 164
  see also roadblocks
Basadur creative problem solving
  profile
inventory 32–4
behavior 2, 4, 13–16, 40
  creative solutions 123
  groups and teamwork 191–2, 194,
    201, 205–7, 212–5
  implementation struggles 268, 275,
    300–1, 310–1
  leadership 240
belief 28, 93, 216, 300, 310
benefits 115, 117, 178, 185, 211, 289
blitzing 96, 98–100
'bogged down, getting' 29, 160
brain functions 132
brainstorming 56, 95–6, 98, 291–2
  process skills 130–3, 137
'broccoli first' principle 111, 121, 123–4
'burning the furniture' 48
business needs 299–300, 311–2, 314–5
business partners 41
buy-ins 4, 256

challenges 14, 19–41, 42, 52, 224–61
  creative solutions 101
  different points of view 141–6
  implementation struggles 256–57,
    263–4, 273, 310–1
  ownership and responsibility 18,
    256–57
  participatory management 64–5
  problem definition 78, 80–94
  process skills 161, 192, 217–22
change 2–6, 30, 33, 55, 80
  accelerated rate of 198
  creative solutions 109, 117–9, 123–4
  fear of 28, 30
  of habits 99–100
  implementation struggles 269, 285,
    300, 310

  leadership 225
  Simplex wheel 59
  unnecessary assumptions 72
clients 189–90, 192, 192, 198–9
closure 111, 121–2
coaching 137, 189, 192, 198–9, 203,
    256–7
  implementation struggles 269, 285,
    310
  team performance benefits 211
cohesiveness, team 202, 209, 213, 215
communication 14–15, 28, 164
  implementation struggles 275, 310
  involving others 268–9, 275, 277–9
  leadership 247
  teamwork 203, 217, 221
competition 2–7, 56, 66, 71–2, 203
  implementation struggles 310
  key challenges 23–4, 31
  leadership 227
conceptualising 20, 33–4, 35–41, 268,
    272–3
concrete experience 272–4
concrete ideas 101
conditioning process 9, 9–11
confidence 28, 37, 205
conflict resolution model 215
consensus 41, 202, 209–11
constructive discontents 58
consultation 200, 257, 305
contacts, outside 275, 279–80
content 16–18, 96, 127, 297
  groups and teamwork 190–1, 203,
    205, 211
  versus process 41–53, 203, 211,
    297–8, 302
convergence *see* active convergence
costs 4, 82, 125–6, 223
  implementation struggles 286,
    307–8
  leadership 233, 241–3, 259
creative problem solving profiles *see*
profiles

creativity 2, 8–18, 154, 213
  implementation struggles 268, 284–83
  key challenges 20–22, 28–10, 32–3, 42
  lack of support 284–6
  leadership 231–2, 255
  problem definition 78
  problem-solving 55–6, 192
  solutions 95–124
credit, giving 118
crises 66, 309
criteria grid method 96, 102–6
critical success factors (CSFs) 309
criticism 98, 198, 278–9
customer expectations 309
customer satisfaction 18, 67, 110, 239–49, 254, 304

deadlines 111, 121, 123
deadlocks 214
debriefing 189–92, 198–9, 213, 284–5
decision-making 18, 22, 101–109, 210
  leadership 238
  process skills 125–6
delegation 254–61
design, organisational 275, 285–6
discontents 58, 68
divergence *see* active divergence
dominant styles 272–4

economic factors 227, 286
efficiency 2, 5–6, 20, 31, 204
  implementation struggles 270–1, 276, 298, 310
  leadership 238–46
ego 68, 71
Employee Involvement (EI) 305
employees 3–4, 53, 188–223, 268–83, 309
  'burning the furniture' 48
  causes for leaving 164
  involvement 302–5

key challenges 30–3, 41
leadership 41, 231–6, 240
problem definition 82–3, 94
suggestion systems 68, 255, 260–1
see also job security; management; teamwork; training
empowerment 3, 200, 205, 254–61
enthusiasm 120
environment 20, 32, 38, 133
  implementation struggles 268–9, 279–80
  meetings 190
evaluation 14, 24–9, 55, 58–9
  challenges 233
  creative solutions 96, 102–109
  implementation struggles 268, 272–4, 286, 288, 290
  problem finding 62, 73–5
  process skills 125–6, 162, 171–3, 184–5
    awareness of 133–4, 139, 155–53
    groups and teamwork 198, 203, 212, 221–3
experience 34, 39, 98, 272–4

facilitators 89, 255–7, 260
  encouraging others as 285–6
  groups and teamwork 189–200, 217, 222
fact finding 15, 38–9, 52, 55, 58, 61–2, 68–76
  challenges 23, 25, 229–30
  delegating responsibilities 256
  implementation struggles 274, 286 7
  invisible facts 227–31
  involving others 273–4
  problem definition 78, 80
  process skills 140–1, 160, 162, 180–4
    groups and teamwork 193, 198, 203, 215–8, 222
failure 19–20, 113, 120–1
fear 20, 28–30, 133, 203, 233

creative solutions 111–3, 120
feedback 189, 192, 198–9, 202, 205, 209–13
  implementation struggles 266, 285
flexibility 2, 5–7, 14–15
  groups and teamwork 192, 204
  implementation struggles 268, 298
forcing connections 96, 98–9
franchisees 217–9
freewheeling techniques 98–9, 130, 216
future, anticipation of 66–7, 164
fuzzy situations 15, 55, 58, 80
  challenges and responsibility 227–30
fear of the unknown 113
  implementation struggles 286
  problem finding 61, 68, 71–2
  process skills 140–1, 164–66, 192, 196–7, 215–6

generating 20, 33–8, 48, 130, 138, 216
  creative solutions 98–9
  implementation struggles 268, 272–4, 288, 290
GMP (Good Manufacturing Practices)
  task force 221–3
goals 4, 18, 31–2, 38, 164
  creative solutions 97, 101, 121, 123
  critical challenges 224–5, 228, 239
  delegation of responsibilities 254–61
  implementation struggles 298, 309
  involving others 268–9, 275–9, 286
  leadership 233, 239, 253, 257
  problem definition 86–94
  problem finding 64–5, 67
  teamwork 202, 205, 221
government regulation 56
groups see teamwork

hitchhiking techniques 98, 129–32
horizontal skills 31, 160–1, 163, 269

human resources see employees; job security; management; teamwork; training

ideation 12–18, 28, 39, 48, 55, 58
  creative solutions 95–109, 112, 117–19
  implementation struggles 275, 277–8, 286, 291
  key challenges 28, 30, 33–4
  leadership 260
  learning and training 288, 290–1
  process skills 130–1, 161–2, 170–2, 183–4
    awareness of 134–5, 138–40, 155, 158
    groups and teamwork 196–7, 207, 221
imperfection, fear of 59, 113, 120–21
implementing 7–8, 34, 38–41, 48, 52, 55
  defining problems 80
  process skills 131–2, 216
  solutions 110–24, 258–9
improvement, continuous 53
incentives 268, 276–7
inflation 312
information 14, 31, 35
  leadership 229–30
  problem finding 61, 66–8, 70
  process skills 135, 138, 164
    groups and teamwork 191, 209–10, 215
infrastructure 298–9, 303, 312
initiator style 274
interest group pressures 56
interfunctional teams 113, 198, 236, 306, 312
  disputes 203
interpersonal skills 202, 207–209, 315
intrapreneuring 3, 301
inventory, Basadur profile 35–6

Japanese organisations 3, 33, 46
  implementation struggles 301
  leadership 255, 258, 261
  problem finding 65, 67–8
jargon 14–15
job roles *see* roles
job security 216, 228, 233, 269, 286
judgment 8, 15, 39, 98, 115
  implementation struggles 266,
    291–2, 297
  leadership 229–30
  problem finding 62, 68, 73–4
  process skills 126, 129–31, 160–76,
    266, 291–2
    awareness of 134–58
    groups and teamwork 192,
      196–7, 209
    process versus content 50–1

key challenges 18, 19–41
killer phrases 82, 131–2, 137–8
  groups and teamwork 196–7, 205,
    215
knowledge 25, 49–50, 68, 71, 131,
    134, 137
  groups and teamwork 189, 204, 208
  implementation struggles 268,
    270–4

language 14–15, 209, 216
leadership 18, 41, 42, 224–61
  groups and teamwork 192, 198,
    200, 205
  implementation struggles 309–11
learning 2, 30–33, 136, 161, 213
  implementation struggles 270–1,
    284
listening 118–9, 202, 206–7, 209, 215,
    269
lists 82–3
logic 8, 35, 68, 137–40, 155

mainstreaming 20, 38–40, 56, 80
  creative solutions 123–4
  implementation struggles 295–6,
    298, 313, 316
  importance of process skills 131–2
  leadership 256, 259
  process versus content 42–3, 52
management 4, 33, 48–9, 316
  groups and teamwork 204–8, 214
  implementation struggles 187, 188,
    202–3, 309–10
  over-management 277–8
  participatory 64–5
Management by Objectives (MBO)
    317–8
mapping 217–23, 225, 228–9, 234–5,
    240–53, 311
  problem definition 78, 87–8, 93
meetings 18, 189–200, 203–4, 215–7,
    285
  key challenges 24, 28
  mandatory 276–7
mental processing 272–4
monitoring 266
morale 233
motivation 65–6, 123–4, 212, 221–3,
    300

negative attitudes 61, 68, 70, 268, 275
'no', saying 112–4
North American organisations 3, 22,
    33, 46–8, 113–4
  leadership 259–60

objections 111, 117, 178
objectives *see* goals
obstacles, key 265–6
open-mindedness 26–9, 39, 102, 210
opinion, differences of 41, 210
  see also viewpoints
opportunities 29, 33, 41, 57, 66–9, 82
  implementation struggles 305

optimising 20, 35–8, 40, 272–4, 307
options 130, 134–5, 138, 156–8
    critical challenges 233
    groups and teamwork 190, 209–10,
        216
overloading 211
ownership 4, 18, 28, 255–7
    creative solutions 118–9
    groups and teamwork 190–2, 198–9
    problem definition 94

paired comparison analysis 96, 102–3,
    105–8
parlour discussion 29
participation 4, 51–2, 189–99
patent barriers 24–6
'pepperoni principle' 111, 122
performance 2, 16–18, 32, 42, 56
    implementation struggles 264, 266,
        290
    key challenges 20, 22, 31–2
    process skills 123–4, 163, 264
    vertical/horizontal leadership
        282–3
    see also appraisal systems,
        performance
personal problems 67–8
personality tests 38
phrases 305
    see also killer phrases
piggyback techniques 98, 131
planning 18, 39, 55, 59, 162
    creative solutions 109, 111–16
    implementation struggles 263–66
    problem definition 87–9`
    process skills 162, 173–7, 185–87,
        193–7, 198–9, 205
points of view see viewpoints
poker situation 179–87
praise 260–1, 284
preconsultation 190, 192–3, 193–5,
    200, 305
present, sensing the 66, 164

pressures 56, 67, 164
prioritising 4, 35–36, 111, 121–2, 130,
    216, 278–9
problem definition 15, 18, 51, 56, 58,
    77–94
    challenges 24–6, 35–36, 38–9, 231–2
    creative solutions 96–8, 101
    critical challenges 239, 247
    delegating responsibility 256
    implementation struggles 307, 311
problem solving 62, 70, 72
    process skills 161–2, 167–70,
        181–2, 192–4
problem finding 7–8, 29, 38, 52, 55–8,
    61–76
    content versus process 42, 46–48
    implementation struggles 274, 288,
        297
    leadership 236, 258–60
    personal problems 67–8, 163
process skills 160, 162–5, 179–80
    the word 'problem' 63–4
problem solving 7–8, 13–15, 18, 55–9,
    95–124
    implementation struggles 268–73,
        288, 291, 295–6, 305, 314–5
    key challenges 20–29, 31, 33–5, 38,
        39
    leadership 225–22, 240, 253
problem definition 80
process skills 131–2, 135–6, 159, 161
    groups and teamwork 190, 192–3,
        198–200, 203, 210, 213, 292
process versus content 41–53, 51–2,
    191
    see also Simplex
process skills 2–8, 18
    creative solutions 98, 117
    implementation struggles 263–66,
        285–6, 305, 310
    key challenges 20–21, 28, 30–1,
        33–40
    problem definition 94

process versus content 42–53, 191
    training 288–96
profiles 20–1, 35–6, 38, 268–75
    Basadur inventory 35–6
    customers' innovation process 273
profitability 3–4, 22, 128, 153, 223,
        233
    implementation struggles 276
    leadership 243, 259
prompter questions *see* questions
psychological roadblocks 111–3,
        121–2

quadrants, process 20–21, 33–8,
        270–1, 274–5, 306–7
quality 3–6, 16, 31, 126–30, 260
    creative solutions 98
    ideation–evaluation 139, 155, 158
    implementation struggles 286,
        300–5
    problem finding 61
    process versus content 41–4, 48, 52
    sensing the present 164
    teamwork 205, 214
Quality Encounter 303–4
questions 66–8, 71–3, 78, 82, 114–5,
        163
    learning process 136
    open-ended 206–7
    teamwork 215–8
    see also why–what's stopping
        analysis

radical ideas 96, 98–9, 131, 139
recognition 260–1
reinforcement systems 4
relationships 48, 263, 294
    forcing connections 96, 98–9
resources 38, 248–50, 269, 305, 309
responsibility
    delegation 253, 254–61
    ultimate 158
reverse–prioritising 111, 121–2
rewards 20, 31–2, 127–8, 258–60

implementation struggles 269,
        276–7, 284–5
    meeting deadlines 111, 123
risks 20, 39, 101, 117, 163
    avoiding 'safe' options 156
    fear of failure 113
    implementation struggles 285, 290
    personal problem finding 67
    sharing 30
roadblocks 70, 78, 80–82, 111–3,
        120–4
    implementation struggles 268, 275,
        284
roles 4, 189–200, 275
role-playing 118

selection 55, 58–9, 62, 96–7, 102–109
    process skills 162, 171–8, 184–5
'self' idea 162
shop floor 33
Simplex 3, 16–7
    implementation struggles 263–5,
        288–96
        involving others 268–75, 286
    key challenges 21, 29–30, 38–40
    leadership 225–6, 233, 236–40, 257
    process skills 126–7, 131–2, 134,
        160–2
        groups and teamwork 190–1,
            196–7, 202–3, 206–7, 214–8,
            222
    process versus content 41, 48–53
skills *see* process skills; social skills
skills progression ladder 294
social skills 191
solutions 7–8, 55–9, 72, 95–124
    implementation struggles 288, 291,
        293–4, 300
    key challenges 20, 24, 28, 31, 34,
        36,41
    problem definition 78, 80, 84, 93–4
    process skills 129–30, 135, 149,
        196–7, 203–4, 214–6

process versus content 49–51
speech 202, 207–9
strategies 18, 87–91, 204, 217–20,
    268–9, 275–9
    implementation struggles 305
    leadership 224, 252–3
strikes 214
structure 4, 21, 255–9, 269, 298
styles 29, 38, 160, 198, 203
    implementation struggles 268,
        272–5, 306–7
    key challenges 20–1, 29–34
success 41, 123–4, 205, 221
    implementation struggles 284–5, 309
suggestion systems 68, 255, 258–61
suppliers 28
support 28, 117, 269, 275
    teamwork 202–3, 207, 209
    training 284–6

T-groups 301
targets 101, 233
TEAM ('Together Everyone Achieves
    More') 302
teamwork 18, 130, 161, 189–223
    creative solutions 110–4
    delegating responsibility 260–1
    implementation struggles 268–9,
        274, 278–81, 305
    key challenges 25–31, 38, 39, 41
    leadership 229–30, 233–5
    problem definition 89
    process versus content 43, 46–47
technical critique 275, 283
technology 4, 43, 52–3, 56, 227, 240,
    306–9
thought processes 2, 35–36, 51–2,
    133–41
    creativity suppression 14–6

implementation struggles 268, 274,
    284–8, 292
key challenges 20, 22, 31–9
saying what you think 68, 70–1
styles 36–8, 307
teamwork 205–6, 209–10, 222–3
unnecessary assumptions 72
time 3, 7, 163, 211
    limitations on 268, 275–6
    wasted 203
total quality control (TQC) 16
total quality management (TQM) 4,
    110, 126–8, 300, 305
Total Quality Process 302–4
training 3, 18, 32, 48, 66
    implementation struggles 269, 275,
        285–96, 313–5
    leadership 240,243, 257
    process skills 127, 136, 164
trust 29, 70, 196–7, 211, 215–21
truth 68, 71
turf issues 275, 283–4

uncertainties 163
unions 214, 305
unknown, fear of 113, 121

vertical skills and goals 31, 51, 160–1,
    196–7, 269, 278–9, 301–2
viewpoints 68–71, 134, 138–58, 210
    teamwork 203, 210–1, 215
visual aids 118, 120

why–what's stopping analysis 78, 79,
    83–94, 149
    implementation struggles 304, 309
    leadership 234–5, 239–51, 253
work stoppages 214

Further titles of interest

ISBN	TITLE	AUTHOR
0 273 60561 5	Achieving Successful Product Change	Innes
0 273 03970 9	Advertising on Trial	Ring
0 273 60232 2	Analysing Your Competitor's Financial Strengths	Howell
0 273 60466 X	Be Your Own Management Consultant	Pinder
0 273 60168 7	Benchmarking for Competitive Advantage	Bendell
0 273 60529 1	Business Forecasting using Financial Models	Hogg
0 273 60456 2	Business Re-engineering in Financial Services	Drew
0 273 60069 9	Company Penalties	Howarth
0 273 60558 5	Complete Quality Manual	McGoldrick
0 273 03859 1	Control Your Overheads	Booth
0 273 60022 2	Creating Product Value	De Meyer
0 273 60300 0	Creating World Class Suppliers	Hines
0 273 60383 3	Delayering Organisations	Keuning
0 273 60171 7	Does Your Company Need Multimedia?	Chatterton
0 273 60003 6	Financial Engineering	Galitz
0 273 60065 6	Financial Management for Service Companies	Ward
0 273 60205 5	Financial Times Guide to Using the Financial Pages	Vaitilingam
0 273 60006 0	Financial Times on Management	Lorenz
0 273 03955 5	Green Business Opportunities	Koechlin
0 273 60385 X	Implementing the Learning Organisation	Thurbin
0 273 03848 6	Implementing Total Quality Management	Munro-Faure
0 273 60025 7	Innovative Management	Phillips
0 273 60327 2	Investor's Guide to Emerging Markets	Mobius
0 273 60622 0	Investor's Guide to Measuring Share Performance	Macfie
0 273 60528 3	Investor's Guide to Selecting Shares that Perform	Koch
0 273 60704 9	Investor's Guide to Traded Options	Ford
0 273 03751 X	Investor's Guide to Warrants	McHattie
0 273 03957 1	Key Management Ratios	Walsh
0 273 60384 1	Key Management Tools	Lambert
0 273 60259 4	Making Change Happen	Wilson
0 273 60424 4	Making Re-engineering Happen	Obeng
0 273 60533 X	Managing Talent	Sadler
0 273 60153 9	Perfectly Legal Competitor Intelligence	Bernhardt
0 273 60167 9	Profit from Strategic Marketing	Wolfe
0 273 60170 9	Proposals, Pitches and Beauty Parades	de Forte
0 273 60616 6	Quality Tool Kit	Mirams
0 273 60336 1	Realising Investment Value	Bygrave
0 273 60713 8	Rethinking the Company	Clarke
0 273 60328 0	Spider Principle	Linton
0 273 03873 7	Strategic Customer Alliances	Burnett
0 273 03949 0	Strategy Quest	Hill
0 273 60624 7	Top Intrapreneurs	Lombriser
0 273 03447 2	Total Customer Satisfaction	Horovitz
0 273 60201 2	Wake Up and Shake Up Your Company	Koch
0 273 60387 6	What Do High Performance Managers Really Do?	Hodgson

For further details or a full list of titles contact:

The Professional Marketing Department, Pitman Publishing, 128 Long Acre, London WC2E 9AN, UK

Tel +44 (0)71 379 7383 or fax +44 (0)71 240 5771

Dear Pitman Publishing Customer

IMPORTANT – Read This Now!

We are delighted to announce a special free service for all of our customers.

Simply complete this form and return it to the address overleaf to receive:

A Free Customer Newsletter
B Free Information Service
C Exclusive Customer Offers – which have included free software, videos and relevant products
D Opportunity to take part in product development sessions
E The chance for you to write about your own business experience and become one of our respected authors

Fill this in now and return it to us (no stamp needed in the UK) to join our customer information service.

Name: Position:

Company/Organisation:

Address (including postcode):

                                               Country:

Telephone: Fax:

Nature of business:

Title of book purchased:

Comments:

---------------------------- **Fold Here Then Staple** ----------------------------

We would be very grateful if you could answer these questions to help us with market research.

1 Where/How did you hear of this book?
☐ in a bookshop
☐ in a magazine/newspaper
(please state which):

☐ information through the post
☐ recommendation from a colleague
☐ other (please state which):

2 Which newspaper(s)/magazine(s) do you read regularly?:

3 When buying a business book which factors influence you most?
(Please rank in order)
☐ recommendation from a colleague
☐ price
☐ content
☐ recommendation in a bookshop
☐ author
☐ publisher
☐ title
☐ other(s):

4 Is this book a
☐ personal purchase?
☐ company purchase?

5 Would you be prepared to spend a few minutes talking to our customer services staff to help with product development? YES/NO

PITMAN PUBLISHING
The Business Publisher

Written for managers competing in today's tough business world, our books will help you get the edge on competitors by showing you how to:

- increase quality, efficiency and productivity throughout your organisation
- use both proven and innovative management techniques
- improve the management skills of you and your staff
- implement winning customer strategies

In short they provide concise, practical information that you can use every day to improve the success of your business.

FINANCIAL TIMES

PITMAN PUBLISHING

the Institute of Management
F O U N D A T I O N
PITMAN PUBLISHING

Free Information Service
Pitman Professional Publishing
FREEPOST
128 Long Acre
LONDON
WC2E 9BR, UK

No stamp
necessary
in the UK